全国高等院校法律英语专业统编教材
法律英语证书（LEC）全国统一考试指定用书

英美法律
文化教程

Anglo-American
Legal Culture Course

张法连 姜芳 主编

北京大学出版社
PEKING UNIVERSITY PRESS

图书在版编目（CIP）数据

英美法律文化教程 / 张法连，姜芳主编 . —北京：北京大学出版社，2018.1
（全国高等院校法律英语专业统编教材）
ISBN 978-7-301-28959-4

Ⅰ.①英… Ⅱ.①张…②姜… Ⅲ.①法律—文化研究—英国—高等学校—教材 ②法律—文化研究—美国—高等学校—教材 Ⅳ.① D956.1 ② D971.2

中国版本图书馆 CIP 数据核字 (2017) 第 300169 号

书　　　名	英美法律文化教程 YINGMEI FALÜ WENHUA JIAOCHENG
著作责任者	张法连　姜　芳　主编
责 任 编 辑	李　娜
标 准 书 号	ISBN 978-7-301-28959-4
出 版 发 行	北京大学出版社
地　　　址	北京市海淀区成府路 205 号　100871
网　　　址	http://www.pup.cn　　新浪微博：@ 北京大学出版社
电 子 邮 箱	编辑部 pupwaiwen@pup.cn　总编室 zpup@pup.cn
电　　　话	邮购部 62752015　发行部 62750672　编辑部 62754382
印 刷 者	河北滦县鑫华书刊印刷厂
经 销 者	新华书店
	787 毫米 ×1092 毫米　16 开本　17 印张　343 千字 2018 年 1 月第 1 版　2024 年 5 月第 4 次印刷
定　　　价	58.00 元

未经许可，不得以任何方式复制或抄袭本书之部分或全部内容。
版权所有，侵权必究
举报电话：010-62752024　电子邮箱：fd@pup.cn
图书如有印装质量问题，请与出版部联系，电话：010-62756370

前　言

　　法律英语是法律科学与英语语言学有机结合形成的一门实践性很强的交叉学科，是 ESP (English for Specific Purposes)最重要的分支之一。法律英语是以普通英语为基础，在立法和司法等活动中形成和使用的具有法律专业特点的语言，是指表述法律科学概念以及诉讼或非诉讼法律实务时所使用的英语。当今世界的发展日新月异，经济全球化进程突飞猛进，国际交流合作日益加强，涉外法务活动空前频繁。中国已经成为经济全球化的引领者。十八届四中全会提出加强涉外法律工作；司法部等四部委办联合印发了《关于发展涉外法律服务业的意见》，对大力发展涉外法律服务业做出全面部署。经济全球化过程中我们所面临的很多问题其实都是法律问题，而这些法律问题中的绝大多数又都属于涉外法律的工作范畴，法律英语则是完成涉外法律工作不可或缺的工具。国家急需明晰国际法律规则、通晓英语语言的"精英明法"复合型人才，法律英语的重要性日益彰显，掌握专业外语已经成为法律人必备的职业素质。法律英语证书（LEC）全国统一考试的成功推出和中央政法委、教育部"卓越法律人才计划"的顺利启动无疑把法律英语的学习和研究推向了高潮。

　　法律英语是高校英语、法学等专业教学改革的新方向。随着高校英语、法学专业教学改革不断深化，国内许多高校在外语、法学院系开设了法律英语课程，有的院系设置了法律英语方向，有些高校大胆创新，开始尝试设置法律英语专业，收到了良好的社会效果。2013年高等教育出版社出版发行《法律英语专业教学大纲》，标志着法律英语专业的诞生，给高校外语、法学院系设置法律英语专业或涉外法律专业指明了方向。本套教材正是以该大纲为重要依据编写而成。

　　语言是文化的载体，法律文化知识是法律英语学习过程中不可或缺的内容。英美法作为西方法律文明的重要分支之一，具有独特的历史传统、文化意蕴、发展路径、表现形式、价值取向以及运作机制。英美法的发展具有历史的连续性；法律、权利与自由之间相互关联。可以说，英国历史上的实践性学徒制法律教育是与其本国的经验主义传统分不开的；而实证主义的产生又对英国法律科学的发展产生深刻影响，它甚至直接促进了英国学院制法律教育的产生与发展。由于受到英国法律文化的影响，学徒制法律教育也曾是美国法律教育的源头；但是在兰代尔主义法律科学思想的影响下，法学院逐渐在美国兴起和变革，美国的法律教育在普通法传统的背景下一度呈现科学化的发展趋势；后来，法律现实主义使美国的法律教育重新回归到对实践性教育的重视。英美法程序正义优于实体正义；在法律价值上，更重视个人、实用和经验。近代以来，特别是改革开放以来，英美法的一些概念、理念和原则被移植到中国，产生了不同程度的影响。深入、系统地研究英美法，对于当代中国合理地借鉴英美法，具有重要的价值。学习英美法，就应该了解英美法的本质特征和法系特点。唯有掌握了这一点，才能理解英美法上的许多看似不合理的制度其实恰恰具有很强的合理性。

本套教材共包括《法律英语精读教程（上、下）》《法律英语泛读教程（上、下）》《法律英语写作教程》《法律英语翻译教程》和《英美法律文化教程》《法律英语视听说》《大学法律英语》以及配套学习使用的《英美法律术语双解》。

编写本书的过程中，编者参考了大量的英美原版法学书籍资料，包括英美法学院教材及大量判例，力求实现教材内容的权威性和丰富性。教材在编写上遵循由总述到具体、由浅入深的原则，基本上达到《法律英语专业教学大纲》提出的目标要求。本书共由三部分组成：第一部分是英国法律文化知识简介；第二部分主要介绍美国法律文化知识；第三部分为选择阅读，主要介绍英美法系的加拿大、澳大利亚及新加坡的法律文化知识。这三部分内容浑然一体，又相互独立。学习本教材不一定要严格按照前后编写顺序进行，教师完全可以根据学生的具体情况挑选合适的内容安排教学。编写本书过程中，我们参考了大量国内外有关资料，在此谨对原作者表示谢忱。

参加本书编写工作的还有河南工业大学杜巧阁副教授、北京信息科技大学赵玉华老师、甘肃政法学院唐丽玲教授、中国音乐学院社科部张桂萍教授等。感谢法律英语证书（LEC）全国统一考试指导委员会将该套教材指定为复习应考LEC的参考用书。

编者

2017年9月于美国印第安纳大学法学院

Indiana University-Indianapolis School of Law

Contents

Part I   **The United Kingdom of Great Britain and Northern Ireland** ········· 1

    Chapter 1   THE BASICS OF LEGAL SYSTEM IN THE UNITED KINGDOM ····· 3

    Chapter 2   THE LEGAL PROFESSION AND JUDICIARY CAREER ········· 16

    Chapter 3   GOVERNING STRUCTURE ········· 39

    Chapter 4   JUSTICE SYSTEM ········· 53

    Chapter 5   HOW THE JUDICIARY IS GOVERNED ········· 78

    Chapter 6   JUDICIAL ACCOUNTABILITY AND INDEPENDENCE ········· 84

    Chapter 7   HISTORY OF THE JUDICIARY ········· 95

    Chapter 8   INTERESTING BRITISH LAWS ········· 105

Part II   **The United States of America** ········· 115

    Chapter 1   BASIC CONCEPTS OF AMERICAN JURISPRUDENCE ········· 117

    Chapter 2   OVERVIEW OF THE U.S. LEGAL SYSTEM ········· 127

    Chapter 3   CONGRESS ········· 140

    Chapter 4   EXECUTIVE BRANCH ········· 156

    Chapter 5   FEDERAL COURTS ········· 166

    Chapter 6   STEPS IN THE FEDERAL CRIMINAL PROCESS ········· 188

    Chapter 7   STATE CONSTITUTIONS AND COURTS ········· 202

    Chapter 8   THE POLICE AND CRIME IN THE U.S. ········· 211

    Chapter 9   U.S. LAW SCHOOLS ········· 220

Chapter 10　PRACTICE LAW IN THE UNITED STATES WITH A

　　　　　　　FOREIGN LAW DEGREE ·· 229

Chapter 11　LEGAL CAREER OVERVIEW ·· 235

Chapter 12　MAJOR DIFFERENCES BETWEEN THE U.S. AND UK

　　　　　　　LEGAL SYSTEMS ·· 245

Part III　Selective Readings ·· **249**

Chapter 1　OVERVIEW OF THE CANADIAN LEGAL SYSTEM ············· 251

Chapter 2　AUSTRALIA'S LEGAL SYSTEM ·· 255

Chapter 3　SINGAPORE'S LEGAL SYSTEM ·· 259

Part I

The United Kingdom of Great Britain and Northern Ireland

Chapter 1
THE BASICS OF LEGAL SYSTEM IN THE UNITED KINGDOM

The United Kingdom of Great Britain and Northern Ireland consists of England, Wales, Scotland and Northern Ireland. It was established in 1801 with the union of Great Britain and Ireland, but only achieved its present form in 1922, with the partition of Ireland and the establishment of the independent Irish Free State (later the Republic of Ireland).

England and Wales have a combined judicial system, while Scotland and Northern Ireland have their own judicial systems.

The Queen is the Head of State, although in practice the supreme authority of the Crown is exercised by the government of the day. The UK legislature is a bicameral parliament, consisting of the House of Commons and the House of Lords. The House of Commons consists of 650 Members of Parliament (MPs) elected by simple majority vote in a general election every five years. The House of Lords has more than 700 members, who fall into three categories: life peers (the largest group), hereditary peers, and bishops; most peers are appointed on the recommendation of the Prime Minister or the House of Lords Appointments Commission.

Sources of UK Law

The three principal sources of UK law are legislation, common law and European Union law. There is no single series of documents that contains the whole of the law of the UK.

Legislation

The principal legislature is the UK Parliament, which is based in London. This is the only body that has the power to pass laws that apply in all four countries. The UK Parliament consists of the House of Commons and the House of Lords.

The House of Commons consists of 650 Members of Parliament (MPs). Each MP represents a defined geographic constituency, whose electors vote using a "first-past-the-post" system. Each elector has one vote, and the candidate with the highest number of votes is elected as MP for that constituency. MPs are only allowed to sit for the lifetime of the Parliament, that is, the length of time between General Elections when a new set of MPs is elected. However, MPs can be reelected a limitless number of times.

The House of Lords consists of nearly 800 peers, of whom 600 are formally appointed by the Queen on the recommendation of the Prime Minister. The other members of the House of Lords are people who have inherited aristocratic titles such as "Lord" or "Lady", and senior bishops of the Church of England.

Notwithstanding its common law heritage, the modern UK legal system relies heavily on statutory law. We should bear in mind that there is no official compilation of all UK statutes currently in force comparable to the United States Code. Nevertheless, consolidated legislation, which incorporates all subsequent revisions and amendments made to the original legislation, is readily accessible from both official and unofficial sources.

Acts of Parliament (Primary Legislation)

Acts of Parliament, sometimes referred to as primary legislation, are the supreme law in the United Kingdom. Most Acts of Parliament fall into one of two broad categories: Public General Acts of universal application and Private Acts affecting only specified localities, entities or individuals. A third category of Hybrid Acts combines elements of both public and private acts. The vast majority of UK legal research involves Public General Acts.

The Scottish Parliament, the Welsh Assembly, and the Northern Ireland Assembly each enact primary legislation for their respective jurisdictions, but only with respect to those matters that have been devolved to them by the national Parliament in London.

Secondary (Delegated) Legislation

Secondary legislation refers to specialized rules and regulations issued by ministers or governmental entities acting under authority delegated to them by an Act of Parliament. Such rules, also known as delegated legislation, have the force of law and are analogous to regulations issued by administrative agencies in the United States.

The most common type of secondary legislation is known as a Statutory Instrument (SI). Other types of secondary legislation include Orders in Council and Orders of Council.

The Scottish Parliament, the Welsh Assembly, and the Northern Ireland Assembly also enact primary legislation that authorizes the creation of secondary legislation applicable within their respective jurisdictions.

Common Law

Common law, also known as case law or precedent, is law developed by judges, courts, and similar tribunals, stated in decisions that nominally decide individual cases but that, in addition, have precedential effect on future cases. Common law is a third branch of law, in contrast to and on equal footing with statutes which are adopted through the legislative process, and regulations which are promulgated by the executive branch. In cases where the parties disagree on what the law is, a common law court looks to past precedential decisions of relevant courts. If a similar dispute has been resolved in the past, the court is usually bound to follow the reasoning used in the prior decision, which is a principle known as stare decisis. If, however, the court finds that the current dispute is fundamentally distinct from all previous cases, which is called a "matter of first impression", judges have the authority and duty to resolve the issue, in which one party or the other has to win, and on disagreements of law, judges make that decision. Resolution of the issue in one case becomes precedent that binds future courts. Stare decisis, the principle that cases should be decided according to consistent principled rules so that similar facts will yield similar results, lies at the heart of all common law systems.

The concept "common law system" refers to a legal system that gives great precedential weight to common law. Common law systems originated during the Middle Ages in England, and from there propagated to the colonies of the British Empire. Today, one third of the world's population live in common law jurisdictions or in systems mixed with civil law. The legal system of England and Wales is a common law one, so the decisions of the senior appellate courts (see below) become part of the law.

EU Law and the European Convention on Human Rights

The UK joined the European Economic Community, the predecessor of the European Union in 1973, since when it has been a requirement to incorporate European Union legislation into UK law and to recognise the jurisdiction of the European Court of Justice in matters of EU law.

The British government led by David Cameron held a referendum on the UK's withdrawal from the EU in 2016, a commonly used term for which is Brexit; a majority voted to leave the EU. On 29 March 2017, Theresa May's administration invoked Article 50 of the Treaty on the European Union in a letter to the President of the European Council. The UK is set to leave by March 2019. The terms of withdrawal have not yet been negotiated, and the UK remains a full member of the EU. May said that the UK government would not seek permanent single market membership, and promised a Great Repeal Bill that would repeal the European Communities Act and would incorporate existing European Union law into the domestic law of the UK.

The Court System

In England and Wales, all criminal cases start in the magistrates' court, but the most serious matters are then sent to the Crown Court. Civil cases are sometimes heard in the magistrates' court, but most are heard by the County Court. Above these courts are the High Court, Court of Appeal and the Supreme Court.

Part I
The United Kingdom of Great Britain and Northern Ireland

The Supreme Court is the final court of appeal for all UK civil cases, and for criminal cases in England, Wales and Northern Ireland. The Supreme Court took over the judicial functions of the Appellate Committee of the House of Lords in October 2009, under the Constitutional Reform Act 2005, thereby making a constitutional separation between the legislature and the judiciary.

A further appellate court is the Judicial Committee of the Privy Council, which hears cases from the British overseas territories and dependencies and some Commonwealth countries, as well as certain highly specialised domestic appeals.

Her Majesty's Courts and Tribunals Service (HMCTS), an executive agency of the Ministry of Justice, is responsible for administration of the court and tribunal system in England and Wales.

The Senior Appellate Courts of the UK

Appellate courts are those that only hear appeals from other courts. The two most senior appellate courts are the Court of Appeal and the Supreme Court.

The Court of Appeal, which encompasses only England and Wales, consists of a Civil Division and a Criminal Division. The Civil Division hears appeals against decisions of the High Court, while the Criminal Division hears appeals about alleged errors of law in the Magistrates' and Crown Courts. Cases are heard by three Lords Justices of Appeal, each of whom reaches an individual decision that may consist of a lengthy speech. The Court's decision may be reached either by unanimity or by a 2:1 majority.

Appeals from the Court of Appeal are heard by the Supreme Court, which is the highest court in the UK. It hears civil appeals from all four countries, and criminal appeals from England, Wales and Northern Ireland. Permission to appeal to the Supreme Court will be given only if a case raises a point of general public importance. Cases are heard by five, seven or nine of the 12 Justices of the Supreme Court, each of whom reaches an individual decision that may consist of a lengthy speech. The Court's decision may be reached either by unanimity or by a simple majority.

Decisions made in the Court of Appeal, the Supreme Court and the Supreme Court's predecessor, the Appellate Committee of the House of Lords become precedents that must be followed by courts in all future cases. This ensures that similar cases are treated similarly, which many people regard as one of the most important aspects of justice.

Traditions of the Courts
The Royal Coat of Arms

The Royal Coat of Arms came into being in 1399 under King Henry IV. It is used by the reigning monarch.

The Royal Arms appear in every courtroom in England and Wales, with the exception of the magistrates' court in the City of London, demonstrating that justice comes from the monarch, and a law court is part of the Royal Court (hence its name).

Judges and magistrates are therefore officially representatives of the Crown.

The presence of the Royal Arms explains why lawyers and court officials bow to the judge or magistrates' bench when they enter the room. They are not bowing to the judge, but to the coat of arms, to show respect for the Queen's justice.

Gavels

Although they're often seen in cartoons and TV programmes and mentioned in almost everything else involving judges, the one place you won't see a gavel is an English or Welsh courtroom—they are not used there and have never been used in the criminal courts.

The Black Cap

The black cap, based on court headgear in Tudor times, was traditionally put on by judges passing sentence of death.

Since the permanent abolition of capital punishment in 1969, there has been no need for the cap to be worn. High Court judges still carry the black cap, but only on an occasion where they are wearing full ceremonial dress.

Red Ribbons

Red or "pink" tape was once used to tie up official papers; indeed, that is where the term "red tape" to describe excessive bureaucracy comes from. The tape is still used by the legal profession for briefs (the documents outlining a case) from private citizens. White tape is used for briefs from the Crown.

Oaths

Judges, magistrates and tribunal members take two oaths when they are sworn in. The first is the oath of allegiance to the reigning monarch, and the second the judicial oath; these are collectively referred to as the judicial oath.

Witnesses giving evidence in court also take an oath, which can be religious (different versions exist for members of different faiths) or secular—where the witness simply affirms that they will tell the truth.

Oaths were used at least as far back as Anglo-Saxon and Roman times.

History of Court Dress

The costumes worn by judges are just about the most distinctive working wardrobe in existence. But that's not altogether surprising: after all, not many uniforms have had seven centuries to evolve….

When Robes and Wigs Weren't Traditional

Strange as it might seem now, when judges first started wearing robes and wigs they probably wouldn't have stood out on the street.

The costume of a High Court judge, for example—a long robe, a full hood with a cowl covering the shoulders and a mantle (or cloak)—was more or less established by the time of Edward III (1327—1377) and was based on the correct dress for attending the royal court.

The material for these robes was originally given to judges as a grant from the Crown, and included ermine and taffeta or silk. The colours were violet for winter and green in summer, with scarlet for best, but the last mention of green robes dates back to 1534.

In 1635 the definitive guide to court dress was published in the Judges Rules. But this didn't introduce new costumes; it just set out what existing robes should be worn, and when.

So after 1635, the correctly-dressed judge would have worn a black robe faced with miniver (a light-coloured fur) in winter, and violet or scarlet robes, faced with shot-pink taffeta, in summer. A black girdle, or cincture, was worn with all robes.

Breaking the Rules?

Not that these guidelines made the matter of correct court dress simple.

By the mid-eighteenth century, the rules of 1635 were not being stuck to as strictly as the author might have hoped.

A less formal version of the robes—a scarlet robe, black scarf and scarlet casting-hood, also known as a tippet or stole, was used for criminal trials, and for civil trials some judges had begun to wear a black silk gown.

When sitting in Westminster Hall, at the time the home of the courts of law, the mantle was not worn; this was now saved for ceremonial wear. And grey taffeta was becoming increasingly popular as an alternative to the pink taffeta used on summer robes.

Plain linen bands began to be worn at the neck, in place of the ruffs associated with Queen Elizabeth I. These were originally wide collars, but by the 1680s had become what we see today: two rectangles of linen, tied at the throat.

Bands are still usually worn with a winged collar, rather than the turn-down collar seen on a typical shirt today.

New Courts, New Codes

Sometimes changes to the court structure itself have had a major effect on what is worn by judges.

The High Court, for example, was created by the Judicature Acts of 1873 and 1875, absorbing the courts of Chancery, Admiralty, Probate and Matrimonial Causes. This led to a new dress dilemma; trial judges in these courts were used to wearing plain black silk gowns.

These judges were allowed to keep the dress code they were used to, and even today, black silk gowns are worn by judges in the Chancery, Probate, Admiralty, Divorce and Family Divisions.

When county courts were created in 1846 the black gown was also worn. However, in 1915 Judge Woodfall suggested that a new robe similar to those worn by High Court judges be introduced.

A violet robe was chosen, faced—to distinguish it from the violet High Court robe—in lilac or mauve taffeta. A lilac tippet and black girdle also formed part of the costume, which due to wartime conditions did not become compulsory until 1919.

A full violet hood for ceremonial occasions was added in 1937, and the creation of the Crown Court in 1971 led to the introduction of a scarlet tippet, to be worn during criminal trials.

However, this was not compulsory; judges could choose to wear a black gown instead. Judges at the Central Criminal Court (the Old Bailey) still wear their black gowns.

The Court of Appeal was created at the same time as the High Court, again combining several existing courts. The Master of the Rolls, head of the Civil Division of the Court of Appeal, and two other members of the Court of Appeal in Chancery were among the new members of this court, which probably explains why a black silk gown was chosen.

The Court of Criminal Appeal, founded in 1908, originally wore the full black, scarlet or violet robes and regalia, but in 1966 the court was abolished and re-formed as the Court of Appeal, namely, Criminal Division. At this point, judges of this court adopted the black silk gown, with the Queen's Bench Division following suit soon afterwards.

Dress at the Top

Elaborate robes of black flowered silk damask, with gold lace and decorations, have been worn by the two senior Chancery judges, the Master of the Rolls and the Lord Chancellor, for ceremonial occasions since the seventeenth century.

After the Judicature Acts, the same dress was adopted by the Lords Justices of Appeal and the President of the Family Division.

These robes cover an equally ornate suit, including a swallow-tail coat, waistcoat and knee breaches, silk stockings and patent leather pumps with buckles. This would have been ordinary dress in the eighteenth century.

Wigs: Following Fashion

Until the seventeenth century, lawyers were expected to appear in court with clean, short hair and beards.

Wigs made their first appearance in a courtroom purely and simply because that is what was being worn outside it; the reign of Charles II (1660—1685) made wigs essential wear for polite society.

The judiciary, however, took some time to convince; portraits of judges from the early 1680s still show judges defiantly sporting their own natural hair, and wigs do not seem to have been adopted wholesale until 1685.

The reign of George III (1760—1820) saw wigs gradually go out of fashion. By the end of the century they were mainly worn by bishops, coachmen and the legal profession, and even bishops were given permission to stop wearing wigs in the 1830s.

Judges wore only full-bottomed wigs until the 1780s, when the less formal, and smaller, bob-wig, with frizzed sides rather than curls, and a short tail or queue at the back, was adopted for civil trials.

The full-bottomed wig continued to be used for criminal trials until the 1840s, but is today reserved for ceremonial dress; smaller wigs are used on a day-to-day basis.

Classification of UK Law

A distinction is made between public law, which governs the relationship between individual citizens and the state, and private law, which governs relationships between individuals and private organizations.

For practical purposes, the most significant distinction is between civil law and criminal law.

Civil law covers such areas as contracts, negligence, family matters, employment, probate and land law. Criminal law, which is a branch of public law, defines the boundaries of acceptable conduct. A person who breaks the criminal law is regarded as having committed an offence against society as a whole.

How Civil Law Is Enforced in England and Wales

A person who believes that another individual or organisation has committed a civil wrong can complete a claim form and send it to the appropriate court. The County Court, which is based at over 200 locations, deals with most claims involving less than 25,000 and claims for less than 50,000 that involve injury to a person. The High Court, which is in London, hears most higher-value cases. In the County and High Courts, each case is heard by a single judge.

The person who starts a civil case is called a claimant, and he or she has the burden of proving that, more probably than not, the defendant committed a civil wrong. If the claimant is successful, the usual remedy is damages, a sum of money paid by the defendant to the claimant. Other remedies, such as a court order that prohibits a person from behaving in a certain way, are available in some circumstances.

Either party to a civil case may appeal to a higher court against the decision.

How Criminal Law Is Enforced in England and Wales

A person who believes that a crime has been committed contacts the police, who conduct an investigation. If, after arresting and interviewing a person, the police believe that he or she has committed the crime, that individual is charged. A report of the case is then sent to the Crown Prosecution Service (CPS).

If the CPS believes that the case has a reasonable prospect of success, and that it would be in the public interest to do so, it will start criminal proceedings against the suspect, who becomes the defendant in the case. In court, the CPS bears the burden of proving, beyond reasonable doubt, that the defendant has committed the crime.

Minor offences, such as speeding, are heard by Magistrates' Courts. Many towns in England and Wales have their own Magistrates' Court, where cases are heard by three magistrates. Magistrates do not need any legal qualifications, and they are advised by a Clerk, who is a qualified lawyer. Magistrates do not state reasons for their decisions.

Very serious offences, such as murder and rape, are heard in the Crown Court. The Crown Court is based in about 90 centres throughout England and Wales. A jury consisting of 12 people chosen at random from the local population will decide, without giving reasons, whether the defendant is guilty of the offence. Usually a jury's decision will be unanimous, but the judge may decide that an 11 to 1 or 10 to 2 majority is sufficient. The jury is advised about the law by the judge, whose role also includes imposing a sentence if the defendant is found guilty.

Some intermediate offences, such as theft, may be tried in a Magistrates' Court or the Crown Court.

The sentences available for criminal offences include fines, payment of a sum of money to the state, imprisonment and community punishments such as unpaid supervised work.

Exercises

I. Identify the following statements as True or False.

1. England and Wales have a combined judicial system, while Scotland and Northern Ireland have their own judicial systems.
2. The UK Parliament is the only body that has the power to pass laws that apply in all four countries.
3. The Scottish Parliament, the Welsh Assembly, and the Northern Ireland Assembly each hold the power of legislation for their respective jurisdictions over a wide range of matters with no need of the devolution from the national Parliament.
4. Stare decisis, the principle that cases should be decided according to consistent

principled rules so that similar facts will yield similar results, lies at the heart of all common law systems.

5. The Supreme Court is the final court of appeal for all civil and criminal cases in the UK.

6. The costumes worn by judges have had an evolution history of nearly seven centuries.

7. The reign of Charles II (1660—1685) made wigs unique wear for bishops, coachmen and the legal profession.

8. What is worn by judges is, sometimes, influenced by changes to the court structure.

9. The person who starts a civil case is called a claimant, and he or she has the burden of proving that, more probably than not, the defendant committed a civil wrong.

10. In the enforcement of criminal justice the function of the jury is to decide, without giving reasons, whether the defendant is guilty of the offence.

II. Questions

1. What are the principal sources of the UK law?
2. Can you introduce the court system in the UK briefly?
3. What do you know about the court traditions in the UK?
4. What is public law?
5. What is private law?
6. What are the basic classifications of the UK law?

III. Topics for Discussion

1. The politics of the UK;
2. Differences between the sources of law in the UK and those in China;
3. The characteristics of common law system.

Chapter 2
THE LEGAL PROFESSION AND JUDICIARY CAREER

Defining the term "legal profession" is more difficult than one may anticipate. It becomes apparent that the simplest definition is perhaps the most befitting. The legal profession is a vocation that is based on expertise in the law and in its applications. Those who pursue this vocation collectively form a body of individuals who are qualified to practice law in particular jurisdictions. The learned occupation of these individuals is to study, promote, uphold and enforce the collection of rules imposed by the authority. They thus form a "legal profession".

Who Are the Legal Professionals?

There are essentially two main branches of the legal profession, namely, solicitors and barristers. Solicitors advise individuals and organizations on legal matters and ensure that their clients act in accordance with the law.

There are over 100,000 practising solicitors within the legal profession in England and Wales, governed by the Solicitors Regulation Authority. Barristers represent clients in court and give specialist opinions on complex legal matters. They generally receive instructions through solicitors.

There are around 14,400 practising barristers within the legal profession in the UK, governed by the Bar Standards Board.

The distinction between solicitors and barristers is not as clear-cut as it once was. Following the Court and Legal Services Act (CLSA) 1990 solicitors have the right to become certified advocates (i.e. represent clients in court). Commentators suggest that barristers have consequently, lost their dominance over advocacy in courts. Although solicitors are taking on a more active advocacy role in the lower courts, barristers still maintain an unrivalled monopoly over the higher courts.

Who Can Enter the Legal Profession?

A consistent requirement for those intent on entering the legal profession is that of high academic achievement. This forms the basic criterion that the vast majority of candidates must meet, before any additional skills they may possess will be considered. Candidates will need a range of skills, which vary depending on the area of the legal profession they wish to specialise in. In order to become a barrister eloquence, excellent articulation, confidence, an analytical mind and persuasiveness are essential requirements. In contrast, the skills demanded of a solicitor lean towards an aptness for problem solving, an enquiring mind and a flair for generating new business and winning clients. It thus becomes clear that in spite of the enactment of the CLSA 1990, solicitors cannot rival or replace barristers given their very separate and distinct roles within the legal profession.

The legal profession is renowned and heavily criticized for its almost impenetrable nature. The first hurdle for many applicants hoping to enter the legal profession is to secure that all-important place at a "redbrick" university, to complete their law degree and then at an equally reputable institution to complete their Legal Practitioner's or Barristers Vocational Course (LPC and BVC). The real competition begins, however upon completion of these two stages. The final hurdle before a student can qualify as a solicitor or barrister is to secure a training contract or pupillage. Of the 6,376 students who passed the LPC in July 2006, only 5,751 secured a training contract in that year. Obtaining a pupillage is substantially tougher. Only 17.5% of BVC students who apply for pupillage are likely to secure one. Notably, the majority of these applicants meet and in some cases surpass the requirements demanded of those pursuing a career in the legal profession, i.e. a 2.1^{+} class degree, a handful of mini pupillages or vacation schemes under their belt and evidence of voluntary work or part time jobs in a legal environment.

Legal Education

Unlike in the U.S., where law is solely a postgraduate pursuit, many UK students study law as undergraduates, earning an LL.B. or a B.A. Others study a different undergraduate subject and then pursue a one-year conversion course—called the "Common Professional Examination" (CPE) or "Graduate Diploma in Law" (GDL)—that covers the basic areas of law: torts, contracts, criminal law, public law, equity and trusts, and European Union law. Next, aspiring lawyers must complete a one-year practical training course, followed by a period of on-the-job training.

The United Kingdom still maintains a distinction between barristers, who advocate for clients in court, and solicitors, who advise clients directly and do not usually appear in court. After their undergraduate law degrees or conversion courses, aspiring solicitors complete a Legal Practice Course. Some law firms cover candidates' LPC costs under training contracts, but many students incur significant debt to pay their own way. Would-be barristers take the Bar Professional Training Course. A mix of private law schools and public universities offer the LPC and BPTC, and some law firms send all of their trainees to one institution. Though top universities do not offer these training courses, some do confer LL.Ms.

After the requisite academic and vocational courses, solicitors and barristers pursue different training periods before qualifying for independent practice. Solicitors complete a two-year training contract with a law firm, while barristers undergo a one-year pupilage with practicing barristers. Placement into both training stages is competitive, with the number of applicants far outpacing available spots.

Contemporary Issues Within the Legal Profession

In addition to its largely inaccessible nature, the legal profession has long been regarded as one of the most closed sectors when it comes to employing ethnic groups. In spite of the rapid progression of a culturally rich Britain, the legal profession is significantly slower in "fostering ethnic talent". Some purport that this is changing given that between 1990 and 2004 there was a 10% increase in the number of students registered with the Law Society from minority backgrounds. This is an unsubstantial development however, considering that between these periods the minority population grew by 53%. Thus, ethnic minority groups remain underrepresented within the legal profession. Although there is evidence of a noteworthy change, there is ample scope for improvement.

In the growing age of technological advancements and the era of the credit crunch, the demand for some professions is decreasing. Some wonder whether the same can be said of the legal profession. Professor Richard Susskind at the University of Oxford argues that the "current market is increasingly unlikely to tolerate expensive [legal professionals] for tasks…that can equally or better be discharged, directly or indirectly, by smart systems and processes." He states that "the jobs of many traditional lawyers will be substantially eroded and often eliminated." With the increasing number of alternative methods available to those needing legal advice, the constant influx of graduates choosing to enter the legal profession, the declining demand for applicants and the increased constraints on our finances, "the market will determine that the legal world is over-resourced." It will "increasingly drive out inefficiencies and unnecessary friction and, in so doing, we will indeed witness the end of outdated legal practice and the end of outdated lawyers." Conclusively, in order for those within the legal profession to safeguard their jobs, they must focus less on maintaining their "fat cat" status and focus more on providing the services that people need at a reasonable cost.

Becoming a Judge

What Makes a Good Judge?

The qualities of a good judge can be well illustrated by the words the Lord Chief Justice spoke at Equality in Justice Day, October 2008:

> *"[When taking the judicial oath, judges and magistrates swear] 'To do right to all manner of people after the laws and usages of this realm without fear or favour,*

affection or ill-will'.

"Ponder the words. I hear them frequently, and they still send a shiver up my spine. It binds my conscience, as it binds the conscience of every judge who takes it.

"Many qualities are required of a judge.... He or she must of course know the law, and know how to apply it, but the judge must also be wise to the ways of the world. The judge must have the ability to make a decision.

"Decisions can be profoundly unpleasant: for example, to say to a mother that her children can be taken away from her, or to say to an individual that he is going to go to prison for the rest of his life.

"Judges must have moral courage—it is a very important judicial attribute—to make decisions that will be unpopular with the politicians or the media and the public, and indeed perhaps most importantly of all, to defend the right to equal treatment before the law of those who are unpopular at any given time.

"...But however you draw up the list, and in whatever order, gender, colour of your skin, religious belief, and social origins are all utterly irrelevant. It is you who is the judge."

Who Appoints Judges?

The Judicial Appointments Commission (JAC) is an independent commission that recommends candidates for judicial office in the courts and tribunals of England and Wales and for some tribunals whose jurisdiction extends to Scotland or Northern Ireland.

Salaried positions have traditionally been full-time, but are increasingly open to part-time and flexible working as well. A legal professional who has taken a salaried role will not be able to return to legal practice.

Fee-paid (part-time) positions are usually similar to the equivalent salaried appointment, but may deal with the less complex or serious cases.

Fee-paid positions, including tribunal appointments, such as recorders and deputy district judges, are paid according to the number of sittings or days worked. The number of sitting days varies depending on the type of appointment, and will generally be at least 15 days a year.

Basic Requirements

Judicial appointments are open only to citizens, including those holding dual nationality, of the United Kingdom, the Republic of Ireland or a Commonwealth country.

There is no upper or lower age limit for candidates, apart from the statutory retirement age of 70 for all judges. However, applicants should be able to offer a reasonable length of service, usually at least five years. Applications from disabled people are welcomed, and reasonable adjustments will be made at every stage to ensure applicants are treated fairly.

Qualifications—Legal Positions

Most judicial posts will require a relevant legal qualification that has been held for either five or seven years.

Government lawyers are eligible to apply for all judicial posts, but when sitting as a fee-paid judge they must not hear cases involving their own department.

For salaried judicial appointments, applicants must normally have served as a fee-paid judicial office-holder for at least two years or have completed 30 sitting days since appointment in a fee-paid capacity.

Work-shadowing

For anyone wanting to find out more about the role they are considering before applying, the Judicial Office runs a Work Shadowing Scheme.

For most shadowing opportunities the scheme is open to any eligible qualified legal practitioner with a minimum of seven years' post-qualification legal experience who may be interested in seeking judicial appointment, within the next two years. The scheme covers the following positions:

- High Court Judge
- Circuit Judge

> District Judge (sitting in civil or family jurisdictions)
> District Judge (Magistrates' Courts)
> Tribunal Judge

A shadower will spend up to three days observing a judge's main duties including, as appropriate, preparing for trial, case management, presiding over court proceedings, hearing actions, sentencing, determining applications and giving judgments.

Becoming a Tribunal Judge

Appointments to tribunals are mainly through the Judicial Appointments Commission (JAC), on the basis of the statutory and non-statutory requirements for that specific post, as well as the qualities and abilities required in any good judge.

The JAC runs appointment competitions for a number of tribunals outside the new tribunal structure, for example, the Residential Property Tribunal Service, as well as for the new First-tier and Upper Tribunals, which absorbed the jurisdictions of a number of tribunals in 2008.

Tribunal office-holders are appointed to either the First-tier Tribunal or the Upper Tribunal, and then assigned to a particular Chamber, for example, Health, Education and Social Care. They may or may not sit in all of the jurisdictions within that Chamber.

Most tribunal appointments are fee-paid, with successful candidates usually expected to sit for at least 15 days each year. For salaried appointment, individuals must normally have served as a fee-paid judicial office-holder for at least two years, or have completed 30 sitting days in a fee-paid capacity.

Basic Requirements

As with the courts judiciary, tribunal appointments are open only to citizens of the United Kingdom, the Republic of Ireland or a Commonwealth country.

There is no upper or lower age limit, apart from the statutory retirement age of 70 for all judges. Applications from disabled people are welcomed.

Legally-qualified Appointments

As with the courts judiciary, most legally-qualified posts will require five or seven years of post qualification experience (the relevant legal qualifications for solicitors or barristers), and legal experience gained during that time.

However, tribunal judges need not always have been solicitors or barristers. The Tribunals, Courts and Enforcement Act (2007) widened the eligibility for many judicial posts, making them open to The Chartered Institute of Legal Executives (CILE), members of the Institute of Trade Mark Attorneys (ITMA) and the Chartered Institute of Patent Attorneys (CIPA).

Applications are also welcomed from non-traditional legal backgrounds, for example, legal academics.

Non-legal Appointments

The varied nature of tribunal work means that there are a number of positions available for non-legal professionals who have expertise in different areas, for example, Employment Tribunals have panel members from employees, or employers' representative backgrounds, and many tribunals include medical professionals.

Requirements for these positions are based on the nature of the tribunal, and candidates must be able to demonstrate the relevant professional experience.

Becoming a Magistrate

The characteristics of being a magistrate are as follows:

- Can be appointed from the age of 18, and retire at 70;
- Are volunteers, and there are around 23,000 from all walks of life;
- Do not need legal qualifications (they are assisted in court by a legal adviser);
- Must be available to carry out at least 26 half-day court sittings a year;
- Although unpaid, can claim expenses, typically for travel to and from court.

Candidates must satisfy the following six criteria:

- Good character;

- Understanding and communication;
- Social awareness;
- Maturity and sound temperament;
- Sound judgement;
- Commitment and reliability.

Because of the need to maintain public confidence in the impartiality of the judiciary, people who work in certain occupations, for example, police officers, cannot become magistrates.

Preparation and Training

Before deciding whether or not to apply, you need to visit a magistrates' court to observe the magistrates sitting.

You will need to visit at least once but preferably two or three times when it is sitting in general session, in the 12 months before you apply. Once they have been selected, all magistrates take the judicial oath—the same oath as that taken by judges.

They are trained before starting to hear cases and throughout their careers as magistrates, and are appraised regularly.

Time and Money

Magistrates need to be able to commit at least 26 half-days per year to sit in court. Employers are required by law to grant reasonable time off work for magistrates.

Magistrates are not paid for their services. However, many employers allow time off with pay for magistrates. If you do suffer loss of earnings you may claim a loss allowance at a set rate. You can also claim allowances for travel and subsistence.

Appointments and Diversity

Judicial Appointments Commission

The Judicial Appointments Commission (JAC) is an independent commission that selects candidates for judicial office in courts and tribunals in England and Wales, and for some tribunals whose jurisdiction extends to Scotland or Northern Ireland.

It selects candidates for judicial office on merit, through fair and open competition, from the widest range of eligible candidates.

The JAC was set up in order to maintain and strengthen judicial independence by taking responsibility for selecting candidates for judicial office out of the hands of the Lord Chancellor and making the appointments process clearer and more accountable. The composition of the JAC is set out in Schedule 12 of the Constitutional Reform Act 2005. There are 15 Commissioners, including the Chairman. Commissioners serve for terms up to five years.

Under the terms of the Constitutional Reform Act 2005, 12 Commissioners including the Chairman are appointed through open competition and three are nominated by the Judges' Council.

Full Diversity Statement

The Lord Chief Justice and the Senior President of Tribunals are convinced of the benefits of a more diverse judiciary and are committed to supporting the development of the judiciary in ways that support greater diversity.

Appointment to judicial office is based solely on merit. The independent JAC must, therefore, be able to select from the widest pool of candidates; and potential applicants must be assured that they will not be disadvantaged by factors such as ethnic origin, gender, disability, sexual orientation or background. They must also be confident that they will be treated fairly after appointment.

The judiciary is therefore committed, not only to encouraging suitable applicants to apply, but also to ensuring that principles of equality and fair treatment apply to all aspects of judicial life. It will therefore have regard to diversity in connection with deployment decisions wherever possible. It is also committed to developing the concept of a judicial career, as envisaged by the independent Advisory Panel on Judicial Diversity chaired by Baroness Neuberger in 2010 (the Neuberger Panel).

Much has already been achieved, including the implementation of many of the recommendations of the Neuberger Panel. The judiciary has long been engaged in an extensive range of activities, many of which are undertaken by judges in their own time, to inform the public about the role of a judge, to improve public confidence in the justice system and to encourage people from non-traditional backgrounds to consider the possibility of a judicial career. The judiciary is continuing to support this work within the resources available and with the goodwill of the individual judges involved.

There is further work to be done. The Lord Chief Justice and the Senior President of Tribunals have therefore commissioned a strategy for encouraging diversity within the judiciary of England and Wales. This will be developed by the Judicial Diversity Committee of the Judges' Council chaired by the Lord Chief Justice.

The direction and purpose of the judicial diversity strategy will be threefold. First, it will be aimed at serving office-holders, supporting those who wish to progress to the more senior levels of the judiciary; at the legal professions, encouraging suitable applicants from all backgrounds to consider applying for judicial office; and at law students and others who may be considering a career in legal practice and have the potential to become the judges of the future. Second, it will remind all judicial office-holders of their responsibilities for promoting diversity, both within their courts and tribunals, and as part of their outreach to the wider community. Third, it will support the work of informing the general public about the role of a judicial office-holder and the justice system so as to improve their understanding of and confidence in the rule of law.

The Neuberger Panel recognized that change must be implemented as a comprehensive package of reform, involving not just the Lord Chancellor, the Lord Chief Justice and the Chairman of the Judicial Appointments commission, but also the leaders of the legal profession (Bar Council, Law Society, and Chartered Institute of Legal Executives [CILEx]) and the Senior President of Tribunals. Responsibility for delivering change rests with these authorities acting individually and cumulatively. They must work together effectively if real progress is to be made.

The Diversity Committee, which is supported by staff in the Judicial Office, will report annually to the Judges' Council and to the Judicial Executive Board, the Senior President of Tribunals and the Tribunals Judicial Executive Board. Reports will include an overview of the costs of diversity initiatives (e.g. the work of the DCRJs). Progress will be measured not simply by improvements to the overall diversity figures for the judiciary but also through analysis of data on trends and through the sharing of qualitative information collected from the Diversity Task Force and other sources. The strategy will be reviewed annually and reissued as appropriate.

What to Call a Judge?

The forms of address for judges vary from court to court, and some of them can seem quite archaic in the modern world. Here is a guide explaining what to call a judge, magistrate or member of a tribunal when you are speaking or writing to them.

Address (in Correspondence)	**Dear…**	**In court**
The Right Honourable The Lord Chief Justice of England and Wales	Lord Chief Justice/Chief Justice	My Lord or My Lady
The Right Honourable The Master of the Rolls	Master of the Rolls	
The Right Honourable The President of the Queen's Bench Division	President	
The Right Honourable The President of the Family Division	President	
The Right Honourable The Chancellor of the High Court	Chancellor	
Retired Head of Division	Title in Private Capacity	N/A

Court of Appeal's Judges

Judges who sit in the Court of Appeal (Lords Justices of Appeal) are Privy Councilors. They are known officially as Lord Justices. They should be addressed as follows:

Address (in Correspondence)	Dear...	In court
The Right Honourable Lord Justice Wells	Lord Justice	My Lord
The Right Honourable Lady Justice Wells DBE	Lady Justice	My Lady

High Court Judges

Members of the High Court are not usually Privy Councilors. Their official designation is as follows:

Office/Position	Address (in correspondence)	Dear...	In court
High Court Judge	The Honourable Mr Justice Wicksteed	Judge	My Lord
High Court Judge	The Honourable Mrs/Ms Justice Wicksteed (whether married or single)	Judge	My Lady

High Court Masters & Registrars

Office/Position	Address (in correspondence)	Dear...	In court
Master	Master Holman (whether male or female)	Master	Master
Registrar	Mr (or Mrs) Registrar Holman	Registrar	Registrar

Circuit Judges

Some Circuit Judges, for example, The Recorder of Liverpool or Central Criminal Court judges, are referred to as "My Lord" or "My Lady".

Address (in correspondence)	Dear...	In court
His Honour Judge Williams (QC if appropriate)	Judge	Your Honour
Her Honour Judge Williams (QC if appropriate)	Judge	Your Honour

District Judges

Address (in correspondence)	Dear...	In court
District Judge Pennington	Judge	Sir or Madam

District Judges (Magistrates' Courts)

Address (in correspondence)	Dear...	In court
District Judge (Magistrates' Courts) Tuff	Judge	Sir or Madam

Magistrates

Dear...	In court
John Curry, Esq JP	Your Worship, or Sir or Madam

Tribunal Judges

Address (in correspondence)	Dear...	In court
First-tier Tribunal Judge/Upper Tribunal Judge (depending on position) Curry	Judge	Sir or Madam

Employment Judges

Address (in correspondence)	Dear...	In court
Employment Judge Collins	Judge	Sir or Madam

Court Dress

Court dress is a style of clothing worn by those in the legal profession when they are working in their official capacity. Though the exact style varies among different levels of the judicial system, long robes are a common basis of court dress. The style and color of the robes, as well as various accessories such as wigs or medallions, have all gone in and out of fashion throughout history.

New Judicial Robes

In July 2007 the Lord Chief Justice announced reforms to simplify judicial court working dress in England and Wales. The changes, which included the introduction of a new civil gown, came into effect on 1 October 2008. Fashion designer Betty Jackson CBE worked on a pro bono basis as the design consultant for the new gown.

Criminal Jurisdiction

From 1 October 2008 High Court judges adopted a single set of red robes for criminal proceedings throughout the year, rather than different sets of robes for summer and winter. Apart from this there was no change to court dress worn by judges when sitting in criminal proceedings.

Civil and Family Jurisdiction—The New Civil Robe

Court of Appeal and High Court judges no longer wear wigs, wing collars and bands when sitting in open court in civil and family proceedings; the new civil robe is worn.

Circuit judges in the County Courts or the Crown Court wear a violet robe with lilac facings, introduced in 1919. As well as a girdle, the judges wear a tippet over the left shoulder—lilac when dealing with civil business and red when dealing with crime.

Since autumn 2008, circuit judges in the County Court have not worn wigs, wing collars or bands; however, circuit judges in the Crown Court retain the wig, wing collars and bands.

In civil and family hearings in open court, all other judges wear the new civil gown.

The design favoured by a judicial working group incorporates coloured bands to identify seniority. The chosen colours are:

- Heads of Division and Appeal Court judges—gold
- High Court judges—red
- District judges—blue
- Masters and Registrars—pink

Financial Implications

These changes were reflected in the dress allowances made to judges and substantial savings resulted. Whilst the one-off cost of supplying the new civil robe to judges was estimated at about 450,000 it was anticipated that annual savings in the region of 200,000 would thereafter be made.

Legal Professionals—Who Does What?

There are several different types of legal professionals, who can help you in different ways. This section provides a brief overview of the main duties and differences between legal professionals in England and Wales.

Arbitrator and Mediator

Arbitration and mediation are non-judicial and alternative ways to resolve disputes, without going to court. Arbitrators and mediators are neutral, which means they will not take sides and cannot provide advice. They are often experts in the field of what the dispute is about, and will reach a decision after hearing from both sides of the dispute.

Barrister

Barristers are legal advisers and courtroom advocates. Barristers put legal arguments to judges, magistrates and juries. They cross-examine witnesses and otherwise attempt to sway the outcome of a court case. Barristers typically have no direct contact with the public. They appear in court when instructed by a solicitor. Only barristers or qualified solicitor advocates may represent clients in the higher courts. Barristers are highly trained courtroom advocates, dealing with the majority of serious and high profile court cases.

Judge

Both solicitors and barristers may be appointed as judges. Judges decide legal cases in certain circumstances or, if a trial involves a jury, judges rule over the proceedings to ensure fairness and that the jury has arrived at their decision in the correct way. The Judicial Appointments Commission selects candidates for judicial office on merit.

Law Costs Draftsman

Law costs draftsmen ensure that a firm's clients are properly charged for work undertaken on the clients' behalf. They also help apportion costs between the two sets of legal advisers at the end of long and complex cases. In some instances, they represent clients in court when there is an issue over costs.

Legal Cashier

Legal cashiers usually work in solicitors' practices. They keep financial records and keep solicitors informed of the financial position of the firm.

Legal Executive

A chartered legal executive can work in a legal office and has the option to later qualify as a solicitor through further vocational training. Fully qualified chartered legal executive lawyers can have their own clients and represent them in court, where appropriate. The main difference between solicitors and legal executives is that the training of legal executives is narrower. Legal executives have studied to the same level as a solicitor, but they have specialised in a particular area of law and completed fewer subjects overall.

Legal Secretary

Legal secretaries provide secretarial and clerical support to solicitors, barristers and the law courts. They deal with large quantities of correspondence and help prepare documents such as wills, divorce petitions and witness statements. Legal secretaries are specialists because legal documents are composed differently from other commercial documents. Positions can usually be found by contacting firms directly or checking with local recruitment agencies.

Notary

Notaries are qualified lawyers appointed by the Archbishop of Canterbury and regulated by the Master of the Faculties. Notaries practice under rules very similar to those of solicitors', including renewing a practicing certificate, keeping client money separate and maintaining insurance. Notaries authenticate and certify signatures and documents, and often also practice as solicitors.

Paralegal

Paralegals assist lawyers in their work. They undertake some of the same work as lawyers but do not give advice to consumers of legal services.

The paralegal is a relatively modern phenomenon in British legal circles. The role has transferred across from the U.S. where paralegals have operated in a support role in law firms for many years.

The duties of a paralegal will vary according to the type of firm and practice area that is worked in. Generic paralegal tasks may include research and drafting documents, attending client meetings and document management. They might prepare reports to help lawyers prepare their case. Some paralegals help to write contracts and mortgages and some help to prepare income tax returns and other financial documents.

Firms usually look for law graduates or non-law graduates who have completed the Common Professional Examination or Graduate Diploma in Law to fill paralegal roles. Some of the larger firms, however, will look for graduates who have also passed the Legal Practice Course.

Paralegal vacancies are generally not well advertised so a good approach is to submit your CV to firms or organizations which you are interested in working for. Publications such as the *Law Society Gazette* run advertisements for these positions.

Solicitor

Solicitors work in many different areas of law and offer many different services. Solicitors are confidential advisers and will often have direct contact with their clients, providing expert legal advice and assistance in a range of situations.

Everyday issues solicitors deal with include:

- providing expert guidance on the issues people regularly face such as buying and selling houses, drawing up wills, and dealing with relationship breakdown;
- promoting business, by helping businesses with the legal side of commercial transactions;
- protecting the rights of individuals by advising people of their rights, ensuring they are treated fairly by public or private bodies, and that they receive compensation when they have been unfairly treated;
- supporting the community by undertaking legal aid work or spending a portion of their time providing free help for those unable to pay for legal services;
- representing clients personally in the lower courts (Magistrates' courts, County Court and tribunals) and with specialist training are also able to represent them in higher courts (Crown Court, High Court, Court of Appeal and the Supreme Court).

The Law Society represents, promotes and supports solicitors in England and Wales.

Usher

Ushers' duties include escorting judges to and from court and preparing and closing courtrooms. A large part of the job is the carrying out of court duties, which includes obtaining names of legal representatives, preparing court lists, maintaining order in the courtroom, administering oaths in court, and handing round exhibits.

Legal Publishers

There have been major changes in legal publishing in recent years. The venerable legal publisher Butterworths has been incorporated into LexisNexis, and the print publishing greatly reduced, academic titles having been sold on to Oxford University Press and many practitioners' titles to Tottel Publishing; Tottel has since been acquired by Bloomsbury and changed its name to Bloomsbury Professional. The other main UK legal publisher, Sweet & Maxwell owned by Thomson Reuters, continues to have an extensive print list.

Other law publishers include Hart, now part of Bloomsbury Publishing; Routledge, owned by Taylor and Francis; Cambridge University Press; Jordan; Palgrave Macmillan; and Wiley.

The leading specialist law publisher for Scotland is W. Green, owned by Thomson Reuters. Some of the UK publishers mentioned above also publish Scottish law titles.

SLS Legal Publications, based at Queen's University, Belfast, was a small publisher specializing in Northern Irish law, but closed at the end of 2012. Books on the law of Northern Ireland are published by Bloomsbury, Hart and other UK publishers.

Case Law Reporting

The modern system of case law reporting in the UK dates from 1865. Listed below are the contemporary UK case law reporters that researchers are most likely to encounter, along with their corresponding citation formats.

The Law Reports. This quasi-official series, published since 1865 by the Incorporated Council of Law Reporting (ICLR) for England and Wales, is widely regarded as the most authoritative. It is currently divided into four sub-series. Appeal Cases (AC) publishes decisions of the Supreme Court and the Court of Appeal, as well as appellate decisions issued by the High Court. The remaining sub-series correspond to the three divisions of the High Court: Chancery Division Cases (Ch); Queen's Bench Division Cases (QB); and Family Division Cases (Fam). The citation format is as follows: party names, [year], sub-series abbreviation, page.

The Weekly Law Reports. This series, also published by the ICLR, appears each week in paperback. The first section of each issue includes cases that are deemed to be worth reporting even though they do not raise new points of law. These cases will not be republished in *The Law Reports*. The second section includes cases of greater significance that eventually will be republished in *The Law Reports*. The citation format is: party names, [year], section number (1 or 2), WLR, page.

All England Law Reports. This commercially published series has broader coverage than *The Law Reports* and *The Weekly Law Reports*. Most practitioners consider the headnotes to be more helpful than the ones published in *The Law Reports*. The citation format is: party names, [year], All ER, page.

In addition to the reporters listed above, there are many specialized reporters published by commercial vendors that focus on particular types of cases. As in the United States, cases often are published in more than one reporter. Citations should be made to most authoritative reporter in which a case appears, with a clear preference given to *The Law Reports*.

Exercises

I. Fill in the gaps with the appropriate words or phrases given in the box.

> A. law   B. specialist   C. advocates   D. barristers
> E. distinction   F. advocacy   G. monopoly
> H. Solicitors Regulation Authority   I. the Bar Standards Board
> J. legal

There are essentially two main branches of the legal profession—solicitors and 1_____. Solicitors, governed by the 2_____, advise individuals and organizations on 3_____ matters and ensure that their clients act in accordance with the 4_____. Barristers, governed by 5_____, represent clients in court and give 6_____ opinions on complex legal matters. The 7_____ between solicitors and barristers is not as clear-cut as it once was. Following the Court and Legal Services Act 1990 solicitors have the right to become certified 8_____ (i.e. represent clients in court). Although solicitors are taking on a more active 9_____ role in the lower courts, barristers still maintain an unrivalled 10_____ over the higher courts.

II. Choose the appropriate answer(s) to each question. There may be more than one choice for some questions.

1. Which of the following requirements are essential for those candidates who are intent to become a barrister?

    A. eloquence and persuasiveness

    B. excellent articulation

    C. confidence

    D. an analytical mind

2. In the sentence that "the final hurdle before a student can qualify as a solicitor or barrister is to secure a training contract or *pupillage*", the italic word "pupillage" means_____.

    A. a minority

    B. the condition of being a pupil or duration for which one is a pupil in primary school

    C. in England and Wales, Northern Ireland and Ireland, the barrister's equivalent of the training contract that a solicitor undertakes

    D. similar to an apprenticeship, during which students build on what they have learnt during the Bar Professional Training Course by combining it with practical work experience in a set of barristers' chambers

3. Which of the following is NOT true for the legal education in the UK?

    A. Many UK students study law as undergraduates, earning an LL.B. or a B.A.

    B. The United Kingdom still maintains a distinction between barristers and solicitors.

    C. Solicitors and barristers pursue different training periods before qualifying for independent practice after the requisite academic and vocational courses.

D. Top universities confer LL.Ms and some offer these training courses.

4. Which of the following are NOT true about judges in the UK?

   A. There is no upper or lower age limit for candidates for judges, apart from the statutory retirement age of 70 for all judges.

   B. The Judicial Appointments Commission selects candidates for judicial office on merit.

   C. Both solicitors and barristers may be appointed as judges.

   D. Tribunal judges need have been solicitors or barristers.

5. Which of the following are true about different types of legal professionals in England and Wales?

   A. Arbitration and mediation are non-judicial and alternative ways to resolve disputes, without going to court.

   B. Paralegals assist lawyers in their work, the role of which has transferred across from the U.S.

   C. Notaries are qualified lawyers appointed by the Archbishop of Canterbury and regulated by the Master of the Faculties. Notaries practice under rules very similar to those of solicitors'.

   D. The main difference between solicitors and legal executives is that the training of legal executives is narrower.

III. Questions

1. What are the differences and similarities between being a barrister and being a solicitor in the UK?
2. What are the basic requirements for becoming a judge in the UK?
3. What criteria should a candidate for a magistrate satisfy in the UK?
4. What do you know about how to call a judge in court?
5. How is the legal profession divided in the UK?

Chapter 3
GOVERNING STRUCTURE

The United Kingdom is a constitutional monarchy with a parliamentary system of governance. Under the uncodified British constitution, executive authority lies with the monarch, although this authority is exercised only by, or on the advice of, the prime minister and the cabinet. The prime minister leads the government and selects all the remaining ministers, most senior ministers of whom belong to the cabinet.

The UK Parliament is the supreme legislative body in the United Kingdom, British Crown dependencies and British overseas territories. It alone possesses legislative supremacy and thereby ultimate power over all other political bodies in the UK and its territories. The government ministers all sit in Parliament, and are accountable to it. The government is dependent on Parliament to make primary legislation.

Until quite recently, the UK's governing structure has been characterized by a high degree of centralization, with power concentrated in Parliament, the national legislature that meets in London. Since 1999, however, some legislative powers have been devolved to a new Scottish Parliament sitting in Edinburgh, a new Welsh Assembly, sitting in Cardiff, and a new Northern Ireland Assembly, sitting in Belfast. Further movement toward a more decentralized governing structure is likely, but a shift to a fully federal system would be difficult to achieve due to the fact that England accounts for nearly 85 percent of the UK's population.

Legislative Authority

Parliament consists of an elected lower chamber, the House of Commons, and an unelected upper chamber, the House of Lords. In the past, the right to sit in the House of Lords was restricted to those who held hereditary titles, known as peerages, and to senior bishops of the Church of England. Today, most members of the House of Lords are life peers, appointed by the monarch on the advice of the prime minister and an independent commission, whose titles are not inherited.

How (Most) Laws Are Made

Most new laws passed by Parliament result from proposals made by the government. Proposals aim to shape society or address particular problems. Normally, they are created over a period of time.

An issue or problem emerges on the government's agenda

Initially, a government's agenda is informed by the general election. Political parties compete for support from British voters by campaigning on their vision for the country and how they would change things. The political party that wins then forms the government, and bases its legislative agenda on its election manifesto. However, where no single political party decisively wins the election—as happened in 2010—two or more parties may form a coalition government. They may have to negotiate a joint vision and agree on which new laws to champion in the upcoming parliament.

Once in government, other events and influences also compete for ministers' attention. Unexpected crises, such as an act of terrorism or a natural disaster, may require an urgent response. The UK's European Union commitments can lead to new legislation. Campaigning by special interest groups, private citizens or other politicians—often through the media—may raise the profile of particular causes or problems. More widely, the media's reporting on issues, government and Parliament all inform and influence Britain's political agenda.

Ideas for addressing an issue are considered

Identifying an issue is one thing. Deciding what to do about it is another. Proposals for addressing particular goals or problems may come from a variety of sources. The political party is one. Governing and opposition parties are expected to have policies on a range of issues, such as taxation, health and education. Recommendations for new laws may also come from public inquiries, civil servants or lobbyist and campaign groups. No matter where a policy idea originates, it normally won't get far without the backing of a government minister. This is because ministers are in a position to champion an idea to government colleagues.

Interested people and groups are consulted

Even a minister's backing, however, isn't enough to guarantee an idea will find its way to Parliament and become a law. Ministers normally—where time allows—shape and inform their proposals by consulting with experts, interest groups and people likely to be affected by the plans. Often, these interested parties are asked to comment on a "green paper"—an initial outline of an idea. Sometimes a "white paper" will be produced, which is a firmer statement of the government's intentions.

Cabinet ministers must agree which proposals to take forward

Having consulted on a proposal, government ministers then aim to persuade colleagues to support the idea. The merits of various policies are debated in cabinet committees, made up of ministers from across government and chaired by a senior member of the cabinet. Even with approval from a cabinet committee, a proposal must still be selected by the committee responsible for drawing up the government's legislative programme. The Legislation Committee makes the final decision as to whether a proposal will be presented to Parliament for scrutiny by MPs and peers.

Proposals are made into "bills"

After a proposal is consulted on and approved by the cabinet, the minister responsible draws up instructions for what should go into the bill. Highly specialised lawyers—called parliamentary counsel—work to translate the principles outlined in the government's proposal into detailed legislation.

All the bills the government intends to introduce in a parliamentary session are announced in the Queen's (or King's) Speech—the main feature of the near-yearly State Opening that opens each new session of Parliament.

Parliament Considers and Scrutinizes Bills

The Houses of Parliament consider proposals, called bills, most of which are introduced by the government. To become law, a bill must be approved by both MPs in the House of Commons and peers in the House of Lords. Bills go through a very similar process in both Houses.

Parliamentary Stages

A bill may begin its journey in either the Lords or the Commons chambers. Any bills that relate to taxation begin in the House of Commons.

First Reading

The bill's title is simply read out in the chamber. The bill is then made available to all members of Parliament.

Second Reading

MPs or peers discuss the main principles of a bill. MPs may vote at the end of this stage, particularly if a bill is controversial. A bill in the House of Lords passes to the next stage without a vote.

Committee Stage

A bill is then considered, line by line, by committees of MPs or peers. Changes—called amendments—are proposed and voted on. Commons bill committees normally consist of around 20 MPs. The entire House of Lords often takes part at this stage.

Report Stage

The bill, with amendments or changes, is "reported" to the House. All members can review the amended bill. Those not involved at the previous stage may suggest further changes.

Third Reading

MPs debate and vote on the bill in its final form. In the House of Lords, further amendments may still be introduced.

A Bill Approved by One Chamber Is Considered by the Other

If a bill begins in the House of Commons—and is approved—it is then sent to the House of Lords, where it goes through the same stages. If the Lords were to make changes to the bill, it would return to the Commons for MPs to consider the Lords' amendments. Both the Commons and Lords must agree on the final shape of a bill before it can become law.

The Monarch's "Assent" Turns a Bill into an Act

With approval from the Lords and the Commons, a bill will also receive formal approval by the monarch—called "Royal Assent". The Monarch always gives their approval on the advice of ministers. A bill then becomes law, and is described as an Act of Parliament.

The House of Lords serves primarily as a venue for scrutinizing and refining proposed legislation. The Lords no longer have the power to block revenue bills, and their ability to reject other types of bills supported by a majority of the House of Commons is limited.

Executive Authority

A cabinet-style government, formed by whichever party (or coalition of parties) commands a majority in the House of Commons, and wields executive power at the national level in the UK.

The head of the national government, known as the prime minister, is the leader of the largest party in the House of Commons. The prime minister appoints the other members of the cabinet, as well as sub-cabinet officials known as ministers.

Most government ministers are members of the House of Commons affiliated with the same political party as the prime minister, but members of the House of Lords also may serve as ministers.

The national government exercises its authority in the name of the sovereign, a hereditary monarch who serves as the head of state, a role that is largely, though not entirely, ceremonial. The current monarch is Queen Elizabeth II.

Judicial Authority

England and Wales share a unified court system, based on common law principles, which originated in medieval England. Scotland and Northern Ireland each have their own judicial systems.

The court system in Northern Ireland closely resembles that of England and Wales, while the Scottish court system is a hybrid model that combines elements of both common law and civil law systems.

The Court System of England & Wales

In England and Wales, most civil cases are heard in the County Court. Many specialist tribunals have been created to resolve particular types of civil disputes, such as those involving taxation and employment, as well as immigration and asylum cases. All criminal cases originate in the Magistrates' Court, but more serious offenses are referred to the Crown Court.

The High Court functions as both a court of first instance for high value civil claims and as an appellate court for civil and criminal cases. It consists of three divisions: the Queen's Bench, the Chancery Division, and the Family Division.

The Court of Appeal functions solely as an appellate chamber. The Civil

Division hears appeals from the High Court and the County Court, and the Criminal Division hears appeals from the Crown Court.

The Supreme Court of the United Kingdom is the final court of appeal for all UK civil cases and for criminal cases that originate in England, Wales, and Northern Ireland. The Supreme Court consists of 12 permanent justices appointed by the Lord Chancellor, a member of the cabinet, at the recommendation of an independent commission.

Prior to the creation of the Supreme Court in 2009, final appeals were heard by the Appellate Committee of the House of Lords (usually referred to as "the Law Lords"), a panel of 12 senior judges appointed to sit as members of the upper chamber of Parliament.

The primary impetus for the creation of an institutionally separate Supreme Court was to provide a clearer separation of powers between the legislative and judicial branches of government.

The tribunals system has its own structure for dealing with cases and appeals, but decisions from different chambers of the Upper Tribunal and the Employment Appeals

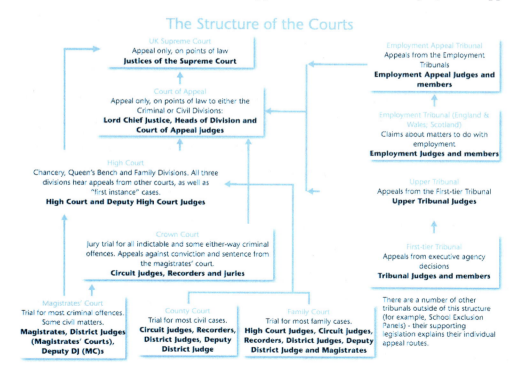

Tribunal may also go to the Court of Appeal.

The diagrams in the link below shows the routes taken by different cases as they go through the courts system, and which judges deal with each.

Tribunals Organisation Chart

The tribunals system covers England, Wales, and in some cases Northern Ireland and Scotland.

UK Constitutional Law

The United Kingdom has never had a written constitution embodied in a single document. The foundational constitutional text for what is now the UK is the Magna Carta issued by King John of England in 1215. Since then, the constitution has evolved organically over time in response to political, economic, and social changes.

The present constitution encompasses both statutory law and landmark judicial opinions, as well as many conventions or unwritten rules of constitutional practice. For example, the residual powers of the monarch and the relationship between the monarch and Parliament are still governed largely by these unwritten but nevertheless binding conventions.

Constitutional law in the UK has undergone significant changes during the past 20 years. Key developments include the incorporation of the European Convention on Human Rights into UK law via the Human Rights Act of 1998, the establishment of devolved legislatures in three of the UK's four constituent nations in 1999(To distinguish it from these new legislatures the United Kingdom Parliament in London is often referred to as "Westminster".), a partial reform of the House of Lords in 2000, and the introduction of a Supreme Court in 2009.

The Scottish independence referendum, held in September of 2014, and the Brexit referendum, held in June of 2016, have strengthened the case for further constitutional reform, with many observers arguing that only a more decentralized, if not a fully federal, system of government can preserve the UK as a unified political entity.

The Ministry of Justice is the government department responsible for the justice system and for certain aspects of constitutional policy. Its head is the Lord Chancellor and Secretary of State for Justice. The Ministry's predecessor was the Department for Constitutional Affairs, which had itself superseded the Lord Chancellor's Department. The Cabinet Office is responsible for many areas of constitutional policy, including devolution, elections and the royal succession.

Features of Britain's Unwritten Constitution

There are a number of associated characteristics of Britain's unwritten constitution, a cardinal one being that in law Parliament is sovereign in the sense of being the supreme legislative body. Since there is no documentary constitution containing laws that are fundamental in status and superior to ordinary Acts of Parliament, the courts may only interpret parliamentary statutes. They may not overrule or declare them invalid for being contrary to the constitution and "unconstitutional". So, too, there are no entrenched procedures (such as a special power of the House of Lords, or the requirement of a referendum) by which the unwritten constitution may be amended. The legislative process by which a constitutional law is repealed, amended or enacted, even one dealing with a matter of fundamental political importance, is similar in kind to any other Act of Parliament, however trivial its subject matter.

Another characteristic of the unwritten constitution is the special significance of political customs known as "conventions", which oil the wheels of the relationship between the ancient institutions of state. These are unwritten rules of constitutional practice, vital to politics, the workings of government, but not committed into law or any written form at all. The very existence of the office of Prime Minister, the head of government, is purely conventional. So is the rule upon which he or she is appointed, being whoever commands the confidence of the House of Commons (the majority party leader, or head of a coalition of parties).

The Monarchy is one of the three components of Parliament (shorthand for the Queen-in-Parliament) along with Commons and Lords. In legal theory, the Queen has absolute and judicially unchallengeable power to refuse her assent to a Bill passed by the two Houses of Parliament. However, convention dictates the precise opposite and in practice she automatically gives her assent to any government Bill that has been duly passed and agreed by Parliament. Another important convention is that government ministers must have a seat in Parliament (and, in the case of the Prime Minister and Chancellor of the Exchequer, specifically in the House of Commons) in order to hold office. This is a vital aspect of what is known as the "Westminster system of parliamentary government", providing a direct form of executive responsibility and accountability to the legislature.

Constitutional Reform

The Lord Chancellor's role changed dramatically on 3 April 2006, as a result of the Constitutional Reform Act 2005. For the first time in almost 900 years, judicial independence is now officially enshrined in law.

The key changes brought in by the act include:

> A duty on government ministers to uphold the independence of the judiciary, barring them from trying to influence judicial decisions through any special access to judges;

> Reform of the post of Lord Chancellor, transferring his judicial functions to the President of the Courts of England and Wales—a new title given to the Lord Chief Justice. The Lord Chief Justice is now responsible for the training, guidance and deployment of judges and represents the views of the judiciary of England and Wales to Parliament and ministers;

> An independent Supreme Court has been established, separate from the House of Lords and with its own independent appointments system, staff, budget and building;

> An independent Judicial Appointments Commission, responsible for selecting candidates to recommend for judicial appointment to the Secretary of State for Justice. The Judicial Appointments Commission ensures that merit remains the

sole criterion for appointment and the appointments system is modern, open and transparent;

➢ An Judicial Appointments and Conduct Ombudsman, responsible for investigating and making recommendations concerning complaints about the judicial appointments process, and the handling of judicial conduct complaints within the scope of the Constitutional Reform Act.

What has not changed is the way judgments are made or given; after all, judges have been independent in the way they work for centuries.

The real differences are in the day-to-day management of the judiciary, the way judges are appointed and the way complaints are dealt with. These are now truly independent, to enhance accountability, public confidence and effectiveness.

Tribunals Reform

The Tribunals Service was created on 3 April 2006, and brought together the administration of a large number of individual tribunals, resulting in a more common and consistent approach for users.

On November 3, 2008, the Tribunals, Courts and Enforcement Act came into force.

This created a new two-tier Tribunal system: a First-tier Tribunal and an Upper Tribunal, both of which are split into Chambers. Each Chamber comprises similar jurisdictions or bring together similar types of experts to hear appeals.

These new super tribunals absorbed over 20 existing smaller tribunals as well as providing a structure to which new appeal rights could be assigned.

Exercises

I. Choose the appropriate answer(s) to each question. There may be more than one choice for some questions.

1. Which of the following is NOT true about the legislative authority in the UK?

    A. The UK's governing structure has been characterized by a high degree of centralization, with power concentrated in Parliament, the national legislature.

    B. Parliament consists of an elected lower chamber, the House of Commons, and an unelected upper chamber, the House of Lords.

    C. Some members of the House of Lords are life peers who held hereditary titles.

    D. Most members of the House of Lords are appointed by the monarch on the advice of the prime minister and an independent commission.

2. Which of the following is NOT true about the executive authority in the UK?

    A. A cabinet-style government, formed by whichever party (or coalition of parties) commands a majority in the House of Commons, wields executive power at the national level in the UK.

    B. The prime minister, the leader of the largest party in the House of Commons, appoints the other members of the cabinet, as well as sub-cabinet officials known as ministers.

    C. Most government ministers are members of the House of Lords.

    D. The national government exercises its authority in the name of the sovereign, a hereditary monarch who serves as the head of state.

3. Which of the following are true about the judicial authority in the UK?

    A. England and Wales share a unified court system, based on common law principles, which originated in medieval England.

    B. Scotland and Northern Ireland have different judicial systems.

    C. The court system in Northern Ireland closely resembles that of England and Wales.

    D. The Scottish court system is a hybrid model that combines elements of both common law and civil law systems.

4. Which of the following are true about the proposal in the law-making process?

    A. The Legislation Committee makes the final decision as to whether a proposal will be presented to Parliament for scrutiny by MPs and peers.

    B. Proposals for addressing particular goals or problems may come from political parties.

C. Ministers normally shape and inform their proposals by consulting with experts, interest groups and people likely to be affected by the plans.

D. It normally won't get far without the backing of a government minister.

5. Which of the following is NOT true about the bill in the law-making process?

   A. After a proposal is consulted on and approved by the cabinet, the minister responsible draws up instructions for what should go into the bill.

   B. Parliamentary counsel work to translate the principles outlined in the government's proposal into detailed legislation.

   C. To become law, a bill must be approved by both MPs in the House of Commons and peers in the House of Lords.

   D. Any bills may begin their journey in either the Lords or the Commons chambers.

6. In England and Wales, most civil cases are heard in the_____.

   A. county courts

   B. High Court

   C. family courts

   D. magistrates' courts

7. The courts in which only appeals are heard are_____.

   A. Court of Appeal

   B. High Court

   C. Crown Court

   D. Supreme Court

8. The courts that exercise both first instance and appellate jurisdiction are _____.

   A. Court of Appeal

   B. High Court

   C. Crown Court

   D. Magistrates' courts

9. _____ may deal with both civil and criminal cases.

   A. Court of Appeal

   B. High Court

   C. Crown Court

   D. Magistrates' courts

10. All criminal cases commence in the _____, but not all cases are tried there.

    A. county courts

    B. High Court

    C. Crown Court

    D. magistrates' courts

11. Which of the following is NOT true about the tribunals system in the UK?

    A. The tribunals system has its own structure for dealing with cases and appeals.

    B. Many specialist tribunals resolve particular types of civil disputes, such as those involving taxation and employment.

    C. Decisions from different chambers of the Upper Tribunal and the Employment Appeals Tribunal may also go to the Court of Appeal.

    D. The tribunals system doesn't cover Northern Ireland and Scotland.

II. Questions

1. What do you know about the British Parliament?

2. What is the legislative process in the UK?

3. Can you tell the difference between a "Bill" and an "Act of Parliament"?

4. What are the five distinct procedures when a Bill is introduced in the House of Commons?

5. Can you summarize the executive authority in the UK?

6. What do you know about the court system of England and Wales?

7. What are the features of Britain's unwritten constitution?

Chapter 4
JUSTICE SYSTEM

The Supreme Court

The Constitutional Reform Act 2005 made provision for the creation of a new Supreme Court for the United Kingdom.

There had been mounting calls for the creation of a new free-standing Supreme Court separating the highest appeal court from the second house of Parliament, and removing the Lords of Appeal in Ordinary from the legislature. On 12 June 2003 the Government announced its intention to do so.

Before the Supreme Court was created, the 12 most senior judges—the Lords of Appeal in Ordinary, or Law Lords as they were often called—sat in the House of Lords.

The House of Lords was the highest court in the land—the supreme court of appeal. It acted as the final court on points of law for the whole of the United Kingdom in civil cases and for England, Wales and Northern Ireland in criminal cases. Its decisions bound all courts below.

As members of the House of Lords, the judges not only heard cases, but were also able to become involved in debating and the subsequent enactment of Government legislation (although, in practice, they rarely did so).

The creation of a new Supreme Court means that the most senior judges are now entirely separate from the Parliamentary process.

It is important to be aware that the new Supreme Court is a United Kingdom body, legally separate from the England and Wales courts as it is also the Supreme Court of both Scotland and Northern Ireland. As such, it falls outside of the remit of the Lord Chief Justice of England and Wales in his role as head of the judiciary of England and Wales.

The new Supreme Court opened for business in October 2009, at the start of the legal year.

Jurisdictions

How different cases are dealt with, and which judges deal with them.

Civil

Civil Justice in England and Wales

Civil justice in England and Wales is mainly dealt with in the county courts and, in the case of more substantial or complex cases, the High Court. The jurisdiction covers a very wide range from quite small or simple claims, for example damaged goods or recovery of debt, to large claims between multi-national companies.

Civil cases involve hearings in open court which the public may attend, hearings in the judge's private room from which the public are excluded, and matters decided by the judge in private but on the basis of the papers alone.

Most civil disputes do not end up in court, and those that do often don't go to a full trial. Many are dealt with through mediation (a process taking place outside a court to resolve a dispute) or by using established complaints procedures. But where a case does go through the courts, the aim is to make it as simple as possible. For smaller claims there is a speedy and cheap way of resolving disputes—through the small claims court.

Judges in the civil jurisdiction do not have the power to imprison a losing party. Ordinarily, but not always, they award financial "damages" to the successful party, the size of which depends on the circumstances of the claim.

A Judge Hearing a Civil Case

Before trying a civil case the judge reads the relevant case papers and becomes familiar with their details.

The vast majority of civil cases tried in court do not have a jury (libel and slander trials are the main exceptions) and the judge hears them on his or her own, deciding them by finding facts, applying the relevant law to them—and there may be considerable argument about what that law actually is—and then giving a reasoned judgment.

Judges also play an active role in managing civil cases once they have started, helping to ensure they proceed as quickly and efficiently as possible.

This includes:

- encouraging the parties to cooperate with each other in the conduct of the case;
- helping the parties to settle the case;
- encouraging the parties to use an alternative dispute resolution procedure if appropriate; and
- controlling the progress of the case.

Occasionally, the parties will have agreed the relevant facts and it will not be necessary for the judge to hear any live evidence. The issues may concern the law to be applied or the terms of the judgment to be given. But more often than not, written and live evidence will be given by the parties and their witnesses and the live witnesses may be cross-examined. The judge ensures that all parties involved are given the opportunity to have their case presented and considered as fully and fairly as possible. During the case the judge will ask questions on any point he or she feels needs clarification. The judge also decides on all matters of procedure which may arise during a hearing.

Judgment

Once the judge has heard the evidence from all parties involved and any submissions (representations) they wish to put forward, he or she delivers judgment. This may be immediately, or if the case is complicated, at a later date.

Civil judges do have the power to punish parties if, for example, they are in contempt of court but, generally, civil cases do not involve the imposition of any punishment.

If the judge decides that the claimant is entitled to damages, he or she will have to go on to decide the amount. Or the claimant may have asked for an injunction—for example, to forbid the defendant from making excessive noise by playing the drums in the flat upstairs in the early hours of the morning, or a declaration—an order specifying the precise boundary between two properties about which the parties had never been able to agree. The task of the judge is to decide on what is the appropriate remedy, if any, and on the precise terms of it.

Costs

When the judgment in the case has been delivered, the judge must deal with the cost of the case. This may include the fees of any lawyers, court fees paid out by the parties, fees of expert witnesses, allowances that may be allowed to litigants who have acted in person (without lawyers), earnings lost and travelling and other expenses incurred by the parties and their witnesses. The general rule is that the unsuccessful party will have to pay the successful party's costs but the judge has a wide discretion to depart from this rule. The judge's decision on this part of the case will be very important to the parties. He or she may decide, for example, that the unsuccessful party should pay only a proportion of the successful party's costs or that each party should bear their own costs. The judge may hear representations about this at the end of the case.

Court of Appeal—Civil Division

The Civil Division of the Court of Appeal hears appeals from all Divisions of the High Court and, in some instances from the County Courts and certain tribunals. The Civil Division is presided over by the Master of the Rolls. Bringing an appeal is subject to obtaining "permission", which may be granted by the court below or, more usually, by the Court of Appeal itself. Applications for permission to appeal are commonly determined by a single Lord Justice, full appeals by two or three judges. The Civil Division of the Court Appeal also deals with family cases.

High Court—Queen's Bench Division—Civil

The President of the Queen's Bench Division presides over that Division, which includes both its criminal and civil jurisdiction. Judges who sit in the Queen's Bench Division of the High Court deal with "common law" business i.e. actions relating to contract except those specifically allocated to the Chancery Division, and civil wrongs (known as tort). They also hear more specialist matters, such as applications for judicial review.

Examples of contract cases dealt with by Queen's Bench Division judges are failure to pay for goods and service and breach of contract.

Judges who sit in the Queen's Bench Division of the High Court deal with actions relating to various different types of tort. These include:
- ➢ Wrongs against the person e.g. defamation of character and libel;
- ➢ Wrongs against property e.g. trespass;
- ➢ Wrongs which may be against people or property e.g. negligence or nuisance.

They also deal with matters that involve both contract and tort, such as personal injury cases which show negligence and breach of a contractual duty of care. Other cases dealt with may be crimes as well as torts, such as assault.

The Queen's Bench Division also contains:
- ➢ The Commercial Court;
- ➢ The Admiralty Courts; and administers;
- ➢ The Technology and Construction Court.

High Court judges who sit in these courts hear cases involving prolonged examination of technical issues, for example, construction disputes.

Judges of the Queen's Bench Division also sit in the Employment Appeals Tribunal.

High Court—Chancery Division

The Chancery Division is a Division of the High Court of Justice. The Division is headed by the Chancellor of the High Court, the Right Honourable Sir Terence Etherton, and is based at the Rolls Building (off Chancery Lane/Fetter Lane).

At the Rolls Building in London, there are currently eighteen High Court Judges attached to the Chancery Division, in addition to the Chancellor of the High Court. The Enterprise Judge, Head of the Intellectual Property and Enterprise Court, is also considered a member of the Division. In addition, there are six judges referred to as Chancery Masters, one of whom is the Chief Master, and five judges referred to as Bankruptcy Registrars, one of whom is the Chief Registrar.

The areas of work that the Chancery Division deals with are:
- Business and property related disputes;
- Competition cases;
- Patents claims;
- Other intellectual property claims, such as trademarks or design;
- Companies' work;
- Insolvency claims, both personal and corporate;
- Trust claims;
- Contentious probate claims;
- General Chancery work, including trade and industry disputes and the enforcement of mortgages.

The Division includes:
- The Bankruptcy and Companies Court;
- The Patents Court;
- Chancery Chambers (Masters);
- The Intellectual Property and Enterprise Court.

The Central London County Court also has a Chancery list.

Circuit Judges—Civil

Circuit judges may deal solely with civil, family, criminal work, or divide their time between the three. Circuit judges deal with a variety of civil and family cases and may specialise in particular areas of law, for example, commercial. Circuit judges generally hear claims worth over £15,000 or those involving greater complexity or importance.

Recorders—Civil

Recorders sit as fee-paid judges in county courts. Some Recorders may also be authorised to deputize for specialist civil circuit judges—for example, in the Chancery Division, the Mercantile Court and the Technology and Construction Court.

The statutory jurisdiction of a Recorder is in general identical to that of a circuit judge, although the usual practice is that Recorders do not hear appeals from district judges. The jurisdiction covers almost the whole field of civil law and is mostly concurrent with that of the High Court. In addition, a number of statutes confer exclusive jurisdiction on the county courts.

Cases listed before a Recorder may include disputes in the fields of housing, commercial landlord and tenant, contract, tort, personal injury or appeals from decisions of local authorities in respect of their exercise of their function regarding homelessness, (Part VII of the Housing Act 1996).

District Judges

District judges are full-time judges who deal with the majority of cases in the county courts of England and Wales.

Their work involves: dealing with civil disputes such as personal injury cases, claims for damages and injunctions; possession proceedings against mortgage borrowers and property tenants, and claims for reasonable provision out of the estates of deceased persons. Many district judges will also deal with bankruptcy petitions, as well as the winding up of insolvent companies.

Deputy District Judges

A deputy district judge is appointed to sit in the county court or in a High Court District Registry to case manage and try civil, family, costs, enforcement and insolvency cases. They try small claims and fast track cases, family ancillary relief hearings, hear interim applications and make procedural directions preparing cases for trial. Their jurisdiction is broadly similar to that of a full time district judge although they have limited authority to deal with family cases involving children.

It is a fee-paid post open to any fully qualified and currently practising solicitor or barrister with at least seven years' experience. There is no minimum age limit for applying although a deputy must retire at 65.

Criminal

Criminal Justice

Most people feel very strongly about crime, and judges and magistrates play a vital role in the criminal justice system—especially when it comes to sentencing.

Criminal cases come to court after a decision has been made by, usually the Crown Prosecution Service, to prosecute someone for an alleged crime. In the vast majority of cases (over 95 percent), magistrates hear the evidence and, as a panel, make a decision on guilt or innocence. For more serious cases a district judge (Magistrates' Court) or a circuit judge in the Crown Court will hear the evidence, and in the case of the latter, this will involve a jury trial. Very serious criminal cases, such as murder and rape, may be heard by a High Court judge.

Both magistrates and judges have the power to imprison those convicted of a crime, if the offence is serious enough. But imprisonment is not the only solution; a judge or magistrate can order a community punishment, or put an individual under some sort of control order where their movements or activities are restricted. Although punishment is a key consideration when sentencing, judges will also have a mind as to how a particular sentence may reduce the chances of an individual re-offending.

A Judge Hearing a Criminal Case

Before a criminal trial starts the judge will familiarise himself or herself with the details of the case by reading the relevant case papers. These include the indictment which sets out the charges on which the defendant is to be tried, witness statements, exhibits and documentation on applications to be made by any party concerning the admissibility of evidence in the trial.

For jury trials in the Crown Court, the judge supervises the selection and swearing in of the jury, giving the jurors a direction about their role in the trial of deciding the facts and warning them not to discuss the case with anyone else.

During the Trial

Once the trial has commenced the judge ensures that all parties involved are given the opportunity for their case to be presented and considered as fully and fairly as possible. The judge plays an active role during the trial, controlling the way the case is conducted in accordance with relevant law and practice. As the case progresses the judge makes notes of the evidence and decides on legal issues, for example, whether evidence is admissible.

Once all evidence in the case has been heard the judge's summing up takes place. The judge sets out for the jury the law on each of the charges made and what the prosecution must prove to make the jury sure of the case. At this stage the judge refers to notes made during the course of the trial and reminds the jury of the key points of the case, highlighting the strengths and weaknesses of each side's argument. The judge then gives directions about the duties of the jury before they retire to the jury deliberation room to consider the verdict.

Sentencing

If the jury find the defendant guilty then the judge will decide on an appropriate sentence. The sentence will be influenced by a number of factors: principally the circumstances of the case, the impact that the crime has had on the victim, and relevant law especially guideline cases from the Court of Appeal. The judge will equally take into account the mitigation and any reports and references on the defendant. Only once the judge has considered all of these factors will the appropriate sentence or punishment be pronounced.

Court of Appeal—Criminal Division

The Lord Chief Justice is President of the Court of Appeal Criminal Division. He is supported in this role by a Vice President. Judges in the Criminal Division hear appeals in criminal matters from the Crown Court.

In the Criminal Division the bench usually consists of a Lord or Lady Justice and usually two High Court judges.

High Court Judges—Criminal Jurisdiction

High Court judges can hear the most serious and sensitive cases in the Crown Court (for example murder) and some sit with Appeal Court judges in the Criminal Division of the Court of Appeal.

Most High Court judges sit in the Queen's Bench Division. They will also deal at first instance with the more serious criminal cases heard in the Crown Court and, relatively early in their careers can be appointed to hear serious criminal matters in Crown Court centres out of London (known as being "on circuit").

Circuit Judges—Criminal

Circuit judges may deal solely with civil, family or criminal work, or divide their time between the three. Most Crown Court cases are heard by circuit judges, although less complex or serious matters may be dealt with by fee-paid Recorders. Some cases from Magistrates' Courts will come to the Crown Court to be heard by a circuit judge—for example, if the defendant has opted for trial by jury, or the magistrates decide they do not have sufficient sentencing powers to deal with a guilty party (magistrates can impose a maximum six-month sentence for a single offence, with a total of 12 months for multiple offences).

Recorders—Criminal

Recorders are fee-paid, part-time judges. For many it is the first step on the judicial ladder to appointment to the circuit bench. Recorders' jurisdiction is broadly similar to that of a circuit judge, but they generally handle less complex or serious matters coming before the court.

It is a post open to any fully qualified solicitor or barrister with at least ten years' practice before the Crown or county courts. They are required to sit for between 15 and 30 days every year with at least one ten-day continuous period. The appointment is for an initial five-year period, extendible for further successive five year terms up to the retirement age of 65.

District Judge (Magistrates' Courts)

The role of a district judge (Magistrates' Courts) is to complement the work of the magistracy. They are legally qualified, salaried judges and they usually deal with the longer and more complex matters that come before Magistrates' Courts. District judges (Magistrates' Courts) also have jurisdiction to hear cases under the Extradition Acts and the Fugitive Offender Acts.

Family

The family justice system exists to help families avoid disputes as far as possible but also, if disputes or problems should arise, to enable them to resolve those problems quickly and with the minimum of pain caused to those involved.

If at all possible the parties are encouraged to resolve their disputes out of court, for example through mediation—on the grounds that they are more likely to stick to any agreement if they themselves have had a role in formulating it.

When disputes do come to the courts, the cases are dealt with by magistrates and judges specially trained to deal with issues affecting families. These disputes often involve very difficult circumstances, for example relationship breakdown or child contact. Judges and magistrates work to make the circumstances of family disputes less adversarial and hearings can often be quite informal with, for example, all parties sitting around a table.

Types of Family Cases

Family law mainly involves two sorts of work: private and public.

Private cases are disputes that involve parents and concern their children, for example, in divorces or separations, who the children should live with, who they should see, where they should go to school or even if they can move to live abroad with one of their parents. The cases can also involve grandparents and other relatives.

Public work is the term used for cases when local authorities take action to remove children from their parents' care because they are being hurt in some way. Such cases can lead to children being adopted and this is also dealt with by a family judge.

Judge's Role in a Family Case

Family circuit judges deal mainly with two sorts of work. They deal with private cases which are disputes involving parents about their children, for instance who they should live with, who they should see, where they should go to school or even if they can move to live abroad with one of their parents. The cases can involve grandparents and other relatives too.

The second sort of case is what is called public work; when local councils take action to remove children from their parents' care because they are being hurt in some way. These cases can lead to those children being adopted and the judge deals with that as well.

The judge will usually have all the papers the day before so will know all about the case before it comes into court. Such cases can take a long time to resolve and it is important that those involved see the same judge throughout the case if possible so that there is a consistent approach to dealing with the problems that are being addressed.

The parties are usually represented by lawyers who have been specially trained to do this difficult and sensitive work. The judges are specially trained too as these cases affect peoples' lives in a very close and sometimes devastating way. The children the judge is dealing with have their own lawyer in public cases and can have a lawyer in private cases if the judge thinks they should. In both cases the judge will have reports from an expert court officer who will talk to the children and get to know their wishes. These cases can take a long time to sort out and it is important to remember that the judge has to put the children's interests and welfare first.

Hearings in the family courts are in private and only those who are involved can attend. The judge does not wear robes and the proceedings are much more informal than those in a criminal court so that people who are often frightened and nervous do not feel intimidated and can tell the judge what they want to say. The people in the cases will know each other, they may be angry and upset and feelings can run high. The case can cause distress and a family judge has to try to keep people calm and be sensitive to everyone's point of view. Sometimes witnesses are too frightened or upset to be in the courtroom and arrangements can be made to help them by using a video link.

High Court—Family

Judges who sit in the High Court have jurisdiction to hear all cases relating to children and exercise an exclusive jurisdiction in wardship.

Judges in the High Court also hear appeals from family proceedings courts and cases transferred from the county courts or family proceedings courts.

Circuit Judge—Family

Designated Family Judges and Nominated Care Judges preside over public law cases, and can make orders for adoption, and the protection, care and supervision of children.

District Judge—Family

District judges are full-time judges who deal with the majority of cases in the county courts of England and Wales and so are heavily involved in family proceedings.

They will preside over both private cases, such as divorce, and public—those dealing with the welfare of children.

District judges of the Principal Registry are considered to be members of the High Court, and can hear both High Court and county court cases. They hear cases relating to divorce (including financial and property adjustment issues and the care and upbringing of children), civil partnerships, care proceedings, and adoption.

Military

This section provides information about the constitutional position, function and history of the Judge Advocate General (JAG), his team of judges, and the staff who support them. It also contains a brief outline of the legal system which underlies the discipline of the British Armed Forces.

This is an informal guide to the Service justice system and is not authoritative as to the law. Service law is to be found in the statutes, statutory instruments, regulations, and reports of cases decided by the superior courts; a brief list of some of the relevant statutes is given below.

Historical Background

The conduct of English soldiers was for many centuries regulated by the Court of the High Constable and Earl Marshal. From 1521 onwards, it was the "Court of the Marshal", and after the standing army had been brought into being in Cromwellian times the office of Judge Advocate General was created in 1666 to supervise "Courts-martial".

It has been held in continuous succession ever since, being expanded to cover Great Britain, and later the United Kingdom, the Royal Air Force, the Royal Navy, and all

British land, air and naval forces overseas. Historically the responsibilities of the Judge Advocate General were very wide and included oversight of both prosecution and defence arrangements as well as the court.

Since 1948, the role has concerned the Court-martial process. From 1661 the office of Judge Advocate of the Fleet (JAF) existed to supervise the Royal Navy Courts-martial system, separately from the JAG. The two historic offices were amalgamated by the Armed Forces Act 2006, with the role of JAF subsumed into JAG. The Armed Forces Act 2006 repealed the three Service Discipline Acts of 1955/57, established a single system of Service law, and created the Court Martial as a standing court. It came into effect on 31 October 2009.

Appointment of Judge Advocate General

The Judge Advocate General is appointed by Her Majesty the Queen by means of Letters Patent, on the recommendation of the Lord Chancellor. He is a Law Officer of the Crown and an independent member of the judiciary and is always a civilian, although he may have served in the armed forces. The JAG is not a General of the Army; the word "general" signifies broad oversight, as in Secretary-General, Attorney-General, etc. The current JAG (from November 2004) is His Honour Judge Jeff Blackett who is also a circuit judge and who formerly served in the Royal Navy.

Judiciary

The JAG has a team of full-time judges comprising the Vice-Judge Advocate General (Judge Michael Hunter) and six Assistant Judge Advocates General, and can also call upon the services of Deputy (part-time) Judge Advocates.

All the judges are civilians, appointed from the ranks of experienced barristers or solicitors in the same way as other district and circuit Judges. When conducting a particular trial they are formally titled "The Judge Advocate", and out of court they are generally referred to and addressed as "Judge". In court the judges wear legal costume, comprising a bench wig and black gown, with a tippet (sash) in army red with navy blue and air-force blue edges.

The JAG and many Judge Advocates also sit in the Crown Court. It is also possible for a High Court judge to be specified to preside in the Court Martial as a Judge Advocate; this is done for exceptionally serious or unprecedented cases, just as in the Crown Court.

Administrative Offices

The administrative staff in the Office of the JAG (OJAG) are part of the Judicial Office, an independent body of civil servants supporting the judiciary. OJAG staff support the judges in the exercise of their judicial functions.

The Military Court Service (MCS) is part of the Ministry of Defence, and maintains four main Military Court Centres at Colchester (Essex), Bulford (Wilts), Catterick (Yorks), and Sennelager (Germany), plus further centres at Aldergrove (N Ireland), Portsmouth (Hants), and Episkopi (Cyprus). MCS arranges, funds and supports trials at these centres and at other ad hoc venues in UK and overseas. Communications about particular cases must be addressed in the first instance to the Court Administration Officer at the MCS Headquarters in Upavon, Wilts.

Services Criminal Justice System

The main elements of the criminal justice system are:

➢ The Court Martial

Serious matters, including both offences against the civilian criminal law and specifically military disciplinary offences, may be tried in the Court Martial, which is a standing court. A Judge Advocate arraigns each defendant and conducts the trial which is broadly similar to a civilian Crown Court trial in all cases, even when dealing with a minor disciplinary or criminal offence.

The jury, known as the board, comprises between three and seven commissioned officers or Warrant Officers depending on the seriousness of the case. Having listened to the Judge Advocate's directions on the law and summary of the evidence, they are responsible for finding defendants guilty or not guilty.

Following a finding or plea of guilty, the board joins the Judge Advocate to decide on sentence. The Court Martial has the same sentencing powers in relation to imprisonment as a Crown Court, including life imprisonment. Most of the sentencing powers in the Criminal Justice Act 2003 are also available in the Court Martial.

➢ Summary Hearings by a Commanding Officer

Minor disciplinary and criminal matters are deal with summarily by the Commanding Officer of the accused. The great majority of matters are disposed of in this way, which forms one of the foundations of the disciplinary system of the armed forces. A Commanding Officer has powers of punishment up to 28 days' detention, which may be extended to 90 days' detention with approval from higher authority. In all cases an accused person may elect for trial in the Court Martial rather than appear before their Commanding Officer, or may appeal to the Summary Appeal Court after the event.

➢ Summary Appeal Court

The accused, if dissatisfied with the outcome of a summary hearing, always has the right of appeal to the Summary Appeal Court, which is conducted by a Judge Advocate accompanied by two officers. This is modelled on an appeal from a Magistrates' Court to the Crown Court.

➢ Court Martial Appeal Court

The avenue of appeal for a convicted defendant, subject to obtaining permission to appeal, is to the Court Martial Appeal Court (as the Court of Appeal Criminal Division is named when dealing with Service cases), and ultimately to the Supreme Court.

➢ Service Civilian Court

Civilians who are officials attached to the Services overseas, or dependants of Service personnel resident overseas (for example in Germany or Cyprus) may be tried for minor offences by the Service Civilian Court, which consists of a Judge Advocate sitting alone, or, for more serious matters, may be tried in the

Court Martial. This is then usually constituted with an all-civilian board acting as a jury; in such cases the Judge Advocate sentences alone.

- Custody, Search Warrants and Arrest Warrants

If a service man or woman is to be detained in custody, or if private premises need to be searched in the course of investigations, or if a person needs to be arrested, the authority of a Judge Advocate is required. The JAG or one of the judges must be satisfied that the continued detention, or the search or arrest, is legally justified. Such cases are often heard by video link and a judge is on duty every day of the year to rule upon urgent applications if required.

Functions of the Judge Advocate General

The duties of the JAG include the following:

- To act as the Presiding Judge in the Services criminal jurisdiction and leader of its judges, thereby supervising the jurisdiction;
- To provide guidance to all stakeholders in the Services criminal justice system on practices and procedures, developments and reforms;
- To monitor the workings of the Services criminal justice system and to advise on its efficiency and effectiveness;
- To be a member of the Services Justice Board;
- To specify judges to conduct specific Court Martial trials in UK or abroad;
- To provide judges to conduct Summary Appeal Courts and Standing Civilian Courts, and to rule upon applications for detention in custody and for search and arrest warrants;
- To act as the trial judge personally conducting some of the most serious, sensitive or controversial trials in the Court Martial (such as murder);
- To refer to the Court Martial Appeal Court cases involving a point of law of exceptional importance;
- To keep the record of proceedings for not less than six years after trial in all cases.

Tribunal

Tribunal Justice

On 3 November 2008, the Tribunals, Courts and Enforcement Act came into force. This created a new two-tier Tribunal system: A First-tier Tribunal and an Upper Tribunal, both of which are split into Chambers. Each Chamber comprises similar jurisdictions or bring together similar types of experts to hear appeals.

The Upper Tribunal primarily, but not exclusively, reviews and decides appeals arising from the First-tier Tribunal. Like the High Court, it is a superior court of record—as well having the existing specialist judges of the senior tribunals judiciary at its disposal it can also call on the services of High Court judges.

Tribunal Hearings

Tribunals usually sit as a panel, incorporating a legally qualified tribunal chairman, as well as panel members with specific areas of expertise. They hear evidence from witnesses but decide the case themselves. Tribunals have limited powers (depending on the jurisdiction of the case) to impose fines and penalties or to award compensation and costs. Other types of tribunal decisions might result in the allowance or disallowance of a benefit; leave or refusal to stay in the UK or about the provision of special educational help for school age children.

Many cases involve individuals putting their own case, without legal assistance, so the system needs to be accessible to all. Tribunal judges often help to ensure this, by guiding non-legally qualified parties through the necessary procedures, if necessary.

There are many different tribunals, covering a wide range of different areas affecting day-to-day life.

Before the Hearing

Before the hearing begins, the Tribunal Judge chairing the hearing reads the papers in the case and considers how to proceed when the hearing begins.

Tribunal judges play an active role in managing tribunal cases once issued, helping to ensure they proceed as quickly and efficiently as possible. This may include:

- Setting appropriate directions to ensure that the right documents and witnesses are available at any hearing;
- Encouraging the parties to cooperate with each other in the conduct of the case, and (where appropriate);
- Helping the parties to settle the case; and generally,
- Controlling the progress of the case.

As many Tribunal hearings are open to the public, parties involved in a Tribunal case are welcome to arrange an early visit to the relevant hearing centre to see another appeal. This will give an insight to how the particular Tribunal conducts an open hearing.

The Hearing

Except in cases which involve national security or evidence of a very personal nature, tribunal cases are held in public.

In many cases, no oath will be administered, and hearsay evidence can be considered. Proceedings are relatively informal and nobody wears robes or wigs. Parties are expected to assist by following directions and providing enough copies of their relevant documents in good time, but the stricter disclosure rules for the ordinary courts may not be applied.

Occasionally, the parties will have agreed the relevant facts and it will not be necessary for the judge to hear oral evidence. The issues may concern the law to be applied or the terms of the decision or judgment to be given. However, more often than not, the parties will give written and oral evidence and their witnesses may be cross-examined (asked questions by the other party) to test their evidence against the other party's case.

The Tribunal Judge ensures that all parties have their case presented and considered as fully and fairly as possible. During the case, the Tribunal Judge or the panel members may ask questions on any point that needs clarification or which will help with his or her decision. The Tribunal Judge also decides on all matters of procedure which may arise during a hearing.

The Tribunal Judge and panel members (if a panel hears the case), will consider the evidence. They are guided and constrained by the statutory powers of their Tribunal to resolve the issue which the claimant has raised. If the case meets the requirements of the statute, the Tribunal can make one of a range of orders set out in the law.

The Tribunal will then hear closing arguments (submissions) from both parties, and make its decision.

The Decision

Tribunal Chairmen or Tribunal Judges may be assisted in their decision-making by other legally qualified members, or by experienced specialist panel members. Specialist members do not act as expert witnesses but bring to the panel their experience of their particular field. All legal matters remain the Tribunal Judge's responsibility. All of the panel members take part in the decision.

The Tribunal's decision is given either at the hearing, or in writing later. In either case, the parties will get a written decision.

After the Hearing

Some tribunals can award costs, but not all.

The ordinary courts enforce tribunal decisions in cases of difficulty, and tribunals do not usually hold funds or order deposits.

Tribunal/Chamber President

The President is responsible for the day-to-day judicial administration of their tribunal or (within the new simplified two tier structure) their chamber. They act as a vital link between the Senior President of Tribunals; the judicial officers of their tribunal, and the senior courts judiciary outside the Tribunals Service.

Tribunal Judges

Tribunal Judges are legally qualified and responsible for ensuring the individual tribunal hearings they chair make the correct decision in law.

Tribunal Members

Tribunal members are the specialist non-legal members of the panel hearing the case. Not every panel includes non-legal members.

Part I
The United Kingdom of Great Britain and Northern Ireland

The Legal Year

The service in Westminster Abbey dates back to the Middle Ages when judges prayed for guidance at the start of the legal term. Judges, whose courts were held in Westminster Hall, left the city and walked to the abbey to take part in the service.

Present Day

The ceremonies now are more or less as they have always been but, instead of the two-mile walk from Temple Bar to Westminster Abbey, the judges now travel by car.

The 45-minute service, which starts at 11:30 am, is conducted by the Dean of Westminster. It includes prayers, hymns, psalms and anthems; the Lord Chancellor reads a lesson.

Around 700 people are invited to attend the service and breakfast. These include judges, senior judicial officers, the Law Officers, Queen's Counsel (QC), government ministers, lawyers, members of the European Court and other overseas judges and lawyers. Judges and QCs wear ceremonial dress.

Disruption of Ceremonies

Although well-established traditions, both ceremonies were cancelled during the last century. In 1940 the service had to be cancelled due to bomb damage in Westminster Abbey; it was not held again until 1946.

In 1953 the ceremony took place in St. Margaret's Church because structures and decorations for the coronation in the abbey had not been removed.

Judicial Sitting Days

During the legal terms, Court of Appeal judges and High Court judges are expected to devote themselves to judicial business throughout the legal year which usually amounts to somewhere in the region of 185—190 days.

Circuit judges are expected to sit for a minimum of 210 days, although the expectation is for between 215—220 per year.

District judges are expected to sit for a minimum of 215 days.

Judges also have out of court duties to perform such as reading case papers, writing judgments, and keeping up to date with new developments in the law.

Coroners

Although the post they hold is judicial, and legal qualifications and experience are often required, coroners are not considered to be members of the courts judiciary.

However, for especially high-profile inquests a judge may be appointed to oversee the proceedings as a deputy coroner.

The office of coroner was formally established in 1194, originally as a form of tax gatherer. In the centuries since, the role has evolved into an independent judicial officer, charged with the investigation of sudden, violent or unnatural death.

The Coroners' System

Unlike the unified courts system, administered by HM Courts and Tribunals Service, there are 92 separate coroners' jurisdictions in England and Wales. Each jurisdiction is locally funded and resourced by local authorities.

Coroners are barristers, solicitors or medical practitioners of not less than five years standing, who continue in their legal or medical practices when not sitting as coroners.

Some 32 coroners are "whole time" coroners and are paid an annual salary regardless of their caseload. The remainder are paid according to the number of cases referred to them.

The coroner's jurisdiction is territorial—it is the location of the dead body which dictates which coroner has jurisdiction in any particular case.

Deputy Coroners

Coroners are required to appoint a deputy or assistant deputy to act in their stead if they are out of the district or otherwise unable to act. Deputies and assistant deputies have the same professional qualifications as the coroner.

In exceptionally high-profile or complex cases, a serving judge may be appointed as a deputy coroner.

For example, in 2007 Lord Justice Scott Baker was appointed as Assistant Deputy

Part I
The United Kingdom of Great Britain and Northern Ireland

Coroner for Inner West London for the purposes of hearing the inquests into the deaths of Diana, Princess of Wales and Emad El-Din Mohamed Abdel Moneim Fayed (Mr Dodi Al Fayed).

Lady Justice Hallett has been appointed Assistant Deputy Coroner for the Inner West London District of Greater London in order to conduct the inquests into the deaths of the 56 people killed in the London bombings on 7 July 2005.

Exercises

I. Choose the appropriate answer(s) to each question. There may be more than one choice for some questions.

1. Which of the following is NOT true after the creation of a new Supreme Court in the UK?

   A. The most senior judges are now entirely separate from the Parliamentary process.

   B. The House of Lords is no longer the supreme court of appeal.

   C. The new Supreme Court is a United Kingdom body having jurisdiction over England, Wales, Scotland and Northern Ireland.

   D. Some cases may be remitted to the new Supreme Court by the Lord Chief Justice of England and Wales.

2. Which of the following is NOT true about the Queen's Bench Division?

   A. It is a division of the High Court.

   B. It has both criminal and civil jurisdiction.

   C. The Division is headed by the Chancellor of the High Court.

   D. Judges who sit in the Queen's Bench Division deal with "common law" business and tort.

3. Which of the following is NOT true about district judges in England and Wales?

   A. They are full-time judges.

   B. Their work only involves dealing with civil disputes.

C. A district judge may hear criminal cases in Magistrates' Court.

D. They deal with the majority of cases in the county courts of England and Wales.

4. Which of the following are true about sentencing in England?

   A. A sentence may be decided on by the judge after the jury find the defendant is guilty.

   B. The sentence will be influenced by relevant law especially guideline cases from the Court of Appeal.

   C. When sentencing, judges will also have a mind as to how a particular sentence may reduce the chances of an individual re-offending.

   D. Only once the judge has considered all of the mitigation and any reports and references on the defendant will the appropriate sentence or punishment be pronounced.

5. Which of the following is NOT true about family cases in England and Wales?

   A. There are two types of family cases: private ones and public ones.

   B Private cases are disputes that involve parents and concern their children, and don't involve grandparents and other relatives.

   C. Hearings in the family courts are in private and only those who are involved can attend.

   D. Public work is the term used for family cases when local authorities take action to remove children from their parents' care because they are being hurt in some way.

II. Questions

1. What do you know about the supreme court in the UK?
2. How are different cases dealt with? And which judges deal with them?
3. What role do judges play in managing civil cases?
4. What actions do judges sitting in the Queen's Bench Division of the High Court deal with?

5. What are the areas of work that the Chancery Division deals with?
6. What cases do circuit judges deal with?
7. What do you know about Recorders in the UK courts?
8. What work do district judges do in the UK?
9. What do you know about deputy district judges in the UK?
10. Can you summarize the criminal justice in the UK?
11. What are the two main types of family cases?
12. What are the main elements of the criminal justice system?
13. What are the duties of the Judge Advocate General?
14. What role do tribunal judges play in managing tribunal cases?

Chapter 5
HOW THE JUDICIARY IS GOVERNED

As part of the constitutional changes of April 2006, the Lord Chief Justice became responsible for some 400 statutory functions, which were previously the responsibility of the Lord Chancellor. For example, the Lord Chief Justice now decides where judges sit, and the type of cases they hear. To do this, the Lord Chief Justice has support from his judicial colleagues, as well as from a small administrative staff.

The Lord Chief Justice has a Judicial Executive Board to help provide judicial direction and a Judges' Council, which is representative of all levels of the judiciary.

Sometimes different levels of judges have their own representative organisations, for example, the Association of Her Majesty's District Judges, or Council of Her Majesty's Circuit Judges. These groups represent the interests of judges from a particular level or jurisdiction.

Finally, judges also have access to administrative support within the court environment, whether this is their own allocated clerk, court staff, or legal advisers for magistrates.

Judicial Executive Board

The Lord Chief Justice exercises executive and leadership responsibilities through, and with the support of, the Judicial Executive Board (JEB).

The Lord Chief Justice chairs JEB, which meets monthly during term time.

Leadership Responsibilities

Judges often hold additional responsibilities over and above their day to day duty.

Local Criminal Justice Board

Each of the LCJB has a circuit judge from the local area as a point of liaison. The judge is independent of the board itself but receives all the minutes and is encouraged to attend the meetings especially when issues relating to the judiciary arise. Often the LCJBs have open days where judges sit on mock trials, which the public are invited to attend, and answer questions about their roles, the law and the court system.

Judge Members of the Probation Board

A Crown Court judge appointed by the Lord Chancellor must sit as a member of a Probation Board in their local area, ideally for around ten meetings a year.

Although the judge is a full time member of the board and can therefore make significant contributions to topics discussed they cannot advise the board on any legal issues that may arise. Instead the judge's role is to spot problems and identify issues that appear whilst ensuring especial attention is paid to the matters in which the court has a particular interest.

The judge should have a pivotal role in advising the board on how resources might best be used and most importantly should highlight to other members changes that are brought about by Acts of Parliament when they relate to the work of the criminal courts or the Probation Service.

The Responsibilities of Resident Judges and Designated Civil and Family Judges

In each area there are arrangements which enable the Resident Judge, Designated Civil Judge and Designated Family Judge to meet with all levels of the judiciary to discuss and reach agreement on issues concerning the administration of justice.

Amongst their other duties some more general responsibilities of a Resident Judge can include:
- Reviewing information relating to the courts, e.g. waiting times;
- Giving guidance for the efficient conduct of the business of the court;
- Ensuring that cases of particular importance or sensitivity are heard by a judge specifically assigned to that case;

Magistrates

The Magistrates Liaison Judge chairs an Area Judicial Forum which deals with judicial matters in relation to the business of the Magistrates' Courts, and coordinates with the Crown Court and other family courts.

Liaison Judges' roles include:

- Helping to ensure that magistrates who sit in the Crown Court are treated in every way as full members of the court;
- Arranging for magistrates to attend the Crown Court from time to time as observers;
- Swearing in new magistrates;
- Ensuring, through consultation with the Designated Family Judge, that there is in place a system for appropriate communication between magistrates sitting in the family jurisdiction and the Designated Family Judge.

Judges' Council

The Judges' Council was first set up under the Judicature Act 1873. It was chaired by the Lord Chancellor and all the Judges of the Supreme Court were members. The Council continued to function until 1981.

Following serious academic debate, the Lord Chief Justice, Lord Lane, set up a new Judges' Council in 1988. This new Council was chaired by the Lord Chief Justice and had a smaller membership of the more senior judges.

In 2002 the council adopted a written constitution and has subsequently widened its membership to include representatives from all areas of the judiciary including the Circuit and District Benches, Magistrates and Tribunals.

In March 2006 the council further revised its constitution and membership following the coming into effect of the Constitutional Reform Act 2005. This Act and the Concordat vest in the Lord Chief Justice very considerable responsibilities in respect of the judiciary and of the business of the courts of England and Wales. The Lord Chief

Justice exercises these responsibilities through the Judges' Council and the Judicial Executive Board.

Role

The primary function of the present Judges' Council is to be a body broadly representative of the judiciary as a whole which will inform and advise the Lord Chief Justice on matters as requested from time to time.

In particular it:

- has a specific statutory responsibility for appointing three members of the Judicial Appointments Commission under the Constitutional Reform Act 2005;
- is consulted to obtain a wide perspective on matters which concern more than one discrete judicial grouping;
- considers and conveys views, ideas or concerns of the wider judicial family;
- provides detailed analysis and consideration of specific matters on which judicial views are sought;
- develops policy and advises the Lord Chief Justice on policy and other matters as requested from time to time by him or the member of the Judicial Executive Board to whom he has delegated the relevant responsibility.

The present council meets three times a year and is chaired by the Lord Chief Justice. The Judicial Executive Board are members of the Judges' Council. The other members are selected by the Judicial Group or constituency which that member represents. Detailed work is carried out through standing committees and working groups.

Other Roles

In 2004 the Council became a member of the European Network of Judges' Councils (ENCJ), an organisation set up to promote judicial independence and to analyse and exchange information on issues of common interest such as case management, judicial conduct and judicial functions.

Judges' Council Publications

The council is supported by its own independent secretariat, publishes regular newsletters to the judiciary and an annual report.

From time to time the Judges' Council responds to government proposals on issues which have a direct impact on the running of the courts. Judges' Council published responses can be found in the publications and reports section of this site.

Exercises

I. Choose the appropriate answer(s) to each question. There may be more than one choice for some questions.

1. Which of the following is NOT within the responsibility of the Lord Chief Justice?

    A. To decide where judges sit.

    B. To decide the type of cases judges hear.

    C. To chair the Judicial Executive Board.

    D. To appoint Crown Court judges.

2. Which of the following are true about the Judicial Executive Board?

    A. It is chaired by the Lord Chief Justice.

    B. It meets monthly during term time.

    C. It helps the Lord Chief Justice provide judicial direction.

    D. It helps the Lord Chief Justice exercise executive and leadership responsibilities.

3. Which of the following are NOT true about the new Judges' Council?

    A. It was set up under the Judicature Act 1873.

    B. It has been chaired by the Lord Chief Justice.

    C. In March 2006 the council further revised its constitution and membership.

    D. It has widened its membership to include representatives from all areas of the judiciary including the Circuit and District Benches, Magistrates and Tribunals.

4. Which of the following are true about the role of the Judges' Council?

   A. The primary function of the present Judges' Council is to be a body broadly representative of the judiciary as a whole.

   B. It has a specific statutory responsibility for appointing three members of the Judicial Appointments Commission under the Constitutional Reform Act 2005.

   C. It considers and conveys views, ideas or concerns of the wider judicial family.

   D. It became a member of the European Network of Judges' Councils (ENCJ), an organisation set up to promote judicial independence and to analyse and exchange information on issues of common interest such as judicial conduct.

II. Fill in the gaps with the appropriate words given in the box.

A. appointment	B. standing	C. proceedings	D. impartial
E. dismissal	F. immunity	G. misconduct	H. presides
I. cabinet	J. convention		

1. His lawyer is representing him in the _____.
2. It is the _____ for American lawyers to designate themselves "Esquire".
3. When he offered to give information to the police, he was granted _____ from prosecution.
4. The _____ of the city treasurer resulted in his being put in prison.
5. They demanded the immediate _____ of Justice William, due to his misbehavior.
6. The Prime Minister invited each member of the _____ to state his view.
7. On his _____ as magistrate, he was involved in a scandal.
8. A judge should give the accused a fair and _____ hearing.
9. Judge White has a ten-year _____ as a practicing barrister.
10. The chairman _____ the meeting with his usual tact.

Chapter 6
JUDICIAL ACCOUNTABILITY AND INDEPENDENCE

This section aims to explain the importance of judicial independence and the consequences of that independence on the notion of judicial accountability. It also aims to explain some of the practical arrangements which govern the way the judiciary of England and Wales operates on a day-to-day basis.

We are all familiar with media reports of a government minister who is forced to resign or dismissed for behaviour which is or is perceived to be inappropriate or for incompetence in the performance of his or her duties. There are also many press headlines which condemn a judge or magistrate, for example, for handing down a "soft" sentence, but there are almost none which announce that the judge in question has resigned or has been dismissed as a result of that criticism. Many may wonder why steps are not taken to dismiss such judges or to force them to resign. Why is it that judges and magistrates appear to be unaccountable in the face of such criticism? Why is it that the way they are treated appears to be different to the treatment of many others, from government ministers and public officials, to the directors and employees of companies?

The truth is that the judiciary is accountable, but in a different manner. The reason for this difference is a fundamental feature of the constitution going to the very heart of that democracy. The difference stems from the need to ensure that judges are impartial and independent of central and local government and from pressures from the media, companies, and pressure groups while exercising their judicial functions. That need is also reflected in the constitutions of all democratic countries.

The extent to which the judiciary in England and Wales are accountable, how they are accountable, and why there is a need for judges to be completely independent from government and other powerful groups, are difficult questions.

With some 35,000 men and women holding judicial office in England and Wales, the answers to these questions have a significant impact.

People's Daily Life

They may affect the confidence people have in the ability of judges to uphold the rule of law. It is a complex area, but we hope that an understanding of some of the issues involved will help to put into perspective the way in which the courts deliver justice.

We aim to explain why judicial independence is a vital element of our democracy and the effect that has on the notion of judicial accountability. This section also looks at the constraints placed on the judiciary by legislation enacted by Parliament, and the ways in which individual judges are accountable.

It considers accountability to more senior judges through the system enabling appeal to a higher court and accountability to the Lord Chief Justice and the Lord Chancellor through the complaints system. It looks at accountability to the public through open access to justice and the publication of the vast majority of judicial decisions. Scrutiny of judges and the judicial system by the media, executive and legislative branches of the state is also considered.

Independence

Independence from Whom and What?

It is vitally important in a democracy that individual judges and the judiciary as a whole are impartial and independent of all external pressures and of each other so that those who appear before them and the wider public can have confidence that their cases will be decided fairly and in accordance with the law. When carrying out their judicial function they must be free of any improper influence. Such influence could come from any number of sources. It could arise from improper pressure by the executive or the legislature, by individual litigants, particular pressure groups, the media, self-interest or other judges, in particular more senior judges.

Why Is Independence Important?

It is vital that each judge is able to decide cases solely on the evidence presented in court by the parties and in accordance with the law. Only relevant facts and law should form the basis of a judge's decision. Only in this way can judges discharge their constitutional responsibility to provide fair and impartial justice; to do justice as Lord Brougham, a 19th Century Lord Chancellor, put it "between man and man" or as Lord Clarke, former Master of the Rolls put it more recently in 2005, "between citizen and citizen or between citizen and the state".

The responsibilities of judges in disputes between the citizen and the state have increased together with the growth in governmental functions over the last century. The responsibility of the judiciary to protect citizens against unlawful acts of government has thus increased, and with it the need for the judiciary to be independent of government.

Independence and the Appearance of Independence

As well as in fact being independent in this way, it is of vital importance that judges are seen to be both independent and impartial. Justice must not only be done—it must be seen to be done. It was for this reason that the House of Lords in the Pinochet case in 1999 held that a decision it had given had to be set aside and the appeal before it heard again by a panel of different Law Lords. It had come to light after the original decision that one of the Law Lords might have given an appearance that he was not independent and impartial because of a connection with a campaigning organisation which was involved in the case. In those circumstances, and even though there was no suggestion that the Law Lord was not in fact independent or impartial, the decision could not stand. Justice demanded that the appeal be heard again before a panel of Law Lords who had and gave the appearance to reasonable well-informed observers that they were independent and impartial.

The Ways in Which Independence Is Protected and Its Limits

Whilst an independent and impartial judiciary is one of the cornerstones of a democracy, the practical ways in which this is given effect are often treated with suspicion. For example, judges are given immunity from prosecution for any acts they carry out in performance of their judicial function. They also benefit from immunity from being sued for defamation for the things they say about parties or witnesses in the course of hearing cases. These principles have led some people to suggest that judges are somehow "above the law".

However, it is not right to say that judges are above the law. Judges are subject to the law in the same way as any other citizen. The Lord Chief Justice or Lord Chancellor may refer a judge to the Judicial Complaints Investigations Office in order to establish whether it would be appropriate to remove them from office in circumstances where they have been found to have committed a criminal offence.

Judicial independence does, however, mean that judges must be free to exercise their judicial powers without interference from litigants, the state, the media or powerful individuals or entities, such as large companies. This is an important principle because judges often decide matters between the citizen and the state and between citizens and powerful entities. For example, it is clearly inappropriate for the judge in charge of a criminal trial against an individual citizen to be influenced by the state. It would be unacceptable for the judge to come under pressure to admit or not admit certain evidence, how to direct the jury, or to pass a particular sentence. Decisions must be made on the basis of the facts of the case and the law alone.

Judicial independence is important whether the judge is dealing with a civil or a criminal case. Individuals involved in any kind of case before the courts need to be sure that the judge dealing with their case cannot be influenced by an outside party or by the judge's own personal interests, such as a fear of being sued for defamation by litigants about whom the judge is required in the course of proceedings or judgment to make adverse comment. This requirement that judges be free from any improper influence also underpins the duty placed on them to declare personal interests in any case before it starts, to ensure that there is neither any bias or partiality, or any appearance of such.

A practical example of the importance of judicial independence is where a high profile matter, which has generated a great deal of media interest comes before the court. Such matters range from the criminal trial of a person accused of a shocking murder, the divorce of celebrities, and challenges to the legality of government policy, for example, the availability of a new and expensive drug to NHS patients. In the 24 hour media age in which we live, it stands to reason that the judge hearing the case will often be under intense scrutiny, with decisions open to intense debate. It is right that this is so. But it is important that decisions in the courts are made in accordance with the law and are not influenced by such external factors. It is also important however to observe one or two points which will have an impact on the outcome of the trial and our understanding of it:

➢ In a Crown Court criminal trial in England and Wales:

The judge does not decide guilt or innocence. That decision is made by the jury, which is made up of resident citizens and registered electors selected at random.

If the jury decides that the defendant is guilty, it is then the task of the judge to pass sentence. In doing so the judge will have to take into account the sentencing scheme which has been enacted in legislation by Parliament, and the various sentencing guidelines which have been agreed and published by the Sentencing Guidelines Council. The guidelines and the decisions of the Court of Appeal (Criminal Division) set out key considerations which must be taken into account by the judge when determining any sentence and provide a framework of appropriate sentences for the judge to apply. The judge is entitled to depart from the guidelines or a decision of the Court of Appeal (Criminal Division) only when the interests of justice require such a departure.

Any sentence that is unduly harsh or in the case of more serious offences is unduly lenient may be corrected by the Court of Appeal, on an appeal by the convicted person or a reference to the Court of Appeal by the Attorney General.

➢ In civil cases any errors by the trial judge may also be corrected by the Court of Appeal and in cases raising important points of law, the decisions of the Court of

Appeal may be appealed to the Supreme Court.

> It is important to recognise that, in both civil and criminal cases, what we read in the papers and see on the news will often only cover a fraction of what has been heard in court. This is not a criticism of journalists. They only have a certain amount of space or time to cover a particular story. It is worth bearing in mind that, for instance, in a criminal case there are often many mitigating or aggravating circumstances surrounding the offence and the offender. These will have had a direct bearing on the sentence handed down and are often difficult for the media to report in full. A good example of this is where a defendant pleads guilty to a crime. In such circumstances Parliament has directed that judges must significantly reduce the sentence.

The purpose of the above examples is not to suggest that judges never get it wrong, or that in criminal cases they have no say in the sentence handed down, but to give an idea of the factors they must consider when making decisions.

The Principles of Judicial Accountability

We have already discussed the peculiar constitutional position of the judiciary and the conventions that protect their independence. In this section we look at the numerous ways in which judges are restrained and which together, ensure that judges are accountable for their actions.

We must first ask what it means to say someone is accountable for their actions. In many areas accountability means that, just like football managers, an individual who fails to perform satisfactorily in their job should be sacked or should resign. Some people have called this form of accountability, "sacrificial accountability", meaning that the only solution is for the individual concerned to no longer continue in their role.

In the case of the judiciary, however, safeguards are needed to ensure that judges are free to make their judicial decisions without fear or favour and thus to preserve their independence. For example, if a politician or senior judge felt able to sack a particular judge, or remove him or her from a case, simply because they did not like the decision reached, the principle of judicial independence would be greatly undermined and there could be no possibility of a fair trial. It could also lead judges to make decisions they felt might be more acceptable to whoever had the right to decide whether they should continue serving as judges or be promoted. If, for instance, the permanent or continued appointment of a part-time temporary judge was in some way determined by one of the parties to the case, there would be a real risk that independent and impartial judicial decision-making could be subverted by self-interest. Prior to 2000 this was the position in Scotland in respect of temporary criminal court judges, or sheriffs, who were appointed for a fixed period of twelve months and the renewal of their appointment was effectively at the discretion of the Lord Advocate, a government minister who is the head of the prosecuting authority. In other words there might well be a risk that such judges could improperly favour the prosecuting authority with an eye to securing a permanent appointment.

This risk is perhaps best demonstrated—albeit as an extreme example—in dictatorships where judges are often appointed specifically because of their loyalty to the regime, and will almost always make decisions in favour of it, regardless of the interests of the individual, the facts and the law. The independence and transparency of the appointments process in England and Wales rebuts any suggestion that such factors could be relevant to the appointment of judicial office holders in this jurisdiction.

We have stated that judges who commit a criminal offence may be subject to an investigation by the Office for Judicial Complaints and may be subject to a disciplinary sanction in accordance with the relevant statutory provisions. Apart from this, however, it is clear that judges are not subject to this "sacrificial accountability". However, they are subject to a different form of accountability, which has been referred to as "explanatory accountability". Put simply this form of accountability means that individuals can be asked to give an account as to why they have behaved in a particular way. The judiciary is subject to this form of accountability in a multitude of ways. Taken together, these ensure a considerable degree of accountability.

Judicial Conduct

The right to appeal exists for those dissatisfied with a judicial decision, but it is also possible for individual litigants to complain about the personal conduct of a judge. Where the Court of Appeal criticises a trial judge, the judgment is always sent to the judge concerned, and where there is any reason for concern about the conduct of the judge it is sent to another more senior judge, in the case of High Court judges the head of that judge's Division, and in the case of circuit judges to the Presiding Judge of that circuit. From time to time, if the Court of Appeal raises particular concerns, judges may be given advice and guidance, or training, or different workloads or types of workload by the responsible senior judiciary. In cases where the judge's conduct is seriously impugned, the relevant Head of Division or Presiding Judge will refer the matter to the Lord Chief Justice and Lord Chancellor. This is another way in which individual judges are accountable.

The Lord Chief Justice and the Lord Chancellor are jointly responsible for considering and determining complaints about the personal conduct of all judges in England and Wales and some judges who sit in Tribunals in Scotland and Northern Ireland. The Office for Judicial Complaints (OJC)—now the Judicial Complaints Investigations Office—was set up on the 3rd April 2006, to handle these complaints and provide advice and assistance to the Lord Chief Justice and Lord Chancellor in their performance of this joint responsibility.

The Lord Chief Justice and the Lord Chancellor take complaints about the judiciary very seriously, and consider it important to maintain public confidence by ensuring such complaints are dealt with by an independent body. For 2012 and 2013 the number of complaints dealt with, and upheld, was very low; across all levels of the judiciary, just 55 cases required any disciplinary action. Further information is available in the JCIO's Annual Report.

The Lord Chief Justice has the right to give a judge formal advice, a formal warning or a reprimand, or to suspend them from office in certain circumstances. The vital principle is, however, that none of these actions can be taken unless the Lord Chancellor and the Lord Chief Justice agree on it. For a government minister to be involved in this way in judicial discipline may appear to strain the principle of judicial independence. However, the procedure helps to dispel any suspicion that judges would not wish to take action against a fellow judge, and also provides a safeguard. Equally, making the responsibility for discipline a joint responsibility of the Lord Chief Justice and the Lord Chancellor ensures that the suspicion cannot arise that judges can be disciplined on political grounds: a further safeguard of judicial independence and the rule of law. The fact that both have a role ensures that the independence of an individual judge is not improperly infringed, either by the executive, or internally by another more senior member of the judiciary.

All complaints are made, or referred, to the Judicial Complaints Investigations Office, which then assesses whether the complaint falls within the system. More than half do not because they are complaints about judicial decisions rather than judicial conduct.

Complaints about judicial conduct are considered by a nominated judge, who will either make a recommendation straight away to the Lord Chief Justice and the Lord Chancellor, or refer the case to an investigating judge. Ultimately a recommendation will be made to the Lord Chief Justice and Lord Chancellor, who will have to decide what action, if any, to take. The judge who is the subject of the complaint has a right to make submissions at every stage and, if he or she is not content with the decision, can refer the case to a Review Body.

Complaints against magistrates, of whom there are about 30,000, follow a different course as they are considered by Advisory Committees of magistrates, which recommend the appropriate action to the Lord Chief Justice and the Lord Chancellor.

It is also possible to ask for the Judicial Appointments and Complaints Ombudsman to review any decision made by the Office for Justice Complaints, thus providing a further route of appeal for those dissatisfied with a judge's personal conduct.

Other Forms of Accountability

These are valuable forms of indirect, explanatory accountability to the public, as they enable scrutiny of individual judicial decisions and the judiciary as an institution.

Individual Judges

Media Reports: The media often reports on the progress and outcome of court cases, as well as upon their views on a judge's performance in particular cases or in general. This form of accountability allows scrutiny through the media of individual judges.

The Judiciary as an Institution

Interviews and media briefings: The media also reports on matters concerning the judiciary as a whole. Additionally, judges from time to time give interviews or media briefings although these will never be to comment on a particular case or decision. Since the time when Lord Taylor was Lord Chief Justice the holder of that office has given press interviews. On occasion, it may also be helpful for judges to provide clarity—in general terms—to the public, via a media briefing, on a particular issue, though this will remain very much the exception rather than the rule. In addition, the Judicial Office press team will, on behalf of the judiciary, sometimes issue media statements where it is felt the judiciary's position needs to be publicly stated.

The Lord Chief Justice's Review of the Administration of Justice in the Courts: After the Constitutional Reform Act came into force in April 2006, the then Lord Chief Justice announced that he would publish a regular review of the areas for which the judiciary is now responsible, and to identify the matters which appeared to him to be of importance to the judiciary and to the administration of justice in England and Wales. The first such review, presented to the Queen as Head of State and Parliament, was published in March 2008.

Court reports: Individual courts also provide an annual report on their own performance throughout the year, including a commentary from the local Resident Judge, Designated Civil or Designated Family Judge.

Exercises

I. Fill in the gaps with the appropriate words or phrases given in the box.

A. powers	B. private	C. courts	D. the rule of law
E. England	F. discretion	G. interests	H. judges
I. life	J. judiciary		

Judicial independence is the concept that the 1_____ needs to be kept away from the other branches of government. That is, 2_____ should not be subject to improper influence from the other branches of government, or from 3_____ or partisan interests. Judicial independence is vital and important to the idea of separation of 4_____.

Different countries deal with the idea of judicial independence through different means of judicial selection, or choosing 5_____. One way to promote judicial independence is by granting 6_____ tenure or long tenure for judges, which ideally frees them to decide cases and make rulings according to 7_____ and judicial 8_____, even if those decisions are politically unpopular or opposed by powerful 9_____. This concept can be traced back to 18th century 10_____.

II. Questions

1. What is judicial independence?
2. Why is judicial independence a vital element of the democracy?
3. What are the consequences of judicial independence on the notion of judicial accountability?
4. What are the constraints placed on the judiciary by legislation enacted by Parliament?
5. What are the ways in which individual judges are accountable in the UK?
6. How are complaints about judicial conduct dealt with in the UK?

Chapter 7
HISTORY OF THE JUDICIARY

When you see a judge or magistrate sitting in court, you are actually looking at the result of 1,000 years of legal evolution.

It is doubtful that anyone asked to design a justice system would choose to copy the English and Welsh model. It is contradictory in places, and rather confusing. However, the judiciary is still changing and evolving to meet the needs of the society, and despite its oddities it is widely regarded as one of the best and most independent in the world.

A Real Ordeal

Justice for the Anglo-Saxons and even after the Norman invasion of 1066 was a combination of local and royal government. Local courts were presided over by a lord or one of his stewards. The King's court—the Curia Regis—was, initially at least, presided over by the King himself.

Today, going on trial in an English and Welsh court is not exactly a comfortable experience. But it is far better than trial by ordeal, used until almost the end of the 12th century to determine guilt or innocence in criminal cases.

Under this system, the accused would be forced to pick up a red hot bar of iron, pluck a stone out of a cauldron of boiling water, or something equally painful and dangerous.

If their hand had begun to heal after three days they were considered to have God on their side, thus proving their innocence. The number of "not guilty" verdicts recorded by this system is not known.

Another, extremely popular "ordeal" involved water; the accused would be tied up and thrown into a lake or other body of water. If innocent, he or she would sink.

There were two problems with this method, which was often used to try suspected witches: the accused was tied right thumb to left toe, left thumb to right toe, which made it almost impossible to sink; and opinion is divided as to whether those who did sink were fished out afterwards.

William II (1087—1100) eventually banned trial by ordeal—reportedly because 50 men accused of killing his deer had passed the test—and it was condemned by the Church in 1216.

Fighting for Freedom?

Criminal and civil disputes could also be decided by trial by combat, with a win held to prove either innocence or the right to whatever property was being disputed. Either side could employ their own champions, so the system wasn't perhaps as fair as it might be.

Trial by combat gradually fell into disuse for civil cases, although it wasn't until someone involved in a dispute in 1818 tried to insist on it that it was realised this was still, technically, an option. Trial by combat was quickly banned, forcing litigants to rely on more conventional routes.

The Earliest Judges

During this period judges gradually gained independence from the monarch and the government. The very first judges, back in the 12th century, were court officials who had particular experience in advising the King on the settlement of disputes. From that group evolved the justices in eyre, who possessed a mixed administrative and judicial jurisdiction.

The justices in eyre were not, to put it mildly, popular. In fact, they came to be regarded as instruments of oppression.

The seeds of the modern justice system were sown by Henry II (1154—1189), who established a jury of 12 local knights to settle disputes over the ownership of land. When Henry came to the throne, there were just 18 judges in the country—compared to more than 40,000 today.

In 1178, Henry II first chose five members of his personal household—two clergy and three lay—"to hear all the complaints of the realm and to do right".

This, supervised by the King and "wise men" of the realm, was the origin of the Court of Common Pleas.

Eventually, a new permanent court, the Court of the King's Bench, evolved, and judicial proceedings before the King came to be seen as separate from proceedings before the King's Council.

Seeds of Change

In 1166, Henry issued a Declaration at the Assize of Clarendon (an assize was an early form of the King's Council; the term later became the name for a sitting of a court).

The Assize of Clarendon ordered the remaining non-King's Bench judges to travel the country—which was divided into different circuits—deciding cases.

To do this, they would use the laws made by the judges in Westminster, a change that meant many local customs were replaced by new national laws. These national laws applied to everyone and so were common to all. Even today, we know them as the "common law".

The system of judges sitting in London while others travelled round the country became known as the "assizes system". Incredibly, it survived until 1971.

Changes evolved slowly; even in the middle of the 14th century, under Edward III, there could be close collaboration between the Court of King's Bench and the King's Council. A third common law court of justice, the Court of Exchequer, eventually emerged as the financial business of the Royal Household was split off to a specialist group of officials.

The First Professional Judges and Magistrates

Martin de Pateshull, Archdeacon of Norfolk and Dean of St Paul's, became a Justice of the bench in 1217. By the time he died in 1229 he was known as one of the finest lawyers in England; even 60 years after his death, his judgments were being searched for precedents.

Like Martin, many judges of this era were members of the clergy—although this did not necessarily mean they were parish priests, performing services, weddings and christenings. In an era when the church was rich and the King poor, joining the clergy was often just seen as a sensible means of support.

By the middle of the 13th century, knights had begun to join clerics on the bench. The first professional judges were appointed from the order of serjeants-at-law. These were advocates who practised in the Court of Common Pleas. Lawrence de Brok, a serjeant, became a judge in 1268, starting the tradition, which lasted until 1875, of serjeants being the group from which judges were chosen.

This was important, because it meant that the judiciary now had real professional experience of the law before moving on to the bench.

Over the years, serjeants were overtaken in popularity by barristers and solicitors, and even today, these are the groups from which the judiciary is appointed.

Growth of Independence

During this era bribes and payments were common, but even so, in the middle of the 13th century the judiciary was openly accused of corruption.

In 1346, judges were obliged to swear that "they would in no way accept gift or reward from any party in litigation before them or give advice to any man, great or small, in any action to which the King was a party himself."

Judicial salaries were also increased, possibly to make them less dependent on other forms of income.

This didn't always help: In 1350 the Chief Justice of the King's Bench, William de

Thorpe, was sentenced to death for bribery (he was later pardoned, but demoted).

The First Magistrates' Courts

Meanwhile, a new type of court began to evolve—that which we now recognise as the magistrates' court. Magistrates' courts hark back to the Anglo-Saxon moot court and the manorial court, but their official birth came in 1285, during the reign of Edward I, when "good and lawful men" were commissioned to keep the King's peace.

From that point, and continuing today, Justices of the Peace (JP) have undertaken the majority of the judicial work carried out in England and Wales (today, about 95 per cent of criminal cases are dealt with by magistrates).

Until the introduction of our modern system of councils in the 19th century, JPs also governed the country at a local level.

Problems with Politics

The 14th century saw members of the judiciary still involved in politics to some extent—for example, for ten years, Edward III's Chancellors were common-law judges.

In 1387, six judges advised Richard II that a parliamentary commission set up to limit his own powers was "invalid and traitorous". They were all impeached, convicted and sentenced to death, although only one was actually executed; the rest were banished to Ireland.

Unsurprisingly, for two centuries after this the judiciary kept almost entirely away from politics.

Moving away from Politics

During the turbulent 15th century—the Wars of the Roses—judges stood apart from both the Houses of Lancaster and York, and were largely unaffected by the changes in government.

From 1540 onwards, Henry VIII had no judges in his Privy Council. His son

Edward VI and daughter Mary I did include judges on their own Privy Councils, but Elizabeth I excluded them for 40 years.

In 1553, Mary I also removed three judges from office, but Elizabeth I made no changes on assuming the throne—although she did remove one later during her reign. The judiciary were becoming separate from the executive. Although it was generally accepted at this time that even the King was subject to the laws of the land, the Reformation added to the sovereign's powers; the state had taken over the Church's privilege to define the laws of God, and had removed the influence of the Pope as the ultimate arbiter on Earth.

So the King remained principal law-maker, with the judges as interpreters of that law; a potentially uneasy relationship.

Meanwhile, by the Elizabethan and early Stuart periods, assize judges on the six circuits in England were mainly dealing with the most serious crimes not normally handled by the local Quarter Sessions, run by JPs.

They also took a role in local administration, although this was much reduced following the English Civil War.

A Risky Business

On the face of it, the judiciary was becoming steadily more independent. In 1642, Charles I was forced to agree to the appointment of judges "during good behaviour", and their salaries were raised from under £200 to £1,000 a year in 1645.

On the restoration of the monarchy in 1660, all judges—and there were just 12 at this point, four in each of the common law courts—remained in office.

But in 1668 the system of appointments "during pleasure" was reintroduced, and in the last 11 years of his reign Charles II sacked 11 of his judges. The next king, Charles's brother James II, sacked 12 in just three years.

This was bound to affect the quality of the judiciary. Judges knew very well their jobs were at risk if the sovereign did not like their judgments.

Part I
The United Kingdom of Great Britain and Northern Ireland

A New Independence

The day after the House of Commons resolved that James II had abdicated, a parliamentary committee drew up Heads of Grievances to be presented to the new King, William III.

This document contained, among other things, items on paying judges' salaries out of public funds, and preventing judges being removed or suspended from office, "unless by due cause of law". These grievances eventually appeared in much the same form in the Act of Settlement (1701) and have remained in place ever since.

When Common Law Failed

Mirroring developments in the role and independence of judges were changes to the avenues of redress open to aggrieved parties. The common law system was an improvement on what had gone before, but it was still slow, highly technical—making procedural mistakes that could ruin a case all too likely—and vulnerable to corruption, especially when juries were used.

Fortunately, those who felt they had been failed by the common law system could still petition the King with their grievances.

Gradually, these cases were delegated to the King's council, and eventually to one individual—the Lord Chancellor.

Because of this, the Lord Chancellor came to be known as the "King's conscience", and began to preside over his own court, the Court of Chancery. This dealt only with civil disputes, for example, property and contract cases, and applied the law of equity—even-handedness or fairness.

By the time of Henry VIII, the Court of Chancery had become a rival to the common law courts.

But as the years went by, the Court of Chancery began to be known for the same problems it had been set up to combat: expense and delay. Also, the Lord Chancellor was free to give whatever ruling he liked in a Chancery court, unbound by the law—which made it almost impossible for lawyers to advise their clients correctly.

Changes to the System

It was not until 1830 that there was any change to the nearly 300-year-old assize courts. By the Law Terms Act of that year, the Court of Great Sessions was abolished and the Welsh counties and Chester were brought into the general circuit system. Shortly afterwards, the new Central Criminal Court was set up, unifying the administration of justice in London and surrounding areas.

In 1856, judges of the Central Criminal Court were also given the right to hear cases outside the court's ordinary jurisdiction, to ensure a fair trial where local prejudice existed or when it could offer an early trial and so avoid the delay involved in waiting for the next assizes.

County courts, dealing with civil cases, were created under the County Courts Act 1846.

The Judicature Act 1873 and After

In 1873, Parliament passed the Judicature Act which merged common law and equity. Although one of the Divisions of the High Court is still called Chancery, all courts could now administer both equity and common law—with equity to reign supreme in any dispute.

The same Act established the High Court and the Court of Appeal and provided a right of appeal in civil cases to the Court of Appeal. Criminal appeal rights remained limited until the establishment of a Court of Criminal Appeal under the Criminal Appeal Act 1907.

The Court of Criminal Appeal sat for nearly 60 years, until its existence as a separate body was ended by the Criminal Appeal Act 1966. Its jurisdiction passed to the Court of Appeal.

The Crown Court Is Created But Still Not Separate

Crown Courts as we know them today were not actually established until 1956, and then only in Liverpool and Manchester. These courts also took over the quarter sessions work in their cities.

The Royal Commission on Assizes and Quarter Sessions, 1966—1969, led to the abolition of courts of assize and quarter sessions and the establishment of a new Crown Court to deal with business from both, under the terms of the Courts Act 1971.

Hundreds of years of evolution may have resulted in an independent judiciary—but that doesn't mean they were entirely separated from government. Chief Justice Lord Mansfield was in the Cabinet between 1757 and 1765, for example and more recently Lord Cave was Home Secretary for a couple of months at the end of the First World War when he was also a serving Lord of Appeal in Ordinary, or Law Lord.

And until 2006, the Lord Chancellor was part of the executive, the legislature and the judiciary. The Lord Chancellor's role changed drastically on April 3, 2006 as a result of the Constitutional Reform Act 2005. This latest major change to affect the judiciary has been described as the most significant since Magna Carta. The Act establishes the Lord Chief Justice as President of the Courts of England and Wales and Head of its Judiciary, a role previously performed by the Lord Chancellor. For the first time an express statutory duty is placed on the Lord Chancellor and other Ministers of the Crown to protect the independence of the judiciary. For the first time in its 1,000-year history, the judiciary is officially recognized as a fully independent branch of the government.

Exercises

I. Identify the following statements as True or False.

1. Trial by ordeal was used until almost the end of the 13th century to determine guilt or innocence in criminal cases in England and Wales.

2. Only civil disputes could be decided by trial by combat, with a win held to prove the right to whatever property was being disputed.
3. The very first judges, back in the 12th century, were court officials who had particular experience in advising the King on the settlement of disputes.
4. Henry II (1154—1189) established a jury of 12 local knights to settle disputes over the ownership of land. The seeds of the modern justice system were sown then.
5. A new permanent court, the Court of the King's Bench, evolved during the reign of Henry II.
6. The system of judges sitting in London while others travelled round the country became known as the "assizes system". Incredibly, it survived until 1971.
7. The Court of King's Bench, the King's Council and the Court of Exchequer were three civil law courts of justice.
8. Magistrates' courts hark back to the Anglo-Saxon moot court and the manorial court, but their official birth came in 1285, during the reign of Edward I, when "good and lawful men" were commissioned to keep the King's peace.
9. The Court of Chancery dealt only with civil disputes and applied the law of equity-even-handedness or fairness. By the time of Henry VIII, the Court of Chancery had become a rival to the common law courts.
10. In 1873, Parliament passed the Judicature Act which merged common law and equity with equity to reign supreme in any dispute.

II. Questions

1. What do you know about trial by ordeal?
2. How did judges gain independence from the monarch and the government?
3. How did the first professional judges come into being?

Chapter 8
INTERESTING BRITISH LAWS

Britain—specifically England—is the origin of the common law and remains a common-law jurisdiction. Thus, unlike on the continent, justice is based heavily on precedent. In other words, if there exists an old case that is substantially similar to the case being decided on, then the ruling in the old case will be followed. Hence, a judge's final ruling for a case will be essentially a law that will bind all later substantially similar cases, unless a decision to overrule (which is rare, and only made by Supreme Court, or in previous eras the House of Lords) is made later. That is why in lawyer movies / TV series, lawyers may have to look up century-old cases for possible precedent which might be helpful for their current case, though mostly for better understanding as the laws created by those cases are readily documented in any references (unless it's so obscure or obsolete like the laws shown below).

It is important to note, however, that the law system in Scotland is very different from the rest of the UK. While laws passed by parliament (e.g. age restrictions and weapon laws) still come into effect, as a result of devolution, the Scottish parliament now passes laws of its own, and some new laws in the UK parliament do not apply. The system of courts and the legal basis for them is also different, and precedent is not as important in determining the law and the High Court of Justiciary (Scotland's highest criminal court) has limited declaratory powers. Even before devolution Scotland had a separate Common Law (Scots Law), as a result of its separate judiciary; unlike the English common law, Scots Law is heavily influenced by the Roman Civil Law (transmitted by French law professors before the House of Stuart inherited the English Crown, thanks to the Auld Alliance).

The law in Scotland also differs in that there are three outcomes possible in court: guilty, not guilty and not proven. Not proven is pretty unique to Scotland and means exactly the same as "not guilty". However, juries have begun applying it to mean that the court pretty much knows that the defendant has committed a crime, they can't actually prove it. The Scottish law system is sufficiently different to the English system that any lawyer wishing to transfer from one to the other is required to complete a one-year transition course.

Some Laws You Should Know
Smoking

It is now illegal to smoke in an enclosed public place, bar some minor exceptions for stage performances. Vaping currently falls outside this law, though some establishments still ban it as it is easy to mistake for actual smoking and it is easier for staff not to have to make judgement calls.

The Age to Buy Alcohol

It is legal to consume alcohol in a pub/bar/restaurant with a meal at 16, but it must be bought by someone at least 18. Only wine or beer, though, no spirits. And it is at the premises' discretion; they are legally allowed to refuse alcohol to 16-to-18-year-olds—actually, all selling of alcohol is at the premises' discretion, so someone can refuse to sell you alcohol even if you are clearly over 18 because they think you are already too drunk, or they are not convinced you are actually old enough (even if you've shown them ID, it might not be real, or yours, after all) which avoids issues if they don't believe what you say your age is.

The legal age to consume alcohol is 5 (you read that correctly), in private with parental supervision. This reflects actual British habits, as it is not considered harmful to give children small amounts of alcohol (not enough for the kid to get drunk on, of course) on certain occasions (particularly Christmas). Below that age, a doctor has to decide that it would be a good idea for some medical reason (rarely invoked, obviously).

Note that carrying an opened container of alcohol in a public place is an offence under various city bye-laws. Check if it applies to you. Normally the worst that will happen is the nice police officer will confiscate your stuff, but if you are egregiously drunk, you may end up spending a night in the cells.

Getting Married

The age to get married is 16 with parental permission, 18 without (except in Scotland, where it is 16 with or without parental consent). In UK works you may expect to run across references of teenage lovers eloping to get married in Gretna. Historically this was the first town you'd come to across the Scottish border and therefore seen as a quick place to get married in. As such it has accrued a bit of a romantic reputation and now has a sizable waiting list for marriages. Still, you can pass your time at the giant outlet mall near the motorway. Gay marriage has been legal for longer in England and Wales than in Scotland, so the reverse was true for gay couples until the Scottish legalization went into effect on 31 December 2014.

Gay marriages are not permitted in Northern Ireland. Gay marriages performed elsewhere in the UK are treated as civil partnerships there. The status of gay marriages performed in the Republic of Ireland (legal starting 2015 under the Thirty-Fourth Amendment to the Constitution of the State) is pending, but are likely to receive the same treatment.

The age of sexual consent is 16. If a person older than that has sex with someone below it, it is now rape of a young child (distinct from and more harshly punished than rape) if the younger partner is under 13 or sexual activity with a minor (if they're between 13 and 16; this carries a lesser punishment). Until recently, the age for male homosexuality was 18 (and before that, 21), and the age for female homosexuality was non-existent, as it had never been banned. They're now both set at 16.

Same-sex Civil Partnerships

Same-sex civil partnerships are legal. The establishment of civil partnerships gives us an excellent insight into the British character. Some people didn't like it, and many more said it couldn't be the same as a marriage. So the government created the term "civil partners" and said on no account was anyone in officialdom to consider civil partnerships as marriages and the terms were not interchangeable; however, the two offer the exact same sets of rights and responsibilities. As soon as the UK population were told not call CPs marriages, everyone did, the average Brit being determined to be bloody minded to the last.

Abortion

Abortion is legal up until 24 weeks if two doctors are satisfied that continuing the pregnancy risks injury to the physical/mental health of the woman (Section C of the Abortion Act) or existing children of the woman (Section D), effectively meaning that anybody determined to have one can. After that, it's the doctor's call.

This is a "conscience issue" in Parliament—MPs will not get told by their parties how to vote on this. This is also a conscience issue for doctors; no doctor has sign off on or carry out an abortion if it conflicts with their own beliefs but in this case they are legally obliged to refer the patient on to a doctor who will and also legally obliged to make sure that this delays the process as little as possible.

Abortion is illegal in Stroke Country and in the Republic of Ireland unless the Mother's life is threatened, but it is not illegal for people in either part of Ireland seeking abortions to travel to Britain to have one for free on the NHS. After a case in Ireland where pro-life doctors refused to allow a young Indian woman an abortion even though it was clear she would die without it, this may soon change for the Republic.

Jaywalk and Nudity

It is not illegal to jaywalk. Many Brits find the idea might be baffling. Even if crossing lights say "Don't Walk" you can happily cross if you can see the way is clear. This applies to all roads except Dual Carriageways and Motorways. Unlike the U.S. pedestrians do not have right of way at crossings or junctions. Many an American tourist in London has had a shock when they expect traffic to stop for them.

It is illegal to be naked in public when it causes distress in a public place (your back garden probably wouldn't count). Nudity is legal on a handful of public beaches.

Cannabis

Cannabis remains illegal, although there is some confusion among the public and the police guidelines will mean that officers will simply confiscate small amounts or hand out a fixed penalty notice.

Cannabis was originally classed with barbiturates in Class B; it was demoted to Class C a couple of years ago to join drugs such as Valium. However, the government has announced it will be returning to Class B (against the advice of their scientific advisory body) due to an increase in the strength of the commonly-available material.

Also related to the previous government's obsession with targets—arrest one person for possession? That is a single crime detection. Warn the whole group he is with (which couldn't be made to stick if arrests were made.) That is one detection for every person in the group.

Incitement to Racial Hatred

Incitement to racial hatred is a criminal offence. Any criminal act that is racially motivated or homophobic will get an increased sentence. Attempts to bring in similar laws for "religious hatred" failed due to concerns over stifling legitimate debate. Similarly, Rowan Atkinson led a campaign to remove a vaguely worded provision against "insulting" language, which it was feared would lead to an even worse stifling.

The Possession of Handguns by Civilians

The possession of handguns by civilians has been illegal since 1998. This was in response to the Dunblane Massacre, a school shooting in which sixteen young children and a teacher were killed and fifteen injured by someone armed with four handguns.

Shotguns require a licence. The licence is a right and it is up to Police to have a reason NOT to issue one. Getting a licence for a rifle requires a "good reason" and it is up to you to show why you should have it. A licence can be issued for specific uses in specific areas, ie "To shoot rabbit on Warren Farm" and you can then only use the weapon for that specific use and no other. (It explicitly cannot be for self-defence, excepted in Norn

Iron), but there is no lower age limit.

Carrying "realistic-looking replica firearms" openly in public is illegal. Airsoft weapons should be stored in a case, unloaded. Since the passing of the Violent Crime Reduction Act 2006, the sale of such is also illegal barring a few specific defences.

Carrying a knife in public is illegal, unless it meets very specific criteria (the blade must be under 3" and not fixed or automatic (i.e. it must fold out of the handle by being pulled on by the user) unless the owner can prove they have a good reason for carrying it, e.g. their job. Until recently any bladed instrument could be owned on private property except for butterfly knives. The sale, import and export of curved swords is now illegal, excepting traditionally manufactured and martial arts swords. Also, you have to be 18 to buy all forms of blades, including butter knives, paper knives and safety scissors, leading to the odd situation of University students without ID being prevented from buying cutlery for their first year away from home.

Exceptions to all weapon laws are made with regards to antiques.

Licences to Watch Broadcast Television

It is illegal to watch broadcast television without a licence. The BBC does not run adverts and is instead funded by these licence fees.

The BBC may not run adverts, and can not make or fund any show with product placement, nor can they show 3rd party shows with obvious product placement, however commercial offshoots (Like BBC America) can show product placement with some limitations.

Furthermore, all "public service broadcasters" (i.e, all of them) are mandated by law to be impartial in all things. Thus, shows like *The Daily Show* or *The O'Reilly Factor* could not be made in Britain, as their hosts offer blatantly partisan comment (though British people can still watch them if they can pick them up). Political debate is supplied by shows such as *Newsnight* and *Question Time*, where politicians of each of the "main" parties are invited on to debate/be grilled by the hosts. This only extends so far—it is at the BBC's discretion which views they may deem "discredited" and thus ignore note.

Part I
The United Kingdom of Great Britain and Northern Ireland

This sometimes causes controversy, such as a recent BBC decision to "review" whether or not the view that "global warming is not occurring/man-made" should still be considered a valid viewpoint.

Driving Licenses

Age to get a driving license for a car is 17; 16 for mopeds or small agricultural tractors. A driving license is not required on private land.

As a general rule, cars keep the same registration number from showroom to scrapyard. Vintage cars lacking the original number are worth substantially less than those that do. Number plates are bought from third-party suppliers rather than supplied by the registration authority. If you are a vain twitnote then you can get a personalized numberplate. There are various rules on what it may say, for instance, S4M would be allowed by P3N15 would not.

Killing the Sovereign

If you design to/attempt to/deliberately kill the Sovereign, any of their family, then you must be tried for treason, not murder or manslaughter (neither of these verdicts, in fact, are available to the court). Duress and marital coercion are not defenses. If it was by accident then manslaughter and negligent homicide are available. The Treason Act 1495 provides that in a civil war between two claimants to the throne, those who fight for the losing side cannot be held guilty of a crime merely for fighting against the winner.

The Old Dumb Laws

Every country in the world seems to have a collection of strange laws that are bizarre, outdated or just plain wrong, even to the people who live there. Britain is no exception and it is quite probable that you may have already heard of some of these as the BBC held a competition some years ago to see which of these laws the public felt were the most stupid.

All men over the age of 14 are required to train with a longbow for two hours every Sunday.

If you meet a Welshman within the city walls of Coventry after dark, it is legal to shoot him with a crossbow. There are multiple variations of this in various cities. They generally involve criteria such as:

> The victim being Welsh or Scottish; which tends to depend which border is nearer;
> It being (or not) a Sunday or under certain circumstances on a Sunday;
> Some specified weapon, usually a bow or crossbow;
> Being within the city limits or a specific area of the city.

Contrary to popular belief, the infamous "Suicide is punished by hanging" law has been repealed for some time.

Several Christmas pastimes, such as eating mince pies on December 25th, are technically illegal due to the efforts of Oliver Cromwell to cancel Christmas after he won the Civil War.

Up until the late Nineties, there were still three crimes which carried the death penalty, even though the death penalty itself had been abolished for most crimes thirty years before. These were treason, piracy on the high seas, and arson in HM shipyards. The last provision is a relic of when Britain's navy was made of wooden ships and so starting a fire in HM dockyards could potentially cripple British military strength. Sort of the equivalent to setting off a fission bomb in Pearl Harbor. The arson in HM shipyards was demoted as separate incrimination in 1971, and folded in the general crime of arson.

Scotland has several old, never abolished laws, specific to the area, for example:

> It is illegal to be drunk and in "control" of a cow. Though this law did actually make a lot of sense when it was passed, as farmers would go to town centres on market day, get sloshed, and then have to drive their unsold livestock back to their farms, except they were now woefully incapable of doing so. The chaos this created makes the law seem rather clever, in hindsight.
> In the city of Glasgow it is illegal to tie your goat to a lamppost.

Notably, while male homosexuality was illegal in Britain until the latter half of the

20th Century, lesbianism was not outlawed because (so legend has it) Queen Victoria refused to believe women would actually do such things and persuaded the Prime Minister of the time to remove references to it from the Act. In truth, as a constitutional monarch, the Queen did not have the power to overrule parliament. Had she tried, there would have been political uproar. There is belief, however, that parliament themselves omitted lesbianism in case including it gave women ideas.

It is illegal to resign from the House of Commons. However, an MP who accepts an "office of profit under the Crown"—that is to say, a paid position in the executive or judiciary of the UK—must immediately stand to be re-elected to Parliament from their constituency in a special by-election or else be disqualified from Parliament. However, positions in the Cabinet and most other executive positions with a Crown salary are exempt from this rule (to spare the expense and annoyance of having to run by-elections for nearly the entire Government as soon as it is formed). Thus in order to resign from Parliament, MPs resort to a legal fiction whereby they are appointed to an office of profit under the Crown that is not exempted (usually either Crown Steward and Bailiff of the Chiltern Hundreds or Steward and Bailiff of the Manor of Northstead, non-jobs with pittance salaries), immediately disqualifying them from serving in Parliament unless they stand again (which, with one notable exception, has not happened since the exemptions were established).

All of these laws (except for the rules about resignation from Parliament, which now largely consists of loopholes large enough to sail a Queen Elizabeth-class carrier through), are now no longer on the books however, as in the 90s a bill was passed in Westminster striking all bylaws and laws over a certain age (made possible by the fact that Sir Robert Peel amalgamated most of the sensible laws into a few, easier to access, acts known as the Peel's Acts) from the books, requiring them to be re-passed. All the old and daft bylaws are gone.

I. Identify the following statements as True or False.

1. The decision to overrule a former judge's final ruling for a case is only made by Supreme Court (or in previous eras the House of Lords).
2. Scots Law is heavily influenced by the Roman Civil Law, so there is no separate common law in Scotland.
3. It is now illegal to smoke in an enclosed public place, bar some minor exceptions for stage performances.
4. The legal age to consume alcohol is 5, in private with parental supervision, while it is 18 in a pub/bar/restaurant.
5. Gay marriage has been legal for longer in England and Wales than in Scotland and Northern Ireland.
6. Smoking as well as vaping in an enclosed public place is now illegal.
7. The possession of handguns by civilians has been legal since 1998.
8. All "public service broadcasters" are mandated by law to be impartial in all things.
9. A driving license is also required on private land.
10. Those who deliberately kill the Sovereign or any of their family must be tried for treason, not murder or manslaughter except that there exists duress or marital coercion.

II. Questions

1. What do you know about the differences between the law system in Scotland and the rest of the UK from the text?
2. What is a method of avoiding precedents mentioned in the text in England?
3. Are there laws on smoking and the age to buy alcohol in your country? If any, give two justifications for these laws.

Part II

The United States of America

Chapter 1
BASIC CONCEPTS OF AMERICAN JURISPRUDENCE

Summary of Basic American Legal Principles

What follows are some of the fundamental principles that comprise the American legal system. Each of these is discussed in greater detail in this and other chapters of this book. They are summarized below in order to give the reader an overview of some of the basics of American common law.

Impact of Precedent—The Principle of Stare Decisis

The defining principle of common law is the requirement that courts follow decisions of higher level courts within the same jurisdiction. It is from this legacy of stare decisis that a somewhat predictable, consistent body of law has emerged.

Court Hierarchy

Court level or hierarchy defines to a great degree the extent to which a decision by one court will have a binding effect on another court. The federal court system, for instance, is based on a three-tiered structure, in which the United States District Courts are the trial-level courts; the United States Court of Appeals is the first level court of appeal; and the United States Supreme Court is the final arbiter of the law.

Jurisdiction

The term "jurisdiction" has two important meanings in American law. One meaning of "jurisdiction" refers to the formal power of a court to exercise judicial authority over a particular matter. Although the term most often is used in connection with the jurisdiction of a court over particular matters, one may also speak of matters being within or beyond the jurisdiction of any other governmental entity.

Second, the federal court system is based on a system of "jurisdictions", the geographic distribution of courts of particular levels. For instance, while there is only one Supreme Court, the court of appeals is divided into 13 circuits, and there are 94 district courts. In addition, each state court system comprises its own "jurisdiction". As indicated above, the jurisdiction in which a case arose will determine which courts' decisions will be binding precedents.

Mandatory / Binding Versus Persuasive Authority

Some of the various sources of law that will be examined are considered to be "mandatory" or "binding", while other sources are considered to be merely "persuasive".

Indeed, a court may completely disregard precedent that is not binding (i.e., not even consider it to be persuasive). The issue of whether authority is mandatory or persuasive relates directly to the application of stare decisis principles.

Primary Versus Secondary Authority

The various sources of law may also be broken down into primary and secondary sources of law. Primary sources of law may be mandatory on a particular court, or they may be merely persuasive. Whether they are binding or persuasive will depend on various factors. Secondary authority is not itself law, and is never mandatory authority. A court may, however, look towards secondary sources of law for guidance as to how to resolve a particular issue. Secondary authority is also useful as a case finding tool and for general information about a particular issue.

Dual Court Systems

The American legal system is based on a system of federalism, or decentralization. While the national or "federal" government itself possesses significant powers, the individual states retain powers not specifically enumerated as exclusively federal. Most states have court systems which mirror that of the federal court system.

Interrelationship Among Various Sources of Law

One of the more complex notions of American jurisprudence is the extent to which the various sources of law, from both the state and federal systems, interrelate with one another. There is a complex set of rules that defines the relative priority among various sources of law and between the state and federal systems.

What Is Common Law?

The term "common law" evokes confusion and uncertainty—which is no surprise given its duality of meaning. The term "common law" may refer to any of the following:

Common Law as Differentiated from Civil Law

The American system is a "common law" system, which relies heavily on court precedent in formal adjudications. In the common law system, even when a statute is at issue, judicial determinations in earlier court cases are extremely critical to the court's resolution of the matter before it.

Civil law systems rely less on court precedent and more on codes, which explicitly provide rules of decision for many specific disputes. When a judge needs to go beyond the letter of a code in disposing of a dispute, the judge's resolution will not become binding or perhaps even relevant in subsequent determinations involving other parties.

Case Law

Common law may refer to "judge-made" law, otherwise known as case law.

Cases are legal determinations based on a set of particular facts involving parties with a genuine interest in the controversy.

Case Law May Be of Several General Types:

- Pure decisional case law—Court called upon to decide cases on the basis of prior court decisions (precedent) and / or policy and a sense of inherent fairness. In cases of pure decisional law, there is no applicable statute or constitutional provision that applies. This type of decisional law is what is referred to as "judicially-created doctrine". Historically, the term "case law" referred to certain areas of law (e.g., torts, property) that began as judge-made, or pure decisional law.

- Case law based on constitutional provisions—Court called upon to consider whether a particular statute or governmental action is consistent with the United

States Constitution or a particular state constitution. Court interpretation may rely upon prior decisional law interpreting the same or some other constitutional provision.
- ➢ Case law based on statutory provisions—Court called upon to interpret a statute. Court interpretation may rely upon prior decisional law interpreting the same or similar statute.

Subsequent Case History:
- ➢ Subsequent Case History defined—What a higher level court has done with respect to a lower-level court decision on appeal.
- ➢ Importance of Subsequent Case History—If a higher level court has taken action on a lower level case, it is the opinion and holding of the higher level court that will constitute the precedent in the case. A higher level court opinion will in effect abrogate the lower level court opinion in the same case.

Subsequent Case Treatment:
- ➢ Subsequent Case Treatment—defined as What other cases have said about the initial case. Has it been followed? Reversed? Distinguished? Applied in a specific way?
- ➢ Importance of Subsequent Case Treatment—It will indicate how the same and other courts interpret the initial case.

A System Based on Advocacy and the Presence of Actual Controversy

The American legal system is adversarial and is based on the premise that a real, live dispute involving parties with a genuine interest in its outcome will allow for the most vigorous legal debate of the issues, and that courts should not have the power to issue decisions unless they are in response to a genuine controversy. Hence, federal courts are prohibited from issuing "advisory" opinions, or opinions that do not involve a live case or controversy. These principles are based on Article III of the U.S. Constitution, which limits federal court jurisdiction to "cases and controversies". Unlike the federal courts, some states do allow for the presentation of cases that are not based on live controversies, and hence do not share the federal court bias against advisory opinions.

Threshold Issues Designed to Preclude Advisory Opinions

Given the prohibition against advisory opinions by the federal courts, there are certain threshold prerequisites which must be satisfied before a federal court hears a case. Issues surrounding the applicability of these prerequisites may also arise in state courts and on petitions for review of agency orders. The principal prerequisites to court review are the following:

Standing—The parties must have an actual, cognizable, usually pecuniary or proprietary, interest in the litigation.

Finality—In the case of appeals or agency review, the action by the trial court or administrative body must be final and have a real impact on the parties.

Exhaustion—The parties must have exhausted any possible avenues for relief available in the trial court or administrative body.

Ripeness—The dispute must present a current controversy which has immediate rather than anticipated or hypothetical effects on the parties.

Mootness—The dispute must not have been resolved. Nor must the circumstances have changed in any way that renders the dispute no longer subject to controversy.

No Political Questions—Courts will not involve themselves in nonjusticiable disputes that are between the other two branches of the federal government and are of a political nature.

While these prerequisites are well-established, the courts tend to apply them in a pragmatic way and allow exceptions to these requirements when warranted by the facts.

Courts Generally Confine Themselves to the Dispute Presented for Resolution

As a jurisdictional matter, courts are supposed to restrict their holdings to the narrowest terms possible in resolving a dispute. This limitation relates to the principle of dictum, under which portions of the opinion not required for the resolution of the precise issues before the court on the facts presented by the parties are of diminished precedential value.

Tendency to Avoid Constitutional Issues When Possible

Federal courts also tend to avoid deciding constitutional issues when they are able to decide a case on a procedural, statutory, or some other ground.

Institutional Roles in the American Legal System

Attorney

Depending upon the circumstances and the needs of the client, the lawyer may be a counselor, a negotiator, and / or a litigator. In each of these roles, the lawyer will need to engage in factual investigation. With respect to each of these roles, the lawyer will do the following:

Counselor: Attorney will help advise the client how to order the client's affairs, how or whether to proceed with a proposed course of action, or how to proceed with respect to pending or potential litigation or settlement. Often, this is when the lawyer will prepare (or ask that someone prepare) an interoffice memorandum of law, which will examine the client's legal position and help the lawyer counsel the client.

Negotiator: Lawyer will work with opposing counsel to try to get a favorable resolution for the client with respect to a pending dispute. The parties may already be in litigation when they negotiate, or the parties, through their attorneys, may be negotiating a resolution to a dispute not yet in court. The art of negotiating involves many techniques individual to particular attorneys and the circumstances. The client always retains the right to accept or reject a settlement negotiated or offered by the opposing party.

Litigator: In litigating, the attorney will help pick a jury and participate in pretrial motions. At trial, the attorney will present evidence through testimony of witnesses, documents and perhaps demonstrative evidence (e.g., charts, diagrams). The lawyer will also present an opening statement and closing argument, and will make and respond to evidentiary objections lodged by the opposing party. The lawyer may also make motions, sometimes supported by a memorandum in support thereof before the court, and propose to the court a set of jury instructions.

Fact Investigator: All of the lawyer's roles require the investigation of relevant facts, including locating and interviewing witnesses.

A lawyer is to be a zealous advocate of his / her client. In this respect, the lawyer must advocate on the client's behalf and avoid conflicts of interest. The lawyer is also an officer of the court and is required to deal fairly and honestly with the court and with its other officers, including the lawyer's opponents.

There are specific ethical rules applicable to these issues, but in most circumstances, when the client's interests and those of the lawyer as officer of the court conflict or otherwise interfere with each other, the lawyer is generally expected to favor his or her role as advocate of the client.

Judge

The judge is the final arbiter of the law. The judge is charged with the duty to state, as a positive matter, what the law is. At trial, the judge takes a passive, "umpire" role in connection with the presentation of evidence by counsel. The judge must also make evidentiary rulings, and charge the jury as to the law to be applied. In addition, the judge is to maintain order in the courtroom. Occasionally, when the parties agree, the judge may also act as trier of fact. This is known as a "bench trial". Judges in federal courts are appointed by the President with the "advice and consent" of the Senate. Many state court judges are elected by popular vote.

Jury

The jury, a group of local citizens, is the fact-finder in most trials. The jury will receive instructions from the judge as to the law, and its members will assess the facts as they perceive them in light of the law as instructed, to return a verdict.

Exercises

I. Choose the appropriate answer(s) to each question. There may be more than one choice for some questions.

1. Which of the following is NOT true about the United States federal court system?

    A. The United States District Courts are the trial-level courts.

    B. The United States Higher Court is the first level court of appeal.

    C. The United States Supreme Court is the final arbiter of the law.

    D. The United States federal court system is based on a four-tiered structure.

2. In American law "jurisdiction" or system of jurisdiction may_____.

    A. refer to the formal power of a court to exercise judicial authority over a particular matter

    B. mean the dual court systems

    C. refer to the power of any other governmental entity to exercise authority over a particular matter

    D. mean the geographic distribution of courts of particular levels

3. Which of the following are true about the dual court systems in America?

    A. The U.S. court system is divided into two administratively separate systems.

    B. For the federal court system, there is only one Supreme Court, the court of appeals is divided into 13 circuits, and there are 93 district courts.

    C. The American legal system is based on a system of federalism.

    D. Most states have court systems which mirror that of the federal court system.

4. Which of the following are true about the term "common law"?

    A. It may refer to "common law" system differentiated from civil law systems which rely less on court precedent and more on codes.

    B. It may refer to "judge-made" law.

    C. It may mean case law.

    D. The defining principle of common law is stare decisis.

5. Case law may present as _____.

   A. judicially-created doctrine

   B. decisional law interpreting prior same or some other constitutional provision

   C. prior decisional law interpreting the same or similar statute

   D. certain areas of law (e.g., torts, property) that began as judge-made, or pure decisional law

6. Subsequent case treatment may take the form of _____.

   A. being followed

   B. being reversed

   C. being distinguished

   D. being applied in a specific way

7. When the client's interests and those of the lawyer as an officer of the court conflict or otherwise interfere with each other, what is the lawyer generally expected to do?

   A. The lawyer is generally expected to favor his/her own interest.

   B. The lawyer is generally expected to favor more substantial interest.

   C. The lawyer is generally expected to favor his or her role as an officer of the court.

   D. The lawyer is generally expected to favor his or her role as advocate of the client.

8. The American legal system is adversarial and is based on the premise that _____.

   A. there is a real, live dispute

   B. parties involved in a dispute have a genuine interest in its outcome

   C. live controversies will allow for the most vigorous legal debate of the issues

   D. courts should not have the power to issue decisions unless they are in response to a genuine controversy

9. Depending upon the circumstances and the needs of the client, the lawyer may take the role of _____.

   A. a counselor

   B. a negotiator

C. a litigator

D. a factual investigator

10. Which of the following are NOT true about the role of the American judge?

    A. The judge is charged with the duty to state what the law is.

    B. The judge must also make evidentiary rulings.

    C. The judge need not charge the jury as to the law to be applied.

    D. The judge is not responsible for maintaining order in the courtroom.

II. Questions

1. Can you summarize the basic American legal principles?
2. In what way is the American legal system regarded as "adversarial"?
3. What are the threshold prerequisites which must be satisfied before a federal court hears a case?
4. What roles does the attorney play in the American legal system?
5. What roles does the judge play in the American legal system?
6. What roles does the jury play in the American legal system?

Chapter 2
OVERVIEW OF THE U.S. LEGAL SYSTEM

The U.S. legal system is a complex organization of federal and state governmental divisions. In order to understand the U.S. legal system, you should first know which laws, rules or regulations control. In other words, which laws have priority or controlling effect.

The U.S. Constitution is the highest law of the land. federal laws enacted by the U.S. Congress come next. This does not mean that the Federal Congress can adopt laws that control states in every situation. It can't unless the law can be applied to the states under the U.S. Constitution and court decisions.

Each state has a legislature that adopts state laws called "statutes". Those statutes are sometimes complied into what is referred to as a code. This is nothing more than a codification of all the applicable statutes.

The U.S. legal system is based on federal law, augmented by laws enacted by state legislatures and local laws passed by counties and cities. Most rights and freedoms enjoyed by Americans are enshrined in the first ten amendments of the U.S. Constitution and popularly known as the "Bill of Rights".

Legal System

The courts enforce statutes and interpret them. They also invalidate unconstitutional statutes, and make law in areas not covered by statutes. Here are some examples of the four main roles played by courts:

Enforcement

The Copyright Act gives a copyright owner the exclusive right to reproduce the owner's work. A copyright infringement suit is an example of court enforcement of a statute.

Interpretation

According to the Copyright Act, the copyright in a work created by an employee within the scope of his or her employment is owned by the employer. The Copyright Act does not define the term "employee". The Supreme Court case that defines the term is an example of court interpretation of a statute.

Invalidation

The courts invalidate unconstitutional laws. Unconstitutional laws are laws that conflict with provisions of the Constitution. The Constitution is the supreme law of the United States. Many "constitutionality" cases involve claims that a law violates the Constitution's Bill of Rights (the first ten amendments). In *Roe v. Wade*, the Supreme Court invalidated a state statute restricting women's access to abortion. According to the Court, the statute violated a pregnant woman's constitutional right of privacy.

Making Laws

The courts create the law for "common law" subject areas. Common law covers areas not covered by statutes. In many states, for example, individuals' rights of privacy and publicity are protected under common law rather than under statutory laws.

Types of Courts

There are several types of courts. The federal and state court systems consist of two levels of courts: trial courts and appellate courts. Cases are tried in trial courts. Appellate courts review the decisions of the trial courts.

The federal court system is divided into 13 judicial circuits. Eleven of the circuits are numbered. Each of the numbered circuits contains more than one state. The Ninth Circuit, for example, covers California, Oregon, Washington, Idaho, Nevada, Arizona, Alaska, and Hawaii. The 12th and 13th circuits are the District of Columbia Circuit and the Federal Circuit. The Federal Circuit handles appeals in patent cases and Claims Court cases.

Each federal circuit has one appellate court. These courts are known as Courts of Appeals or Circuit Courts. The Supreme Court reviews the decisions of the Courts of Appeals.

Each federal circuit is divided into judicial districts. A district can be as small as one city or as large as an entire state. The trial courts are known as the United States District Courts.

The Federal Courts

A separate system of federal courts operates alongside state courts and deals with cases arising under the U.S. Constitution or any law or treaty. Federal courts also hear disputes involving state governments or between citizens resident in different states. Cases falling within federal jurisdiction are heard before a federal district judge. Appeals can be made to the Circuit Court of Appeals and in certain cases to the U.S. Supreme Court.

The Civil and Criminal Courts

There's a clear separation and distinction between civil courts, which settle disputes between people, such as property division after a divorce, and criminal courts that prosecute those who break the law. Crimes are categorised as minor offences ("misdemeanors") or serious violations of the law ("felonies"). Misdemeanors include offences such as dropping litter, illegal parking or jay-walking, and are usually dealt with by a fine without a court appearance. Felonies, which include robbery and drug dealing, are tried in a court of law and those found guilty are generally sentenced to prison (jail). In many counties and cities, there are often eccentric local laws, usually relating to misdemeanors rather than felonies.

People who commit misdemeanors may be issued a summons (unsuspecting foreigners who violate local by-laws may be let off with a warning), while anyone committing a felony is arrested. An arrest almost always involves being "frisked" for concealed weapons, handcuffed and read your rights. You must be advised of your constitutional (Miranda) rights when arrested. These include the right to remain silent, the right to have a lawyer present during questioning, and the right to have a free court-appointed lawyer if you cannot afford one. You will be asked if you wish to waive your rights. This isn't recommended, as any statement you make can then be used against you in a court of law.

It is better to retain your rights and say nothing until you have spoken with a lawyer. At the police department, you are charged and have the right to make one telephone call. This should be to your embassy or consulate, a lawyer or the local legal aid office, or (if necessary) to someone who will stand bail for you. You are then put into a cell until your case comes before a judge, usually the same or next day, who releases you (if there is no case to answer) or sets bail. Bail may be a cash sum or the equivalent property value. For minor offences, you may be released on your "personal recognisance". In serious cases, a judge may oppose bail.

Jurisdiction

The federal courts have jurisdiction over cases involving federal statutes (the Copyright Act, for example) and other "federal questions". They also have jurisdiction over cases in which the party filing the suit and the party being sued reside in different states. This type of federal jurisdiction is known as "diversity" jurisdiction.

Other types of cases must be brought in state courts.

Litigation

Litigation is an American tradition and national sport, and every American has a right to his day in court (as well as to his 15 minutes of fame). There are 15 to 20 million civil suits a year, which leads to a huge backlog of cases in all states and even the Supreme Court. One of the most unusual aspects of the U.S. law is that lawyers are permitted to work on a contingency fee basis, whereby they accept cases on a "no-win, no-fee" basis. If they win, their fee is as high as 50 per cent of any damages. If you must hire a lawyer on a non-contingency basis, the cost is usually prohibitive.

Many people believe this system helps pervert the cause of justice, as a lawyer's only concern is winning a case, often irrespective of any ethical standards or the facts of the matter. The contingency-fee system is responsible for the proliferation of litigation cases, which lawyers are happy to pursue because of the absurdly high awards made by the U.S. courts.

The litigation system is primarily designed to make lawyers rich, while ensuring that almost everyone else ends up a loser. Not only must individuals have liability insurance to protect against being sued, but everyone from doctors to plumbers must have expensive malpractice insurance to protect themselves against litigious patients or customers. The whole U.S. economy and legal system is underpinned by litigation, in which it seems half the population are directly employed and the other half are plaintiffs or defendants.

Everyone except lawyers agrees that litigation is out of control and is seriously undermining the U.S.'s competitiveness. Nobody, however, seems to know what to do about it. Meanwhile, lawyers spend their time dreaming up new and lucrative areas of litigation. They even follow ambulances in an attempt to be first in line to represent accident victims, hence the term "ambulance chasers"!

In many states, there are hair-raising product liability, personal liability and consequential loss laws. Some of these have limited liability, while others don't, which means that multiple warnings are printed on the most unlikely articles. In fact, most companies attempt to anticipate the most ridiculous and implausible events in order to protect themselves against litigation. Taken to ridiculous extremes a bottle of beer would have warnings about drinking and driving, choking on the stopper, breaking the glass and cutting yourself or someone else, swallowing broken glass, taking alcohol where it is prohibited, drinking under age or giving a drink to someone under age, alcoholism, carrying alcohol in your car or over certain state borders, being mugged or falling over while drunk, etc. —and this is hardly an exaggeration!

In fact, alcohol does carry a number of health warnings regarding cancer risk and other health problems, birth defects, driving and operating machinery. In Colorado, a barman must insure himself against being sued for serving someone who is later involved in a car accident. In the U.S., you can sue a tobacco company for causing your cancer, a car manufacturer for causing an accident, a ski firm for contributing to your ski accident, or a computer software company for fouling up your tax return. In fact anything that can (however remotely) be blamed on someone else, will be!

If you are the victim of an accident, you must never discuss your injuries with anyone connected with the other party and must never sign any documents they present to you without legal advice. Put the matter in the hands of an experienced litigation lawyer and let him handle everything. And in case you might forget, there are television adverts advising you of your rights to sue in accident situations, by attorneys claiming special competence at winning huge settlements.

Most companies and professionals are so frightened of the courts that many cases don't go to trial, e.g. personal injury and medical malpractice cases, which, apart from the cost of losing, are bad for business. This adds to the proliferation of law suits, as it is expensive to fight a legal battle even if you win, and litigants know that most companies are happy to settle out of court. If you are in business and not being sued by at least 100 people, it is usually a sign that you are broke and therefore not worth suing. If someone sues you for your last dime, don't take it personally—it is simply business.

Not surprisingly there are a lot of lawyers in the U S. The chief role of lawyers is to make themselves (very) rich and to make business as difficult as possible for everyone else. Never forget that lawyers are in business for themselves and nobody else and, although they may be representing you, their brief never strays far from the bottom line (i.e. how much they will be paid).

Many social service agencies provide free legal assistance to immigrants (legal and illegal), although some may serve the nationals of a particular country or religion only. There are help lines and agencies offering free legal advice in most towns and cities, many with legal aid societies (offering free advice and referral on legal matters), Better Business Bureaux (dealing with consumer-related complaints, shopping services, etc.) and departments of consumer affairs (who also handle consumer complaints).

Civil and Criminal Cases

A criminal case is brought by the federal government or a state to prosecute a defendant (the party sued) for violations of the government's criminal laws. Murder and burglary are examples of violations of criminal laws. If the defendant in a criminal case is found guilty by the jury, he or she is sentenced by the court to serve a jail sentence or pay a fine as punishment for the crime.

A civil case is a case brought by one party (the "plaintiff") against another party (the "defendant") to resolve a legal dispute involving rights based on statutory law or common law. A copyright infringement case is an example of a civil case involving statutory law. A suit seeking damages for a writer's breach of a contract (in which the writer promised to create a script for a movie but failed to do so) is an example of a civil case involving common law rights.

While certain violations of the Copyright Act and the Lanham Act (the federal trademark statute) are criminal violations, multimedia developers and publishers will be concerned primarily with civil cases.

Civil Lawsuits

There are several stages in civil lawsuits, from initiation to trial and then on to stages of appeal. We will discuss these stages in this section.

Initiation

A civil lawsuit is initiated when the plaintiff files a "complaint" against the defendant alleging that the defendant has wronged the plaintiff in some way recognized by the law. In most civil lawsuits, the plaintiff asks the court to award the plaintiff "damages" (a remedy for the defendant's wrongdoing—usually money) or to order the defendant to do something.

The defendant responds to the allegations in the complaint by filing an "answer" (a document in which the defendant admits or denies the complaint's allegations and states defenses). The defendant can also file a "counterclaim" against the plaintiff (allegations that the plaintiff has wronged the defendant).

Trial

If the parties do not "settle" the case (reach their own agreement on how to resolve the dispute), the case eventually goes to trial. In most types of civil cases, the Constitution gives the parties a right to a jury trial. The role of the jury is to decide questions of fact. However, in some complex cases, the parties choose to dispense with the jury and have the case decided by the judge.

Appeal

If the losing party in a civil lawsuit is not satisfied with the decision of the trial court, the losing party can appeal the case to the appropriate appellate court.

In the federal court system, the appeal generally must be filed with the Court of Appeals for the judicial circuit in which the trial was held. A case tried in the United States District Court for the Northern District of California, for example, must be appealed to the Court of Appeals for the Ninth Circuit.

An appellate court's job in reviewing a trial court's decision is to look for "mistakes of law" made by the trial court. Appellate courts do not "second guess" factual issues decided by trial courts. In American legal system, factual issues are supposed to be resolved by the jury, not by the appellate court. So long as there is adequate factual evidence to support the verdict, an appellate court will not reverse a trial court's decision or "remand" the case (send it back to the trial court for retrial) unless they find that the trial court made a "mistake of law".

Filing an appeal is probably a waste of money unless a losing party can reasonably hope to convince the appellate judges that there is insufficient evidence to support the trial court's decision, or that the trial court misapplied the law.

Example: Plaintiff's lawsuit alleges that the defendant infringed the copyright on the plaintiff's song by copying the melody of the song. The jury found that the defendant did not infringe the plaintiff's copyright. If the jury reached its decision after being told by the judge that a song's melody is not protected by copyright (a mistake in the applicable law, copyright law), the plaintiff has a good basis for appeal. However, if the jury reached its decision after listening to the defendant's song and concluding that the melody of the defendant's song is not similar to the melody of the plaintiff's song, the plaintiff does not have a strong basis for appeal. (Whether or not the songs have similar melodies is a factual determination.)

Appellate courts generally issue written opinions explaining how they have reached their conclusions on whether to affirm (uphold), reverse, or remand a case. These opinions are important parts of the development of the law because the legal system is based on "precedent" (reliance on previously decided cases).

Precedent

An appellate court's decision on an issue is binding on lower courts in the appellate court's jurisdiction. Thus, an appellate court's decisions are "precedent" that the lower courts in the appellate court's jurisdiction must follow (apply).

Example: In *Effects Associates, Inc. v. Cohen*, the United States Court of Appeals for the Ninth Circuit held that the grant of a nonexclusive copyright license can be implied from the copyright owner's conduct. This decision is binding on the federal district courts located in the Ninth Circuit. Those courts are not free to decide that a nonexclusive copyright license cannot be implied from conduct.

A lower court's decision is not binding on a higher court. In fact, appellate courts frequently reverse decisions made by trial courts to correct the trial courts' "mistakes of law".

Because the United States Supreme Court is the "highest court in the land", the Supreme Court's decisions are binding on all courts in the United States.

Example: In *Community for Creative Nonviolence v. Reid*, the Supreme Court decided how to apply the Copyright Act's "Work Made for Hire" rule to works created by independent contractors. That decision is binding on all courts in the United States.

A court's decision may "be persuasive" outside its region. For a decision to "be persuasive" means that other courts, while not compelled to follow it, choose to follow it.

For example, if the Court of Appeals for the Eleventh Circuit has never decided whether a nonexclusive copyright license can be implied from the copyright owner's conduct but the Ninth Circuit has, the Eleventh Circuit may reach the same conclusion as the Ninth Circuit when it decides that issue because it believes that the Ninth Circuit's decision was correct.

Earlier court decisions are generally "followed" by the deciding court in all later cases involving the same issue.

For example, if the Ninth Circuit decides a case that involves the same legal issues that were involved in a previous case, it is likely to decide those issues as it did in the previous case.

The reliance that our courts put on previously decided cases in deciding new cases is known as stare decisis. That is Latin for "let the decision stand". The doctrine of stare decisis does not prevent a court from "overruling" its own previously decided cases. However, stare decisis discourages rapid and radical changes in the law. As Supreme Court Justice William O. Douglas once wrote in the *Columbia Law Review*, "stare decisis provides some moorings so that men may trade and arrange their affairs with confidence....It is the strong tie which the future has to the past."

The doctrine of stare decisis is the reason that an attorney performs legal research hoping to find cases supporting the attorney's position on a legal issue.

Finding the Law

Because law is made by the courts on a precedent basis following the doctrine of stare decisis, and also made by Congress and the state legislatures, knowing the law on a given topic generally requires a review of both statutory law and case law.

Statutes

Federal and state statutory laws can be found by consulting published "codifications" of laws in law libraries maintained by law schools, law firms, courts, and bar associations. To find a federal law such as the Copyright Act, for example, you would look in the

Part II
The United States of America

United States Code, which is divided into "titles". Federal and state statutory laws can also be obtained "on-line" from Westlaw or Lexis, two computerized legal research services.

Recently adopted laws may not be included in the published codifications of statutes. While the publishers of these codifications add new material regularly (in "pocket parts" inserted at the back of appropriate volumes), even the pocket parts may not include laws adopted in the most recent session of the legislature.

Court Decisions

Court decisions, also known as "case law" can be found in publications called "reporters". For example, decisions of the United States Supreme Court are published in *the United States Reports, the Supreme Court Reporter,* and *the Lawyers Edition* (three different "reporters" from three different publishers).

These decisions are also available from computerized services such as Westlaw and Lexis, which provide on-line research assistance for locating cases on desired topics. "Digests" that divide decided cases into topics are also helpful for locating relevant cases. Other research resources help lawyers determine whether cases in which they are interested have been reversed by a higher court or overruled (modified by a later decision of the same court).

Various publishing companies publish "annotated" statutory codes, which bring statutes and relevant court decisions together in one source. West Publishing Company, for example, publishes *the United States Code Annotated*, which lists the court decisions enforcing or interpreting each provision of the United States Code.

Arbitration

Court of Appeal Judge

The parties to a dispute sometimes choose to resolve a dispute through arbitration rather than through court litigation. In arbitration, a dispute is resolved by a neutral arbitrator rather than by a judge or jury.

Arbitration is generally quicker and cheaper than court litigation. Specially qualified

137

arbitrators are often used to resolve technical disputes.

Both parties must agree to submit their dispute to arbitration. Many contracts require that disputes be resolved through arbitration rather than through litigation.

In the United States, many arbitration cases are handled by arbitrators approved by the American Arbitration Association, which has offices in a number of cities. Arbitration is similar to a trial in that both parties present their cases to the arbitrator, who renders a decision. Appeals of arbitrators' decisions are generally possible only if the arbitration was conducted improperly.

Exercises

I. Fill in the gaps with the appropriate words or phrases given in the box.

A. Bill of Rights	B. The U.S. Constitution	C. enacted
D. adopt	E. unless	F. code
G. legislature	H. federal laws	I. rights and freedoms
J. the U.S. Congress		

1_____ is the highest law of the land. Federal laws enacted by 2_____ come next. This does not mean that the Federal Congress can 3_____ laws that control states in every situation. It can't 4_____ the law can be applied to the states under the U.S. Constitution and court decisions.

Each state has a 5_____ that adopts state laws called "statutes". Those statutes are sometimes complied into what is referred to as a 6_____. This is nothing more than a codification of all the applicable statutes.

The U.S. legal system is based on 7_____, augmented by laws 8_____ by state legislatures and local laws passed by counties and cities. Most 9_____ enjoyed by Americans are enshrined in the first ten amendments of the U.S. Constitution and popularly known as the "10_____".

II. Questions

1. Can you put forward some examples to show the four principal roles that courts play in the U.S.?
2. Can you summarize the court system in the U.S. briefly?
3. What jurisdiction do the federal courts have?
4. What do you know about the litigation in the U.S.?
5. How many stages are there in civil lawsuits in the U.S.? And what are they?
6. What does "precedent" mean under the U.S. legal system?
7. If a decision is labeled as "persuasive", what does it imply?
8. How can an attorney know the law on a given topic?
9. What do you know about the arbitration system in the U.S.?

Chapter 3
CONGRESS

The United States Congress makes up the legislative branch of the federal government. It consists of two houses, the Senate and the House of Representatives. Senators serve in the Senate and Representatives serve in the House. Both are chosen through direct election. Congress was created by Article I, section 1, of the Constitution, adopted by the Constitutional Convention on September 17, 1787. The primary duty of Congress is to debate and pass bills, which are then sent to the president for approval.

The first Congress under the Constitution met on March 4, 1789, in the Federal Hall in New York City. Members of the House of Representatives are elected for two-year terms. To be eligible for election individuals must be at least 25 years old, should have been citizens of the United States for at least seven years, and must be residents of the state from which they are elected. The House of Representatives is led by the Speaker of the House. Members of the House of Representatives are apportioned among the states according to their populations in the federal census.

Senators on the other hand are elected for six-year terms. They must be at least 30 years old, must have been the U.S citizens for at least nine years, and legal residents of the state from which they are elected. The Vice President has formal control over the Senate and he presides over the Senate for important ceremonies or to cast a tie-breaking vote. The President pro tempore, member of the majority party in the Senate, is elected by the Senate and presides over the day-to-day operations of the Senate.

The House and the Senate have equal power in the legislative process because legislation cannot be enacted without the consent of both chambers. Congress mainly passes legislation on national policies and directs government spending. The Senate is uniquely empowered to ratify treaties and to approve top presidential appointments. Revenue bills must originate in the House of Representatives.

Legislative Process

The legislative process is a series of steps that a legislative body takes to evaluate, amend, and vote on a proposed legislation. The U.S. Congress, state legislatures, county boards, and city councils are machineries engaged in the legislative process. Most legislation in the United States is enacted by the Congress and state legislatures. The following is a step by step description of how a proposed legislation or a bill is passed into law.

Step 1—Introduction

Only a member of the House of Representatives or Senate can introduce the bill for consideration. The Representative or Senator who introduces the bill becomes the "sponsor" of the bill. A bill may also have cosponsors, who are other legislators who support the bill or work on its preparation. Usually, important bills have several cosponsors. There are four types of legislations that are considered by Congress. They are bills, simple resolutions, joint resolutions, and concurrent resolutions. The bill or resolution that has officially been introduced in either House is assigned a number (H.R. # for House Bills or S. # for Senate Bills), and printed in the *Congressional Record* by the Government Printing Office.

Step 2—Committee Consideration

All bills and resolutions that are officially introduced in the House of Representatives or Senate are then "referred" to one or more House or Senate standing committees. Major legislations are usually referred to more than one committee.

Step 3—Committee Action

Once referred to it, the committee considers the bill in detail. A bill can be referred to a subcommittee or considered by the committee as a whole. It is at this point that the bill is examined carefully and its chances for passage are determined. If the bill must go through more than one committee, the first committee must refer it to the second committee. The subsequent committee can then only act on the bill. If the committee does not act on a bill, it is equivalent to killing the bill. If the committee approves the bill, it moves on in the legislative process.

Step 4—Subcommittee Review

Usually, the committee sends bills to a subcommittee for further study and public hearings. Hearings based on the bill provide the executive branch, experts, other public officials, supporters and opponents of the bill, an opportunity to put on record their views regarding the bill. Anyone having an interest in the bill can give their testimony either in person or in writing. Notice regarding these hearings, as well as instructions for presenting testimony is officially published in the *Federal Register*.

Step 5—Mark Up

After the hearings on the bill are completed, the subcommittee may make changes and amendments to the bill, and decide to report or recommend it back to the full committee for approval. This process is called "Mark Up". If the subcommittee decides not to report a bill to the full committee, the bill dies there.

Step 6—Committee Action—Reporting a Bill

After the subcommittee reports or recommends the bill back to the full committee for approval, the full committee reviews the deliberations and recommendations of the subcommittee. The committee may also conduct further review, hold more public hearings, or simply vote on the report from the subcommittee. The full committee then prepares and votes on its final recommendations to the House of Representatives or Senate. Once a bill has successfully passed this stage it is said to have been "ordered reported" or simply "reported".

Step 7—Publication of Committee Report

Once a bill has been reported, a written report about the bill is published. The report will include the intent and scope of the bill, its impact on existing laws, budgetary considerations, and any new taxes or tax increases that will be required by the bill. The report may also contain transcripts from public hearings on the bill, as well as the opinions of the committee for and against the bill.

Step 8—Scheduling Floor Action

Once the bill has been reported with a favorable report and published, it will be placed in chronological order on the legislative calendar of the House of Representatives or Senate and scheduled for "floor action" or debate before the full membership. The House of Representatives has several legislative calendars. The Speaker of the House and House Majority Leader decide the order in which reported bills will be debated. However, the Senate has only one legislative calendar. During its wait for floor action, the bill is subject to a motion to refer it again to the same committee or any other committee for reconsideration. This is a classic method of defeating a bill without taking it to the stage where it is put for final vote.

Step 9—Debate

When a bill reaches the floor of the House of Representatives or the Senate, debate for and against the bill proceeds before the full House or Senate according to strict rules which determine the conditions and amount of time allocated for general debate on the bill.

Step 10—Voting

Once debate on the bill has ended and any amendments to the bill have been approved, the full membership will vote for or against the bill. Voting is done either by a voice vote or a roll-call vote.

Step 11—Bill Referred to Other Chamber

A bill approved by one chamber of Congress (House of Representatives or Senate) is then sent to the other chamber where they will usually follow the same track of committee to debate to vote, as described in steps 2 to 10 above. The other chamber may approve, reject, ignore, or amend the bill as it deems appropriate.

Step 12—Conference Committee

If only minor changes are made to the bill by the other chamber, the bill will go back to the first chamber for concurrence. However, if the second chamber makes significant changes to the content of the bill, a "conference committee" made up of members of both chambers, usually three to five members from each chamber will be formed. The conference committee will have to work to reconcile the differences between the Senate and House versions of the bill. If the committee cannot agree, the bill simply dies. If the committee succeeds in reaching a compromised version of the bill, they should prepare a conference report detailing the changes they have proposed. Both the House of Representatives and Senate must approve the conference report. If the bill is not approved, it will be sent back to the conference committee for further work.

Step 13—Final Action Enrollment

Once both the House of Representatives and Senate have approved the bill in identical form, it becomes "enrolled" and sent to the President of the United States. The President may sign the bill into law. If the President signs the bill, from then on the enrolled bill becomes an act, a written law. The President can also take no action on the bill for ten days while Congress is in session and the bill will automatically become law. If the President is opposed to the bill, he can "veto" it. If the President takes no action on the bill for ten days after Congress has adjourned their second session, the bill dies. This action is called a "pocket veto".

Step 14—Overriding the Veto

Congress can attempt to "override" a presidential veto of a bill and force it into law, by a 2/3 vote by a quorum of members in both the House of Representatives and Senate.

Bills

A bill is a proposed new law or a proposed amendment to an existing law which has been introduced in either the House of Representatives or the Senate. After a bill is passed by both chambers of Congress, it has to be approved by the President of the United States to become enforceable.

The first step in the legislative process is to introduce a bill in either chamber of Congress. Only a member of the House of Representatives or Senate can introduce a bill for consideration. The Representative or Senator who introduces the ill becomes the "sponsor" of the bill. A bill may also have cosponsor(s). Any bill that has officially been introduced in either chamber is then assigned a number. Bills originating in the House of Representatives will have "H.R. #" and bills originating from the Senate will have "S. #".

Once the bill is formally introduced, it will be referred to one or more House or Senate standing committees. The committee may consider the bill in detail or may further refer it to a subcommittee. The subcommittee conducts hearings based on the bill. Anyone having an interest in the bill can give their testimony either in person or in writing. After hearings on the bill have concluded, considering its outcome, the subcommittee may make changes and amendments to the bill. The subcommittee then reports or recommends the bill back to the committee for approval. If the subcommittee does not report a bill to the committee, the bill dies there.

The committee, after reviewing the deliberations and recommendations of the subcommittee, may conduct further review and hold more public hearings, or may simply vote on the report from the subcommittee. The committee then sends its recommendations to the House of Representatives or Senate. Once a bill has been reported, a written report about the bill is published. Then the bill is scheduled for "floor action" or debate before the full membership by placing it in chronological order on the legislative calendar of the House of Representatives or Senate. When the bill reaches the floor of the House of Representatives or the Senate, debate for and against the bill is conducted, and amendments may be made to the bill. Once debate is concluded and any amendments to the bill have been approved, the full membership will vote for or against the bill.

A bill approved by one chamber of Congress is then sent to the other chamber. The other chamber may approve, reject, ignore, or amend the bill. If only minor changes are made to the bill by the other chamber, the bill will go back to the first chamber for concurrence. However, if the second chamber makes significant changes to the content of the bill, a "conference committee" will be formed to reconcile the differences between the Senate and House versions of the bill. If the committee succeeds in reaching a compromised version of the bill, it will prepare a conference report detailing the changes that have been made. Both the House of Representatives and Senate must approve the conference report.

Once both the House of Representatives and Senate have approved the bill in identical form, it becomes "enrolled" and sent to the President of the United States. The President may sign the bill into law. If the President is opposed to the bill, he can "veto" it.

Congressional Powers

Article 1 of the U.S. Constitution defines the powers of the American Congress. The U.S. Congress consists of two houses: the Senate and the House of Representatives. The states are empowered over the conduct of federal elections by Section 4 of Article 1 of the U.S. Constitution. However, the Congress has the power to alter such regulations. The American Congress, being a legislative body, has certain inherent powers. The Congress has the power to investigate legislative needs.

Section 8 of Article 1 of the U.S. Constitution provides a list of congressional powers over financial and budgetary matters such as collection of taxes, duties, imposts and excises, repayment of common defense and general welfare debts. Proper allocation of funds also comes under powers of the Congress. This power provides proper control over the executive branch. Section 8 also empowers the Congress with the authority to borrow money on the credit of the United States.

The Congress plays an important role in national defense. It has the power to maintain the armed forces and make rules for the military. The Congress is vested with the power to declare war. Establishment of inferior courts, post offices and post roads, issuance of patents and copyrights, fixation of standards of weights and measures, also come under Congress's powers. The Congress can admit new states in to the American Union and allow impeachment to remove the President. It can also remove federal judges or federal officers. Above all, the Congress is also given the power to make all laws necessary to execute the foregoing powers, and all other powers granted by the Constitution of the United States.

The U.S. Constitution does not clearly define the implied powers of Congress. However, the Constitution permits the American Congress to make any law that is necessary and proper to carry out its enumerated powers. This is also interpreted as "elastic clause" by jurists.

House of Representatives

United States Congress consists of two Houses, namely, the United States Senate and the United States House of Representatives ("House"). Senate is the upper house, and the House of Representatives is the lower house. House of Representatives derive its powers from Article 1 of the Constitution. Article 1 of the Constitution lays down the composition and structure of the House.

Members of the House are comprised of representatives from each state. The manner of election, and the time and place to elect the representatives is decided by each state legislature. Congress shall not interfere with that process unless required. If a vacancy occurs in the House due to a fall out of representation from a state, the executive authority sends a Writ of Election to the respective state to fill the vacancy. All the officers within the House and the Speaker of the House are chosen by the members. The House also has sole power to impeach them.

The House meets in Washington D.C. The Speaker is the presiding officer of the House. Apart from the rules, the proceedings of the House are dependent on custom, tradition and precedents. The House meetings are held on weekdays. The House requires a quorum, which is the minimum number of members to conduct the session. Generally, the quorum is assumed to be there. The Speaker regulates the sessions. During debates, only the members called upon by the Speaker can speak. All debates and speeches are addressed to the Speaker. Other members are addressed in the third person. When addressing the Speaker or other members the member should take good care and address them with respect, for example, "Mr. Speaker", or "Madam Speaker", and "Gentleman" or "Gentlewoman" when referring other members. The proceedings of the House are recorded in a journal called *Journal of Proceedings*. This journal is published in timely intervals. However, parts of proceedings requiring secrecy are not published. The meeting of Congress (joint sitting of both the Houses) takes place at least once a year and shall happen on the first Monday of December.

All bills relating to revenue originate in the House. Debate on passing a bill is always confined to one hour. Debates are between the majority and minority party. The floor manger allocates the time for debates and each member who wishes to speak may be granted 30 seconds to 1 minute to make a point. On conclusion of the debate the motion is put to vote. There are three modes of voting, electronic device vote, teller vote and roll call vote. The Speaker is also allowed to vote like other members.

Members of the House

The tenure of a member of the House is two years. The election to the House is conducted every two years. The members are elected by the citizens of every state who are qualified to elect the members. The number of member representatives in the House is based on the population of the state. Minimum number of representation is one, and more than one representative will be permitted if the population is high. For every thirty thousand people, there shall be one representative. Likewise, the State of New Hampshire is entitled to choose three, Massachusetts eight, Rhode Island and Providence Plantations one, Connecticut five, New York six, New Jersey four, Pennsylvania eight, Delaware one, Maryland six, Virginia ten, North Carolina five, South Carolina five, and Georgia three.

Qualifications required to become a member are:

> Shall be at least 25 years in age;
> Should have been a citizen of United State for the past seven years;
> And, shall, when elected, be an inhabitant of that state in which he/she shall be chosen.

Apart from the above qualifications, the member of the House shall not hold any other civil offices under United States. If holding such an office, then the person shall resign the office before becoming a member. The manner of election, and the time and place to elect the representatives is decided by the state legislature. The congress shall interfere only if required.

The members are paid a compensation for the services they provide. The amount of compensation is ascertained by law. This compensation is paid out of the United States treasury. The members enjoy certain privileges. The members shall not be arrested while they are attending the session in the house, or while going to or returning from the House. Further, they shall be questioned only when making a speech or debate and not elsewhere. Despite of all the privileges enjoyed, the members can get expelled from the House, if he/she consistently shows disorderly behaviors. A representative can be expelled from the House with the concurrence of two-third of the total strength of the House. Members after their service, enjoy benefits such as pension, health benefits and social security benefits. The members are often referred with a prefix 'honorable' and known as congressman/woman or representative.

If at any time a shortage of representation from any state occurs, the executive authority sends a Writ of Election to the respective state to fill the vacancy. Members choose the officers and the Speaker of the House. The House enjoys the sole power to impeach them.

Passage

The first step in the legislative process is the introduction of a bill to Congress. Anyone can write it, but only members of Congress can introduce legislation.

After being introduced, a bill is referred to the appropriate committee for review. There are 17 Senate committees, with 70 subcommittees, and 23 House committees, with 104 subcommittees. Each committee oversees a specific policy area, and the subcommittees take on more specialized policy areas.

A bill is first considered in a subcommittee, where it may be accepted, amended, or rejected entirely. If the members of the subcommittee agree to move a bill forward, it is reported to the full committee, where the process is repeated again. Throughout this stage of the process, the committees and subcommittees call hearings to investigate the merits and flaws of the bill.

If the full committee votes to approve the bill, it is reported to the floor of the House or Senate, and the majority party leadership decides when to place the bill on the calendar for consideration. If a bill is particularly pressing, it may be considered right away.

When the bill comes up for consideration, the House has a very structured debate process. Once debate is over, the votes of a simple majority passes the bill.

A bill must pass both houses of Congress before it goes to the President for consideration. Depending on where the bill originated, the final text is then enrolled by either the Clerk of the House or the Secretary of the Senate, and presented to the Speaker of the House and the President of the Senate for their signatures. The bill is then sent to the President.

When receiving a bill from Congress, the President has several options. If the President agrees substantially with the bill, he or she may sign it into law, and the bill is then printed in the Statutes at Large. If the President believes the law to be bad policy, he may veto it and send it back to Congress. Congress may override the veto with a two-thirds vote of each chamber, at which point the bill becomes law and is printed.

There are two other options that the President may exercise. If Congress is in session and the President takes no action within 10 days, the bill becomes law. If Congress adjourns before 10 days are up and the President takes no action, then the bill dies and

Congress may not vote to override. This is called a "pocket veto", and if Congress still wants to pass the legislation, they must begin the entire process anew.

Senate

The United States Senate is the upper house of the United States Congress. The House of Representatives is the lower house. The composition and powers of the Senate are established in Article 1 of the Constitution. Each state has two senators and they are elected directly by the people.

Article 1, Section 3 of the Constitution sets three qualifications for Senators: 1) each senator must be at least 30 years old, 2) must have been a citizen of the United States for at least the past nine years, and 3) an inhabitant (at the time of election) of the state he or she seeks to represent.

The term of a senate is six years and the terms are staggered so that approximately one-third of the seats are up for election every two years. The staggering of the terms is arranged to ensure that both seats from a given state are never contested in the same general election except when a mid-term vacancy is being filled. The Vice President of the United States shall be President of the Senate and he has the authority to preside over Senate's session, however, he votes only to break a deadlock. The Constitution authorizes the Senate to elect its own officers and also a President pro tempore to preside in the absence of the Vice President. Other elected officers include a chaplain, secretary of the Senate, and sergeant at arms, who are not senators. The President pro tempore shall be the member of the political party with the largest representation in the House.

The Senate may expel a senator by two-thirds vote. The Chief Justice of the United States presides over the impeachment trial of President of the Senate. If an impeached person is found guilty, he or she can be removed from office and forbidden to hold federal office again. The Senate cannot impose any other punishment, but the person may also be tried in regular courts.

The Senate publishes journals with regard to its proceedings and it also lists the bills passed, amendments offered, motions made, and votes taken. President shall have power to fill up all vacancies that may happen during the recess of the Senate, by granting commissions. The Senate will consider the nominations when it returns to session.

Powers reserved to the Senate include:

➢ Confirming or rejecting treaties;

➢ Confirming or rejecting presidential appointments to office, including the Cabinet, other officials of the executive branch, federal judges, including Supreme Court justices, and ambassadors;

➢ Trying a government official who commits a crime against the United States.

The Senate uses committees for a variety of purposes, including the review of bills and the oversight of the executive branch. The appointment of committee members is formally made by the whole Senate, but the choice of members is actually made by the political parties. Each Senate committee and subcommittee is led by a chairman, usually a member of the majority party. The chamber of the United States Senate is located in the north wing of Capitol building, in Washington, D.C.

Senators

A senator is the member or legislator of a senate who possessing legislative powers. Article 1, Section 3, Clause 5 of the United States Constitution provides that no person shall be a senator of the U.S. Senate who shall not have attained the age of thirty years, who has not been nine years a citizen of the United States and who shall not when elected, be an inhabitant of that state that person representing. Generally, the elected member to the United States Senate, before seated is called "senator-elect" and appointed to a seat is called a "senator-designate".

There are two houses for the United States Congress. The upper house of the United States Congress is the Senate and the lower house is the House of Representatives. There are two senators representing each state aggregating 100 senators for the United States Congress. Here the weight of population is ignored to ensure equal representation of each state of the United States. The Chamber of United States Senate is located at Washington, D.C.

The Vice President of the United States is the President of the Senate and exercises voting right if there is a tie. In general practice, the President of the United States Senate occasionally presides over the Senate sessions.

The Presiding Officer of the Senate is the President pro tempore. The President pro tempore is elected by the Senate. Generally, the most experienced senator of the majority party is selected as the President pro tempore of the Senate.

In 1913, the Seventeenth Amendment standardized the election to the Senate nationally. The senators of 48 states are elected by the plurality voting system. However, the qualifying senator candidate for the States of Georgia and Louisiana must attain the majority of votes cast. If any of the senator candidates fails to attain the majority votes, the senator is selected by a second election.

Article 1, Section 3 of the Unites States Constitution establishes three qualifications for a senator:

➢ The candidate must be more than 30 years of age;
➢ The candidate must be a citizen of United States for at least nine years; and
➢ The candidate must be a resident of the state of representation.

The tenure of a senator is six years. Approximately the term of one-third senators expires in every two years. Elections to the senate are held on the first Tuesday of November in every even-numbered year. The senator is selected for the state as a whole.

The senators are considered as important political icons because they are few in number, long tenure in service, represent larger constituencies, more sittings in committees, and supported with more personnel.

Exercises

I. Identify the following statements as True or False.

1. The United States Congress makes up the legislative branch of the federal government, which consists of two houses, the Senate and the House of Representatives.

2. The number of member representatives in the House and that of senators representing each state in the Senate are based on the population of the state.

3. The Vice President has formal control over the Senate and he presides over the day-to-day operations of the Senate or to cast a tie-breaking vote.

4. The House and the Senate have unequal power in the legislative process because the Senate is uniquely empowered to ratify treaties and to approve top presidential appointments.

5. Four types of legislations that are considered by Congress are bills, simple resolutions, joint resolutions and concurrent resolutions.

6. Only a member of the House of Representatives or Senate can introduce a bill for consideration. The Representative or Senator who introduces the bill becomes the "sponsor" of the bill. A bill must have cosponsor(s).

7. Before a proposed legislation or a bill is passed into law, public hearings held by subcommittees are imperative.

8. After the hearings on the bill are completed, the subcommittee may make changes and amendments to the bill, and decide to report or recommend it back to the full committee for approval. This process is called "Mark Up".

9. Once the bill has been reported with a favorable report and published, it will be placed in chronological order on the legislative calendar of the House of Representatives or Senate and scheduled for "floor action" or debate before the full membership.

10. Congress can attempt to "override" a presidential veto of a bill and force it into law, by a 2/3 vote by a quorum of members in both the House of Representatives and Senate.

II. Fill in the gaps with the appropriate words or phrases given in the box.

A. equal	B. enacted	C. grants	D. impeached
E. revenue-raising	F. legislative	G. states	H. vested
I. ratifies	J. decides		

Article One of the United States Constitution 1_____, "All 2_____ Powers herein granted shall be 3_____ in a Congress of the United States, which shall consist of a Senate and House of Representatives." The House and Senate are 4_____ partners in the legislative process—legislation cannot be 5_____ without the consent of both chambers. However, the Constitution 6_____each chamber some unique powers. The Senate 7_____treaties and approves presidential appointments while the House initiates 8_____bills. The House initiates impeachment cases, while the Senate 9_____impeachment cases. A two-thirds vote of the Senate is required before an 10_____person can be forcibly removed from office.

III. Questions

1. Can you introduce the U.S. Congress in a brief way?
2. What are the qualifications required to become a member of the House?
3. What are the qualifications for senators under the U.S. Constitution?
4. How can a proposed legislation be passed into law?
5. What are the congressional powers provided by the U.S. Constitution?
6. What are the differences between the composition and structure of the House and that of Senate?
7. What are the differences between the powers of the House and those reserved to the Senate?

Chapter 4
EXECUTIVE BRANCH

The executive branch of the United States Government consists of the President, Vice President and fifteen Cabinet-level executive departments. The power of the executive branch is vested in the President of the United States, who also acts as head of state and Commander-in-Chief of the armed forces. The Vice President is also part of the executive branch, who assumes the office of the President should the need arise. The Cabinet and independent federal agencies are responsible for the day-to-day enforcement and administration of federal laws. The executive branch employs more than 4 million Americans.

The President is both the head of state and head of government of the United States of America, and Commander-in-Chief of the armed forces. The President is responsible for implementing and enforcing the laws written by Congress. The President appoints the heads of the federal agencies, including the Cabinet. The President also appoints the heads of more than 50 independent federal commissions, such as the Federal Reserve Board or the Securities and Exchange Commission, as well as federal judges, ambassadors, and other federal offices. The executive branch conducts diplomacy with other nations, and the President has the power to negotiate and sign treaties.

The primary responsibility of the Vice President of the United States is to be ready at a moment's notice to assume the Presidency in case of the President's death, resignation, or temporary incapacitation, or if the Vice President and a majority of the Cabinet judge that the President is no longer able to discharge the duties of the presidency. The Vice President also serves as the President of the United States Senate, where he or she casts the deciding vote in the case of a tie. Except in the case of tie-breaking votes, the Vice

President rarely actually presides over the Senate.

The Executive Office of the President (EOP) created in 1939 by President Franklin D. Roosevelt provides support to the President to govern effectively. The EOP consists of the immediate staff to the President, along with entities such as the Office of Management and Budget and the Office of the United States Trade Representative. The EOP has responsibility for tasks ranging from communicating the President's message to the American people to promoting trade interests abroad. The current EOP employs around 1800 people.

The Cabinet is an advisory body consisting of the heads of the 15 executive departments. These departments and agencies have missions and responsibilities as widely divergent as those of the Department of Defense and the Environmental Protection Agency, the Social Security Administration and the Securities and Exchange Commission. All the members of the Cabinet take the title Secretary, excepting the head of the Justice Department, who is designated as Attorney General.

Executive Office of President

The Executive Office of the President (EOP) is created to assist in supervising the executive branch of the government. The enactment of the Reorganization Act in 1939 gave the President the power to appoint an additional confidential team to restructure the executive branch.

The staff of the EOP includes the President's immediate staff supported by a multi level reporting team. The Executive Office of the President is the direct reporting agency to the President. Initially, the White House Office and the Office of Management and Budget (formerly known as Bureau of the Budget) were included as subunits of the EOP. Some other major units are:

Council of Economic Advisors (created in 1946);

National Security Council (created in 1947);

Office of the U.S. Trade Representative (created in 1963);

Council on Environmental Quality (created in 1970);

Office of Science and Technology Policy (created in 1976);

Office of Administration (created in 1977);

Office of National Drug Control Policy (created in 1989);

Office of Homeland Security (created in 2001);

Office of Faith-based and Community Initiatives (created in 2001).

The White House Chief of Staff is the head of the Executive Office of the President. He is considered the "Second-Most Powerful Man in Washington". There are three divisions of Executive Staff in the Office of the President. The Assistant to the President is the head of senior staff, the Deputy Assistant to the President heads the second-level staff and the Special Assistant to the President heads third level staff. The appointment of White House Staff does not require any approval from the Senate.

President

The President of the United States is the head of state and head of government of the United States. The President is the highest political official in the United States. The President leads the executive branch of the federal government.

Pursuant to Article II of the U.S. Constitution, the President has the duty to "faithfully execute" federal law. Article II also makes the President commander-in-chief of the United States armed forces, allows the President to nominate executive and judicial officers with the advice and consent of the Senate, and allows the President to grant pardons and reprieves.

The President is indirectly elected by the people through the Electoral College to a four year term. Forty three individuals have been elected or succeeded to the office of President, serving a total of 56 four year terms.

The first power conferred upon the President by the U.S. Constitution is the legislative power of the presidential veto. Any bill passed by Congress should be presented to the President before it can become law. Once the legislation has been presented, the

President has three options. The President can

- sign the legislation; the bill then becomes law.
- veto the legislation and return it to Congress with his objections; the bill does not become law, unless each House of Congress votes to override the veto by a two-thirds vote.
- take no action. The President can neither sign nor veto the legislation. After 10 days, not counting Sundays, two possible outcomes emerge:

1) If Congress is still convened, the bill becomes law.

2) If Congress has adjourned, thus preventing the return of the legislation, the bill does not become law.

The role of the commander-in-chief of the United States armed forces is perhaps the most important of all presidential powers. While the power to declare war is constitutionally vested in Congress, the President commands and directs the military and is responsible for planning military strategy.

The President also directs the foreign policy of the United States. The President is responsible for the protection of Americans abroad and of foreign nationals in the United States. The President decides whether to recognize new nations and new governments, and negotiates treaties with other nations, which become binding on the United States when approved by two-thirds of the Senate. The President may also negotiate executive agreements with foreign powers that are not subject to Senate confirmation.

The President, being the head of the executive branch of the government, is the chief executive of the United States. The President is responsible for the execution and enforcement of the laws created by the Congress. Appointments to various executive branch such as ambassadors, members of the Cabinet, and other federal officers, are made by the President with the "advice and consent" of a majority of the Senate. Generally, the President may remove purely executive officials at his discretion. However, Congress can curtail and constrain the President's authority to remove commissioners of independent regulatory agencies and certain inferior executive officers by statute.

The President also has the power to nominate federal judges, including members of the United States Courts of Appeals and the Supreme Court of the United States, upon Senate confirmation. Although the President has the power to appoint judges for the United States district courts he will often defer the power to Senate. The President also has unlimited power to extend pardons and clemencies for federal crimes, except in cases of impeachment.

The President has the ability to withhold information from the public, Congress, and the courts in matters of national security. While the President cannot directly introduce legislation, he can play an important role in shaping it, especially if the President's political party has a majority in one or both houses of the Congress. The President may convene either or both houses of the Congress. Conversely, if both houses fail to agree on a date of adjournment, the President may appoint a date for the Congress to adjourn.

There are three principal qualifications for eligibility to the office of the President. The President must

- be a natural born citizen of the United States;
- be at least thirty-five years old;
- have been a permanent resident in the United States for at least fourteen years.

A person who meets the above qualifications is still disqualified from holding the office of President under any of the following conditions:

- No eligible person can be elected the President more than twice;
- The Senate has the option, upon conviction, of disqualifying convicted individuals from holding other federal offices, including the Presidency;
- The Constitution prohibits an otherwise eligible person from becoming the President if that person swore an oath to support the Constitution, and later rebelled against the United States.

The term of office of the President is two four year terms, but until the 22nd Amendment to the Constitution, ratified in 1951, a President could serve an unlimited number of terms. The office of the President may become vacant under several possible

Part II
The United States of America

circumstances: death, resignation and removal from office. Article II, Section 4 of the Constitution allows the House of Representatives to impeach high federal officials, including the President, for "treason, bribery, or other high crimes and misdemeanors". The Vice President becomes the President upon the removal from office, death or resignation of the preceding President. If the offices of the President and Vice President both are either vacant or have a disabled holder of that office, the next officer in the presidential line of succession, the Speaker of the House, becomes Acting President. The line extends to the President pro tempore of the Senate after the Speaker, followed by every member of the Cabinet in a set order.

The President and the First Family live in the White House in Washington, D.C. which is also the location of the President's Oval Office and the offices of the his senior staff. When the President travels by plane, his aircraft is designated Air Force One. The President may also use Marine Corps helicopter known as Marine One while the President is on board. The President uses an armored presidential limousine for ground travels.

The Presidential Cabinet

The United States Cabinet was established by Article II, Section 2 of the Constitution. It is usually referred to as the "President's Cabinet" or just the "Cabinet". The Cabinet is an advisory body and its role is to advise the President on any subject that he may require. The Cabinet consists of the Vice President and the heads of 15 executive departments. These departments are the Departments of Agriculture, Commerce, Defense, Education, Energy, Health and Human Services, Homeland Security, Housing and Urban Development, Interior, Labor, State, Transportation, Treasury, and Veterans Affairs, along with the Attorney General.

Members of the Cabinet are nominated by the President and appointed upon confirmation by the Senate with a simple majority. All members of the Cabinet, except the head of the Justice Department are known by the title "Secretary". The head of the

Justice Department is known as the "Attorney General".

In addition to running major federal agencies, the Cabinet plays an important role in the presidential line of succession. After the Vice President comes the Speaker of the House and Senate President pro tempore, and then the line of succession continues with the Cabinet offices in the order in which the Departments were created.

Vice President

The Vice President of the United States is second highest executive officer of the United States government, after the President. The Vice President is the first person in the presidential line of succession, who will take over as the President of the United States upon death, resignation, or removal of the President. The Vice President is also the President of the Senate. The Vice President presides over the Senate, but is allowed to vote in the Senate only when it is necessary to break a deadlock. The Vice President also presides over joint sessions of Congress.

The Vice President, together with the President of the United States, is indirectly elected by the people through an Electoral College for a term of four years. The Twelfth Amendment states that "no person constitutionally ineligible to the office of President shall be eligible to that of Vice President of the United States." Therefore, to serve as Vice President, an individual must:

➢ Be a natural born citizen, or a citizen of United States;

➢ Have attained the age of thirty five years; and

➢ Have resided within the United States for a period of at least fourteen years.

Duties of the Vice President are:

➢ To cast a tie-breaking vote when the Senate is in deadlock;

➢ To preside over and certify the official vote count of the U.S. Electoral College;

➢ To preside over most of the impeachment trials of federal officers;

➢ To perform certain executive duties assigned either by President or Congress.

Article 1, Section 3 Clause 6 of the Constitution gives the Senate the power to remove impeached officials from office, given a two-thirds vote to convict. No Vice President has ever been impeached.

Section 2 of the Twenty-fifth Amendment provides that whenever there is a vacancy in the office of the Vice President, the President nominates a Vice President who takes office upon confirmation by a majority vote of both Houses of Congress.

The Vice President is a member of the National Security Council and serves on the board of the Smithsonian (which is an educational institution). The Vice President is the first person in the presidential line of succession. Upon incapacity, death, resignation, or removal from office of the President, the Vice President acts as the President of the United States.

Office of the United States Trade Representative

The Office of the U.S. Trade Representative (U.S.TR) is the executive branch of the government that aids the Office of the U.S. President in developing its trade policies. The United States is constantly extending its trade relations all over the world, and discussions on trade policies are ongoing with many countries. The U.S.TR assists the Office of the President in conducting bilateral and multilateral trade negotiations. The U.S.TR has two sub-agencies called the Trade Policy Staff Committee (TPSC) and Trade Policy Review Group (TPRG) to co-ordinate the trade policy with the Government.

The office of the U.S.TR was established under the Trade Expansion Act of 1962. The Office was initially named Office of the Special Trade Representative (STR). The head of the Office is called the U.S. Trade Representative. The position is equivalent to that of a Cabinet member, although not within the Cabinet. The U.S. Trade Representative is the President's chief advisor on trade policies, principal negotiator on the government's behalf and the spokesperson on the country's trade policies. Mr. Ron Kirk is the current U.S. Trade Representative.

Key responsibilities of the U.S.TR are:

➤ Bilateral, regional and multilateral trade and investment issues;

- Expansion of market access for American goods and services;
- International commodity agreements;
- Negotiations affecting the U.S. import policies;
- Oversight of the Generalized System of Preferences (GSP) and Section 301 complaints against foreign unfair trade practices, as well as Section 1377, Section 337 and import relief cases under Section 201;
- Trade, commodity, and direct investment matters managed by international institutions such as the Organization for Economic Cooperation and Development (OECD) and the United Nations Conference on Trade and Development (UNCTAD);
- Trade-related intellectual property protection issues;
- World Trade Organization (WTO) issues.

The U.S.TR and the Congress work in close conjunction. The Office of the U.S.TR is advised on trade policy by congressional members. Five members from each House are chosen to be the congressional advisors. Additional members may be appointed for advice on particular issues.

Exercises

I. Fill in the gaps with the appropriate words or phrases given in the box.

A. head	B. Pursuant	C. enforcement	D. faithfully execute
E. responsible	F. Executive	G. commander-in-chief	
H. government	I. highest	J. nominate	K. executive
L. Congress	M. advisory	N. Vice President	O. legislative

The 1_____ branch of the United States Government consists of the President, 2_____ and fifteen Cabinet-level executive departments.

The President of the United States is the 3_____ of state and head of 4_____ of the United States. The President is the 5_____ political official in the United States. 6_____ to Article II of the U.S. Constitution, the President has the duty to "7_____" federal law, thus being 8_____ for the execution and 9_____ of the laws created by the 10_____. The first power conferred upon the President by the U.S. Constitution is the 11_____ power of the presidential veto while the most important of all presidential powers is perhaps the role of the 12_____ of the United States armed forces. The President also directs the foreign policy of the United States and has the power to 13_____ federal judges.

The Cabinet is an 14_____ body and its role is to advise President on any subject that he may require. The Cabinet consists of the Vice President and the heads of 15_____ departments.

II. Questions

1. What are the powers conferred upon the President by the U.S. Constitution?
2. How many options does the President has once a bill has been passed by Congress and presented to him/her?
3. What are the three principal qualifications for eligibility to the office of President of the U.S.?
4. What do you know about the Presidential Cabinet of the U.S.?
5. Can you introduce the Vice President of the U.S. briefly?
6. What are the three principal qualifications for being eligible to the office of Vice President of the U.S.?
7. What are the duties of the Vice President of the U.S.?

Chapter 5
FEDERAL COURTS

Supreme Court

The United States Supreme Court is seated in Washington D.C. The Supreme Court is the highest court in the United States and is the head of the judiciary branch of the federal government. The Supreme Court derives its authority from Article III of the Constitution and the Judiciary Act of 1789. It consists of the Chief Justice and eight Associate Justices. The number of Associate Justices is fixed by the Congress, which is now fixed at eight. Any six justices together constitute a quorum.

The President nominates and appoints all the justices including the Chief Justice with the consent and advice of the Senate. The President can make temporary recess appointments when the Senate is on recess. However, once the Senate is back in session, the temporary appointee justice will need the approval of Senate to continue in service.

All justices are paid compensation for the service they perform. The justices enjoy their office for a lifetime, and they may be removed from the position only if convicted of a crime.

Other officers of the Supreme Court are: Counselor to the Chief Justice, Clerk, Librarian, Marshal, Reporter of Decisions, Court Counsel, Curator, Director of Data Systems, and Public Information Officer. The main duty of all the court officers is to assist the Court in its daily proceedings and work operations. The Chief Justice appoints the Counselor to the Chief. Some of the remaining officers are appointed by the Court and others by the Chief Justice with the Court's assistance.

The Supreme Court decides cases relating to:

➢ The Constitution of the United States;

- Laws of the United State (federal law), and treaties made by the United States;
- U.S. Ambassadors and other public ministers, and consuls;
- Admiralty and maritime jurisdiction;
- Cases where the United Sates is a party;
- Cases between two or more states;
- Cases between citizens of a state and another state;
- Cases between citizens of different states (diversity jurisdiction);
- Cases between same state citizens but claiming lands under grants of different states;
- Cases between state or citizen and foreign states, or citizens.

The Supreme Court has two types of jurisdiction: original and appellate jurisdiction. The Supreme Court exercises original jurisdiction on cases dealt by it directly, for example, cases relating to U.S. Ambassadors and other public ministers, and consuls. Appellate jurisdiction is exercised on those cases coming before it from lower courts. For example, cases between citizens of different states. Judicial review and judicial activism are the other two powers exercised by the Supreme Court. Judicial review is the power to declare any law or executive action as unconstitutional if found that the law or executive action contradicts the provisions of the Constitution. Judicial activism is the power of the Supreme Court to create new laws on a point which is not covered by any law created by the legislature.

Apart from the power to decide cases, the Supreme Court has some administrative power. The Supreme Court determines the rules or procedure to be followed by the lower federal courts of the United States.

A term/year in the Supreme Court is between October of a year to October of the next year. During a term roughly 10,000 petitions are filed in the Supreme Court. The Supreme Court functions during five days of the week, which is Monday to Friday from 9 a.m. to 4:30 p.m. The Supreme Court is open to the public during its work hours. The Supreme Court does not work on listed federal holidays, and it stays closed during the holidays. The Supreme Court library is open to the Bar members, attorneys representing different federal department and agencies, and the Congress members.

Supreme Court Clerks Office

The Supreme Court has four statutory officers and the Court Clerk is one of them. The other three statutory officers are the Marshal, the Librarian, and the Reporter of Decisions.

Huge numbers of cases are filed in the Supreme Court. The Court Clerk's office maintains the records of the filing, and filing procedure. The Clerk's office keeps the Supreme Court records and dockets. Apart from the above, the Court Clerk collects certain amount such as fees, costs, and other related court income, and pays it to Treasury. The Court Clerk prepares and submits annual returns of the amounts thus collected to the Supreme Court. The Court Clerk is appointed by the Supreme Court, and the Clerk's compensation is fixed by the Supreme Court. The Supreme Court has the power to remove the Court Clerk. The Court Clerk's office consists of Deputy Clerks, Assistants, and Messengers. The Deputy Clerks are appointed, and their compensations are fixed by the Supreme Court. There may be one or more Deputy Clerks, based on the need. The Court Clerk has the power to remove the Deputy Clerks with the Supreme Court's or the Chief Justice's approval. Likewise, the Court Clerk also can fix their compensation. The Court Clerk, with approval of the Chief Justice, can appoint and fix the required compensations for the Assistants, and Messengers.

The Court Clerk is to be distinguished from Law Clerks. Unlike the Court Clerk, the Law Clerks are involved in assisting justices in making the case decisions.

The Clerk of the Supreme Court is an officer of the Supreme Court, who is responsible for overseeing filings with the Court and maintaining its records. The position of the Clerk was authorized by Congress on September 24, 1789. The purpose of creation of the post was to enter and record all the orders, decrees, judgments and proceedings of the said court.

The Judicial Code provides that the Clerk is appointed, and may be removed, by order of the Supreme Court. The Clerk's duties are prescribed by the statute and by Supreme Court Rule 1, and by the Court's customs and practices.

Decisions

In the Supreme Court, after the oral arguments of both parties are over, the case is submitted for decision. Cases are decided by majority vote of the justices. The general practice of the Supreme Court is to issue decisions in all cases argued in a particular term by the end of that term. Within that term, however, the Court is under no obligation to release a decision within any set time after oral argument. At the conclusion of oral argument, the justices retire to another conference at which the preliminary votes are tallied, and the most senior justice in the majority assigns the initial draft of the Court's opinion to a justice on his or her side. Drafts of the Court's opinion, as well as any concurring or dissenting opinions, circulate among the justices until the Court is prepared to announce the judgment in a particular case.

It is possible that sometimes the Court divides evenly on a case. If that occurs, then the decision of the Court below is affirmed, but does not establish binding precedent. For a case to be heard there must be a quorum of at least six justices. If a quorum is not available to hear a case and a majority of qualified justices believes that the case cannot be heard and determined in the next term, then the judgment of the Court below is affirmed as if the Court had been evenly divided. For cases brought directly to the Supreme Court by direct appeal from a United States District Court, the Chief Justice may order the case remanded to the appropriate U.S. Court of Appeals for a final decision there.

Justices

The Supreme Court is the nation's highest court. Eight Associate Justices and one Chief Justice comprise the membership of the Court. Article II of the United States Constitution gives the President power to appoint justices "by and with the advice and consent of the Senate". Supreme Court justices serve lifetime appointments serving "during good behavior". The term "good behavior" means that justices may serve for the remainder of their lives, although they can voluntarily resign or retire. Justices are also removed from office only through congressional impeachment and conviction. The Constitution also provides that the pay of federal judges "shall not be diminished during their continuance in office". Article III of the Constitution gives Congress the power to fix the number of justices. When the Senate is in recess, the President may make a temporary appointment without the Senate's advice and consent. Such a recess appointee to the Supreme Court holds office only until the end of the next Senate session. When the Chief Justice is unable to discharge his functions, or that office is vacant, his duties are carried out by the most senior Associate Justice until the disability or vacancy ends.

Article I, section 3 of the U.S. Constitution states that the Chief Justice shall preside over impeachment trials of the President of the United States in the U.S. Senate.

The main duties of the Chief Justice are:
- Serving as the head of the Judiciary;
- Serving as the head of the Judicial Conference of the United States, the chief administrative body of the United States;
- Appointing sitting federal judges to the membership of the United States Foreign Intelligence Surveillance Court;
- Appointing the members of the Judicial Panel on Multidistrict Litigation, a special tribunal of seven sitting federal judges responsible for selecting the venue for coordinated pretrial proceedings in situations where multiple related federal actions have been filed in different judicial districts;
- Serving ex officio as a member of the Board of Regents;
- Supervising the acquisition of books for the Law Department and Library of Congress.

Supreme Court Review

There are two ways to get a case reviewed by the U.S. Supreme Court: by appeal and by certiorari. The losers in certain types of cases, for example, cases involving claims that state statutes are unconstitutional, have a right to appeal to the Supreme Court.

For most cases, though, there is no right of appeal to the Supreme Court. However, a party who has lost a case at the federal Court of Appeals level can file a petition for certiorari with the Supreme Court. A petition for certiorari is a document explaining why the Supreme Court should review a case. If the Supreme Court grants certiorari, the appeal proceeds. If the Court denies it, the Court of Appeals' decision stands.

Thousands of petitions for certiorari are filed each year and most are denied. The Supreme Court is likely to grant certiorari on a case only if the case involves a matter of national interest or the Court believes that it must decide the case to resolve conflicts among the Circuit Courts and create uniformity in federal law.

U.S. Sentencing Commission

The United States Sentencing Commission is an independent ongoing agency within the judicial branch of the U.S. government. The Commission was created by the Sentencing Reform Act provisions of the Comprehensive Crime Control Act of 1984. The work of the Commission has a tremendous impact on the nation's criminal justice system. The first task of the Commission was to develop a uniform set of sentencing guidelines for federal courts. The constitutionality of the Commission was challenged on several occasions on the ground that it was a congressional encroachment on the power of the executive. However, in 1989 the U.S. Supreme Court upheld the constitutionality of the Commission. The principal functions of the Sentencing Commission are the following:

- ➢ To establish a uniform set of sentencing policies and practices for federal courts; This includes providing appropriate guidelines regarding the form and severity of punishment for offenders convicted of federal crimes;
- ➢ To advise and assist Congress and the executive branch in the development of effective and efficient policies related to crime and criminal acts;
- ➢ To collect, analyze, research, and distribute information on federal crime and sentencing issues, so as to serve as an information resource for Congress, the executive branch, courts, criminal justice practitioners, the academic community,

and the general public.

The Sentencing Commission consists of seven voting members who are appointed by the President and confirmed by the Senate. The members have a six year term. At least three of the commissioners shall be federal judges and no more than four may belong to the same political party. The Attorney General is an ex officio member of the Commission. The Commission staff is divided into five offices: General Counsel, Education and Sentencing Practice, Research and Data, Legislative and Public Affairs, and Administration. The director of each office reports to the staff director who in turn reports to the chair. The staff director supervises and coordinates all functions of the agency.

The Sentencing Commission is charged with the ongoing responsibility of evaluating the effects of sentencing guidelines on the criminal justice system and making appropriate recommendations to Congress. The sentencing guidelines provide federal judges with fair and consistent sentencing ranges to consult at sentencing. While developing the guidelines, the Sentencing Commission takes into account both the seriousness of the criminal conduct as well as the defendant's criminal record.

Administrative Office of the United States Courts

The Administrative Office of the United States Courts is the administrative agency of the United States federal court system. It was established in 1939. The Administrative Office provides administrative, legal, financial, management, program, and information technology services to federal courts. It provides support and staff counsel to the Judicial Conference of the United States and its committees, and implements and executes Judicial Conference policies, as well as applicable federal statutes and regulations. The Administrative Office also facilitates communications within the Judiciary and with Congress, the Executive Branch, and the public on behalf of the Judiciary.

The aim of the Administrative Office of the United States Courts is to:

➤ Aid the development and implementation of Judiciary policies and procedures;

> Deliver administrative, legal, and technological services to various courts;
> Seek, on behalf of the Judiciary, needed resources, legislation, and other assistance from Congress and the Executive Branch;
> Promote accountability to the public and perform required oversight.

The Administrative Office prepares budgets for courts and submits them to the Judicial Conference for approval by Congress. It analyzes legislation from Congress that will affect the courts' operations or personnel, and interprets and applies new laws. The Administrative Office also provides administrative help to members of courts in the form of clerks, probation and pretrial services officers, court reporters, and public defenders.

The Director of the Administrative Office is the chief administrative officer for the federal courts and secretary to the Judicial Conference of the United States. The Director is appointed by the Chief Justice of the United States, who serves as the head of the Judicial Conference. Other senior managers in the Administrative Office are an Associate Director for Management and Operations, an Associate Director, and a General Counsel. The Administrative Office is directly supervised by the Judicial Conference of the United States.

Federal Judicial Center

The Federal Judicial Center is the research and education agency for the federal courts of the United States. It was established by an Act of Congress in 1967, on the recommendation of the Judicial Conference of the United States.

The main duties of the Federal Judicial Center include:

> Conducting and promoting orientation and continuing education and training for federal judges, court employees, and others;
> Developing recommendations about the operation and study of federal courts;
> Conducting and promoting research on federal judicial procedures, court operations, and history.

The Chief Justice of the United States is ex officio Chair of the Federal Judicial

Center's board. The board also includes the Director of the Administrative Office of the United States Courts and seven judges elected by the Judicial Conference. The board appoints the Center's Director and Deputy Director. It is the Director who then appoints the Center's staff. The Director's Office is responsible for the Center's overall management and its relations with other organizations. Its Systems Innovation & Development Office provides technical support for the Center's education and research program. The Communications Policy and Design wing edits, produces, and distributes all Center print and electronic publications, operates the Federal Judicial Television Network, and with the aid of the Information Services Office maintains a specialized library collection of materials on judicial administration.

The Education Division of the Federal Judicial Center plans and produces educational programs, services, and resources for judges and nonjudicial court personnel. The Research Division, at the request of either the Judicial Conference or its committees, the courts, or other groups in the federal system undertake research programs on federal judicial processes, court management, and sentencing and its consequences. The Federal Judicial History Office develops programs relating to the history of the judicial branch and assists courts with their own judicial history programs. The Interjudicial Affairs Office provides information about federal courts to officials of foreign judicial systems and acquires information about foreign judicial systems.

Courts of Appeals

The United States courts of appeals are the intermediate appellate courts of the United States federal court system. The 12 regional circuits are organized from the 94 U.S. judicial districts. Each of these regional circuits, along with the Federal Circuit, has a United States court of appeals. A court of appeals hears and decides on appeals from the district courts located within its federal judicial circuit as well as appeals from decisions of federal administrative agencies and other designated federal courts. The decisions of the court of appeals are binding on the district courts located within its circuit.

There are currently thirteen United States courts of appeals. There are other tribunals such as the Court of Appeals for the Armed Forces which hear appeals in court martial cases that are also designated as the court of appeals. The First Circuit to the Eleventh Circuit and the District of Columbia Circuit are geographically defined. The Thirteenth Court of Appeals is the United States Court of Appeals for the Federal Circuit, which has nationwide jurisdiction over certain appeals based on a variety of subject matters, including international trade, government contracts, patents, trademarks, certain money claims against the United States government, federal personnel, and veterans' benefits. Appeals to this Court come from all federal district courts, the United States Court of Federal Claims, the United States Court of International Trade, and the United States Court of Appeals for Veterans Claims. The court also takes appeals of certain administrative agencies' decisions, including the United States Merit Systems Protection Board, the Boards of Contract Appeals, the Board of Patent Appeals and Interferences, and the Trademark Trial and Appeals Board. Decisions of the United States International Trade Commission, the Office of Compliance of the United States Congress and the Government Accountability Office Personnel Appeals Board are also reviewed by the Court of Appeals for the Federal Circuit.

The other courts of appeals also hear appeals from some administrative agency decisions and rule-making.

28 U.S.C 48 (a) provides that the courts of appeals shall hold regular sessions at the places listed below:

Circuits	Places
District of Columbia	Washington
First Circuit	Boston
Second Circuit	New York
Third Circuit	Philadelphia
Fourth Circuit	Richmond, Asheville
Fifth Circuit	New Orleans, Fort Worth, Jackson

Sixth Circuit	Cincinnati
Seventh Circuit	Chicago
Eighth Circuit	St. Louis, Kansas City, Omaha, St. Paul
Ninth Circuit	San Francisco, Los Angeles, Portland, Seattle
Tenth Circuit	Denver, Wichita, Oklahoma City
Eleventh Circuit	Atlanta, Jacksonville, Montgomery
Federal Circuit	District of Columbia and in any other place listed above as the court by rule directs.

28 U.S.CS 43 (a) provides that there shall be a court of appeals in each circuit. Such court of appeals shall be a court of record, known as the United States Court of Appeals for the Circuit.

Circuits

Circuits are the regional division under the United States federal courts system. There are 12 regional circuits organized from the 94 U.S. judicial districts. The Thirteenth Circuit is the Federal Judicial Circuit, which has nationwide jurisdiction over certain appeals based on subject matter.

Pursuant to 28 U.S.CS 41 the thirteen judicial circuits of the United States are constituted as follows:

Circuits	Composition
District of Columbia	District of Columbia
First Circuit	Maine, Massachusetts, New Hampshire, Puerto Rico, Rhode Island
Second Circuit	Connecticut, New York, Vermont
Third Circuit	Delaware, New Jersey, Pennsylvania, Virgin Islands
Fourth Circuit	Maryland, North Carolina, South Carolina, Virginia, West Virginia
Fifth Circuit	District of the Canal Zone, Louisiana, Mississippi, Texas
Sixth Circuit	Kentucky, Michigan, Ohio, Tennessee

Seventh Circuit	Illinois, Indiana, Wisconsin
Eighth Circuit	Arkansas, Iowa, Minnesota, Missouri, Nebraska, North Dakota, South Dakota
Ninth Circuit	Alaska, Arizona, California, Idaho, Montana, Nevada, Oregon, Washington, Guam, Hawaii
Tenth Circuit	Colorado, Kansas, New Mexico, Oklahoma, Utah, Wyoming
Eleventh Circuit	Alabama, Florida, Georgia
Federal Circuit	All Federal Judicial Districts

Under 28 U.S.CS 44 (a), the President appoints the circuit judges for the several circuits by and with the advice and consent of the Senate, which is as follows:

Circuits	Number of Judges
District of Columbia	11
First Circuit	6
Second Circuit	13
Third Circuit	14
Fourth Circuit	15
Fifth Circuit	17
Sixth Circuit	16
Seventh Circuit	11
Eighth Circuit	11
Ninth Circuit	29
Tenth Circuit	12
Eleventh Circuit	12
Federal Circuit	12

28 U.S.CS 44 (c) provides that each circuit judge shall be a resident of the circuit for which appointed at the time of his appointment and thereafter while in active service. An exception to this rule is District of Columbia.

Federal District Courts

Federal district courts are the general trial courts of the United States federal court system. These district trial courts were established by Congress. The federal court system includes 94 district courts in the 50 states, Washington, D. C., Puerto Rico, Guam, U.S. Virgin Islands, and Northern Marinara Islands. A federal district court is a court of law, equity, and admiralty where civil and criminal cases are heard. Each federal district also has a bankruptcy unit, as district courts have exclusive jurisdiction over bankruptcy cases.

There are 89 such federal judicial districts in the United States. Most states have only one federal judicial district. Larger states can have between two and four districts. For the purpose of a proper federal judicial administration, a number of federal judicial districts are further divided into federal judicial divisions. Each federal judicial district has at least one federal judicial court. In some federal districts and divisions, there are more than one federal district trial courts. However, it is not constitutionally mandatory that there must be a district court at every federal judicial district.

Federal district courts generally have jurisdiction to hear cases involving federal law and those involving citizens of different states. If a party in a state case can prove that a federal district court has jurisdiction to hear a case, the party may remove the case to the federal court. However, the federal court may abstain from hearing a case that involves questions of both federal law and state law. A situation may also arise where a federal district court may no longer have jurisdiction to hear a case because of changes in the parties to the suit. If a case has been removed to a federal district court and the federal district court lacks jurisdiction, the court on motion of one of the parties will remand the case to the appropriate state court.

Other Federal Courts

Other federal courts in the United States federal judicial system are the United States Court of International Trade, the United States Court of Federal Claims, the United States Court of Appeals for the Armed Forces, the United States Court of Appeals for

Veterans Claims, the United States Tax Court, the United States Bankruptcy Courts, and the United States Territorial Courts.

Congress has created a number of courts in the federal system that have specialized jurisdiction. Unlike constitutional courts, judges appointed to legislative courts do not enjoy lifetime tenure, unless Congress specifically authorized a life term. Moreover, judges in legislative courts do not enjoy the constitutional prohibition against salary reductions of judges. A summary of these courts is as follows:

- The United States Court of International Trade has jurisdiction to hear cases involving customs, unfair import practices, and other issues regarding international trade. This court is a constitutional court, so its judges have lifetime tenure and protection against salary reduction.
- The United States Court of Federal Claims has jurisdiction to hear a broad range of claims brought against the United States. The court was called the United States Claims Court from 1982 to 1992. Many cases brought before this tribunal are tax cases, though the court also hears cases involving litigants who were federal employees and other parties with monetary claims against the United States. Judges sitting on this court enjoy neither life tenure nor protection against salary reduction. An adverse decision in this court is appealed to the United States Court of Appeals for the Federal Circuit.
- The United States Court of Appeals for the Armed Forces reviews court martial convictions from the armed forces. Only the Supreme Court of the United States can review its cases. Judges sitting on this court enjoy neither life tenure nor protection against salary reduction.
- The United States Court of Appeals for Veterans Claims reviews decisions of the Board of Veteran Appeals. Appointments of judges last 15 years. An adverse decision in this court is appealed to the United States Court of Appeals for the Federal Circuit.
- The United States Tax Court is a legislative court that resolves disputes between

citizens and the Internal Revenue Service. Appointments of judges last 15 years. Adverse decisions are appealed to a court of appeals in an appropriate regional circuit.

➢ The United States Bankruptcy Courts are federal courts that have jurisdiction over all bankruptcy cases. Bankruptcy cases are not filed in state courts. All of the 94 federal judicial district courts handle the bankruptcy matters. In 1979, the United States Congress created the separate system of bankruptcy courts.

➢ The United States Territorial Courts are courts with similar jurisdictional power that of the U.S. federal district courts. These courts are formed by the U.S. Congress under Article I and established in territories of the United States. The United States territorial courts are District Court for the Northern Mariana Islands, United States District Court for the District of Guam, and United States District Court for the U.S. Virgin Islands.

Territorial Courts

Article 1 Section 8 Clause 9 of the U.S. Constitution empowers the U.S. Congress to create tribunals inferior to the Supreme Court. The powers enjoyed by territorial courts are similar to the powers of federal district courts. However, unlike federal courts, Congress enjoys some power over the territorial courts. Congress can set restrictions on the tenure of the members of the territorial courts. A majority of the territorial courts that were initially established have been extinguished because the territories have been admitted to the Union as states. The territorial courts now in existence are:

➢ United States District Court for the Northern Mariana Islands

➢ District Court of Guam

➢ District Court of the Virgin Islands

Since the territories do not have separate bankruptcy courts, the territorial courts also have bankruptcy jurisdiction. Decisions from the District Court of the Virgin Islands are appealable to the Third Circuit Court of Appeals. Decisions from the District Court of Guam and the District Court for the Northern Mariana Islands are appealable to the

Ninth Circuit Court of Appeals.

Although the District of Columbia and Puerto Rico are not states, the district courts there are not the U.S. territorial courts but federal district courts.

U.S. Court of International Trade

United States Court of International Trade (U.S.CIT) is a national court established under Article III of the United States Constitution. It constitutes nine judges appointed by the President with the advice and consent of the Senate. The judges are appointed for life. The chambers of the judges, courtrooms and offices of the U.S.CIT are located in New York City at the Courthouse of the U.S.CIT. The old United States Customs Court has been replaced as United States Court of International Trade with more powers.

The U.S.CIT hears and decides cases which arise anywhere in the United States. It is also authorized to hold hearings in foreign countries. The court has limited subject matter jurisdiction. It hears only cases involving particular international trade and customs law. Pursuant to the Customs Courts Act of 1980, the U.S.CIT has the jurisdictional authority to decide any civil action against the United States, its officers, or its agencies arising out of any law relating to international trade. The U.S.CIT has full powers in law and equity, similar to those enjoyed by courts of the United States. Accordingly, the court may grant any relief appropriate to the case before it. The relief granted may include money judgments, writ of mandamus and preliminary or permanent injunction.

The court hears disputes relating to:
- International and customs law;
- U.S. customs and border protection;
- Trade adjustment assistance by the United States Department of Labor or United States Department of Agriculture;
- Customs broker licensing, and disputes relating to determinations made by the United States International Trade Commission;
- The Department of Commerce's International Trade Administration regarding antidumping and countervailing duties;

> Import transactions mainly revenue from imports or tonnage; tariffs, duties, fees, or other taxes on the importation of merchandise.

Appeals from the U.S.CIT decisions may be taken to the United States Court of Appeals for the Federal Circuit, and from there to the Supreme Court of the United States.

U.S.CIT has its own rules prescribing the practices and procedures before the court. These rules are patterned after and follow the arrangement and numbering used in the Federal Rules of Civil Procedure.

The Chief Judge of the U.S.CIT is a statutory member of the Judicial Conference of the United States. Policies concerned with the administration of the United States Court are made in the Judicial Conference of the United States. The Chief Judge periodically organizes a judicial conference of the Court of International Trade in order to consider businesses and improve the administration of justice.

Usually, a case before the U.S.CIT is heard by a single judge to whom the case is assigned by the Chief Judge. However, if a case challenges the constitutionality of a U.S. law or has important implications regarding the administration or interpretation of the customs laws, the Chief Judge assigns the case to a three-judge panel.

All decisions of the Court of International Trade shall be preserved and open to inspection. The court shall forward copies of each decision to the Secretary of the Treasury or his designee and to the appropriate customs officer for the district in which the case arose. The Secretary publishes these decisions on a weekly basis.

U.S. Court of Federal Claims

The United States Court of Federal Claims (COFC) was recreated pursuant to Article I of the United States Constitution in October of 1982, by the Federal Courts Improvement Act. The court consists of sixteen judges nominated by the President and confirmed by the Senate for a term of fifteen years. The court hears non-tort monetary claims against U.S. Government. The United States Court of Federal Claims is situated on Madison Place in Washington D.C.

The court exercises nationwide jurisdiction over various money claims against the United States. It also conducts proceedings in other courts around the country for the convenience of the parties. In addition, the court makes extensive use of alternative dispute resolution.

The main functions of the court are:

- To review agency decisions under various federal compensation programs;
- To advise Congress, when requested, on private relief bills;
- To hear suits on government contracts, constitutional claims, tax refunds, Indian claims, civilian and military pay claims, patent and copyright matters, and vaccine injury claims;
- To accommodate litigants, trials may be held at local courthouses where the disputes arise;
- To hear congressional reference cases (cases referred by house of Congress to the court). The hearing officer (judge) will submit a report to a panel of judges who will review and forward the report to the chamber of Congress;
- Special jurisdiction, to hear claims for money arising from the United States Constitution, federal statutes, executive regulations or an express or implied in fact contract (form of implied contract) with the United States Government;
- To exercise concurrent jurisdiction in matters involving contracts with the Federal government. In this a contractor has the option of choosing between filing suit within one year with the court or within 90 days before the Agency Board of Contract Appeals;
- To exercise concurrent jurisdiction with the U.S. district courts when the claim is for less than $10,000.

All trials at the court are bench trials (trials without a jury). The court only hears cases against the government and the United States is always the defendant in cases before the COFC. Judgments of the court may be appealed to the United States Court of

Appeals for the Federal Circuit.

U.S. Tax Court

The U.S. Tax Court is a federal court that decides cases involving tax related disputes. It operates as an independent judicial body within the legislative branch of the government and is a trial court of record. The U.S. Tax Court was established by the Congress utilizing the powers granted to it by Article I of the U.S. Constitution. Section 8 of the Article permits the Congress to "constitute tribunals inferior to the Supreme Court."

Certain notable points about the U.S. Tax Court are as follows:

- Its jurisdiction is limited to cases involving federal income, death, and other taxes.
- It is an administrative court.
- It handles disputes between tax payers and Internal Revenue Service.
- There are no jury trials.
- The time limit to file a petition is within 90 days of receiving a statutory notice from the Internal Revenue Service.
- It is the only forum to litigate without paying the tax to the department. The full payment rule is inapplicable here.

The U.S. Tax Court was initially created as the U.S. Board of Tax Appeals by the Revenue Act of 1924. The Tax Reform Act of 1969 changed its name to the U.S. Tax Court.

The term of a U.S. Tax Court judge is 15 years. The U.S. Tax Court's office is situated in Washington D.C. There is also a field office on Los Angeles, California. Its sessions are conducted wherever practicable in the U.S. depending on the taxpayer's convenience.

Part II
The United States of America

Exercises

I. Choose the appropriate answer(s) to each question. There may be more than one choice for some questions.

1. Which of the following about the United States Supreme Court is NOT true?

    A. The Supreme Court is seated in Washington D.C.

    B. The Supreme Court is the highest court in the United States and is the head of the Judiciary branch of the federal government.

    C. The Supreme Court derives its authority solely from Article III of the Constitution.

    D. The Supreme Court has two types of jurisdiction: original and appellate jurisdiction.

2. Which of the following is NOT true about the justices in United States Supreme Court?

    A. Any six justices together constitute a quorum.

    B. The President nominates and appoints all the justices including the Chief Justice with the consent and advice of the Senate.

    C. All justices are paid compensation for the service they perform.

    D. The Justices enjoy their office for a lifetime, and they may be removed from the position only if charged of a crime.

3. Which of the following fall(s) within the power of the United States Supreme Court?

    A. To decide cases between same state citizens but claiming lands under grants of different states.

    B. To declare any law or executive action as unconstitutional.

    C. To create new laws on a point which is not covered by any law created by the legislature.

    D. To determine the rules or procedure to be followed by the lower federal courts of the United States.

4. Which of the following are true about the decision made by the United States Supreme Court?

   A. In the Supreme Court cases are decided by majority vote of the justices.

   B. If the Court divides evenly on a case, then the decision of the court below is affirmed, but does not establish binding precedent.

   C. Drafts of the Court's opinion, as well as any concurring or dissenting opinions, circulate among the justices until the Court is prepared to announce the judgment in a particular case.

   D. The general practice of the Supreme Court is to issue decisions in all cases argued in a particular term by the end of that term.

5. Which of the following are true about the Court of Appeals in the United States?

   A. The decisions of the Court of Appeals are binding on the district courts located within its circuit.

   B. The Thirteenth Court of Appeals is the federal judicial circuit, which has nationwide jurisdiction over certain appeals based on subject matter.

   C. Each of the 13 regional circuits, along with the Federal Circuit, has a United States Court of Appeals.

   D. A Court of Appeals hears and decides on appeals from the district courts located within its federal judicial circuit as well as appeals from decisions of federal administrative agencies and other designated federal courts.

II. Identify the following statements as True or False.

1. A petition for certiorari is a document explaining why the Supreme Court should review a case. If the Supreme Court grants certiorari, the appeal proceeds.

2. The Supreme Court has four statutory officers and the Law Clerk is one of them.

3. The first task of the United States Sentencing Commission is to develop a uniform set of sentencing guidelines for federal courts.

4. The Administrative Office is directly supervised by the Judicial Conference of the

United States.

5. The Federal Judicial Center is the research and education agency for the federal courts of the United States.
6. The Eleventh Circuit is the federal judicial circuit, which has nationwide jurisdiction over certain appeals based on subject matter.
7. A federal district court is a court of law, equity, and admiralty where civil and criminal cases are heard.
8. There are 91 federal judicial districts in the United States. Most states have only one federal judicial district. Larger states can have between two and four districts.
9. It is constitutionally mandatory that there must be a district court at every federal judicial district.
10. The U.S. Constitution empowers the U.S. Congress to create a number of courts in the federal system that have specialized jurisdiction. Judges appointed to legislative courts also enjoy lifetime tenure with no exception.

III. Questions

1. Can you introduce the U.S. Supreme Court briefly?
2. What kind of cases does the U.S. Supreme Court decide?
3. What jurisdiction does the U.S. Supreme Court have?
4. What are the principal differences between the Court Clerk and the law clerks?
5. What do you about the Clerk of the U.S. Supreme Court?
6. How does the U.S. Supreme Court decide a case?
7. What are the main duties of the Chief Justices?
8. In what ways can a case be reviewed by the U.S. Supreme Court?
9. What is the aim of the Administrative Office of the United States Courts?
10. What are the main duties of the Federal Judicial Center?
11. Can you introduce the U.S. Courts of Appeals briefly?
12. What do you about the federal district courts?

Chapter 6
STEPS IN THE FEDERAL CRIMINAL PROCESS

In this section, you will learn mostly about how the criminal process works in the federal system. Each state has its own court system and set of rules for handling criminal cases. Here are a few examples of differences between the state and federal criminal processes:

State cases are brought by prosecutors or district attorneys; federal cases are brought by United States Attorneys. State court trial judges have a range of titles, but federal judges are called district court judges.

Federal magistrate judges are used in federal cases to hear initial matter, such as pre-trial motions, but they do not usually decide cases.

The use of grand juries to charge defendants is not required by all states, but it is a requirement in federal felony cases unless the defendant waives the grand jury indictment.

States and the federal government have laws making certain acts illegal, and each jurisdiction is responsible for setting punishments for committing those crimes. A state may punish a certain crime more harshly than the federal government, or vice versa, but a defendant can be charged and convicted under both systems.

The federal rules for criminal cases can be found in the Federal Rules of Criminal Procedure, which govern all aspects of criminal trials. Each state has its own similar rules.

The steps you will find here are not exhaustive. Some cases will be much simpler, and others will include many more steps.

Important steps in the federal criminal process:

Investigation

In the federal government, there are agencies that employ criminal investigators to collect and provide information to the United States Attorneys in the respective district. The following are some of the agencies:

Federal Bureau of Investigation (FBI)

Drug Enforcement Administration (DEA)

Bureau of Alcohol, Tobacco, Firearms and Explosives (ATF)

United States Secret Service (U.S.SS)

Homeland Security Investigation (DHS/HSI)

The investigators at these agencies investigate the crime and obtain evidence, and help prosecutors understand the details of the case. The prosecutor may work with just one agency but, many times, several investigating agencies are involved.

Part of the investigation may involve a search warrant. The Fourth Amendment to the Constitution usually requires that police officers have probable cause before they search a person's home, their clothing, car, or other property. Searches usually require a search warrant, issued by a "neutral and detached" judge. Arrests also require probable cause and often occur after the police have gotten an arrest warrant from a judge.

Depending on the specific facts of the case, the first step may actually be an arrest. If the police have probable cause to arrest a suspect, as is the case if they actually witnessed the suspect commit a crime, they will go ahead and make an arrest.

Direct Evidence

A prosecutor evaluates a case, and uses all the statements and information he has to determine if the government should present the case to the federal grand jury—one in which all the facts lead to a specific person or persons who have committed the crime. However, before the prosecutor makes that conclusion, he has to look at both direct and circumstantial evidence. Direct evidence is evidence that supports a fact without an inference. Testimony of an eyewitness to a crime would be considered direct evidence because the person actually saw the crime. Testimony related to something that happened before or after the crime would be considered circumstantial.

Circumstantial Evidence

The second type of evidence is circumstantial evidence—statement(s) or information obtained indirectly or not based on first-hand experience by a person. Circumstantial evidence includes people's impressions about an event that happened which they didn't see. For example, if you went to bed at night and there was no snow on the ground but you awoke and saw the snow, while you didn't actually see it snowing, you assume that it snowed while you slept.

Charging

After the prosecutor studies the information from investigators and the information he gathers from talking with the individuals involved, he decides whether to present the case to the grand jury. When a person is indicted, he is given formal notice that it is believed that he has committed a crime. The indictment contains the basic information that informs the person of the charges against him.

For potential felony charges, a prosecutor will present the evidence to an impartial group of citizens called a grand jury. Witnesses may be called to testify, evidence is shown to the grand jury, and an outline of the case is presented to the grand jury members. The grand jury listens to the prosecutor and witnesses, and then votes in secret on whether they believe that enough evidence exists to charge the person with a crime. The grand jury may decide not to charge an individual based upon the evidence, no indictment would come from the grand jury. All proceedings and statements made before the grand jury are sealed, meaning that only the people in the room have knowledge about who said what about whom. The grand jury is a constitutional requirement for certain types of crimes (meaning it is written in the United States Constitution) so that a group of citizens who do not know the defendant can make an unbiased decision about the evidence before voting to charge an individual with a crime.

Grand juries are made up of approximately 16—23 members. Their proceedings can only be attended by specific persons. For example, witnesses who are compelled to testify before the grand jury are not allowed to have an attorney present. At least twelve jurors must concur in order to issue an indictment.

States are not required to charge by use of a grand jury. Many do, but the Supreme Court has interpreted the Constitution to only require the federal government to use grand juries for all felony crimes (federal misdemeanor charges do not have to come from the federal grand jury).

After the defendant is charged, he or she can either hire an attorney or if he or she is indigent he or she may choose to be represented by an attorney provided by the government—a public defender—at no or minimal charge. The defendant's attorney is referred to as the defense attorney. He or she assists the defendant in understanding the law and the facts of the case, and represents the defendant just as the prosecutor will represent the government.

Venue

The location where the trial is held is called the venue, and federal cases are tried in a United States district court. There are 94 district courts in the United States including the District of Columbia and territories. Many states have more than one district court, and within each district, there may be several courthouse locations.

Initial Hearing / Arraignment

Either the same day or the day after a defendant is arrested and charged, he or she is brought before a magistrate judge for an initial hearing on the case. At that time, the defendant learns more about his or her rights and the charges against him or her, arrangements are made for him or her to have an attorney, and the judge decides if the defendant will be held in prison or released until the trial.

In many cases, the law allows the defendant to be released from prison before a trial if he or she meets the requirements for bail. Before the judge makes the decision on whether to grant bail, he or she must hold a hearing to learn facts about the defendant including how long the defendant has lived in the area, if he or she has family nearby, his or her prior criminal record, and if he or she has threatened any witnesses in the case. The judge also considers the defendant's potential danger to the community.

If the defendant cannot "post bail" (pay the money), the judge may order him or her remanded into the custody of the U.S. Marshals pending trial.

The defendant will also be asked to plead guilty or not guilty to the charges.

Discovery

Before a prosecutor begins a trial, there is much work to be done. The prosecutor has to become familiar with the facts of the crime, talk to the witnesses, study the evidence, anticipate problems that could arise during trial, and develop a trial strategy. The prosecutor may even practice certain statements he or she will say during trial.

Meanwhile, the defense attorney is preparing in the same way.

One of the first steps in preparing for trial is talking to witnesses who could be called to testify in court. A witness is a person who saw or heard the crime take place or may have important information about the crime or the defendant.

Both the defense and the prosecutor can call witnesses to testify or tell what they know about the situation. What the witness actually says in court is called testimony. In court, the witness is called to sit near the judge on the witness stand. In order to testify, witnesses must take an oath to agree or affirm to tell the truth.

There are three types of witnesses:

> A lay witness—a person who has watched certain events and describes what he/she has seen. It is the most common type of witness.
> An expert witness—a specialist, who is educated in a certain area. He/she testifies with respect to his/her specialty area only.
> A character witness—someone who knows the victim, the defendant, or other people involved in the case. Character witnesses usually don't see the crime take place but they can be very helpful in a case because they know the personality

of the defendant or victim, or what type of person the defendant or victim was before the crime. Neighbors, friends, family, and clergy are often used as character witnesses.

To avoid surprises at trial and to determine which of the witnesses to call to testify, the prosecutor talks to each witness to find out what they may say during trial. These conversations will help the prosecutor decide whom to call as a witness in court.

Another important part of trial preparation is reading every report written about the case. Based on information in the reports and the information from witnesses, the prosecutor determines the facts of the case.

Prosecutors must also provide the defendant copies of materials and evidence that the prosecution intends to use at trial. This process is called discovery, and continues from the time the case begins to the time of trial. A prosecutor has a continuing obligation to provide the defendant documents and other information which may reflect upon the case. A failure of the prosecutor to do so can expose the prosecutor to fines/sanctions by the court. Further, the prosecutor is required to provide the defense with evidence that may hurt his/her case, called exculpatory evidence. This evidence could show the defendant's innocence. If the prosecution does not provide it to the defense, it may require a new trial.

Plea Bargaining

When the government has a strong case, the government may offer the defendant a plea deal to avoid trial and perhaps reduce his/her exposure to a more lengthy sentence.

A defendant may only plead guilty if he/she has actually committed the crime and admits to doing so in open court before the judge. When the defendant admits to the crime, he/she agrees they are guilty, and he/she agrees that they may be "sentenced" by the judge presiding over the court—the only person authorized to impose a sentence. Sometimes the Government will agree, as part of a plea agreement, not to recommend an enhanced sentence, such as additional time in prison for certain reasons, but it is left up to the judge to determine how the defendant will be punished.

If a defendant pleads guilty, there is no trial, but the next step is to prepare for a sentencing hearing.

Preliminary Hearing

Once the defendant has entered a plea of not guilty, a preliminary hearing will often be held. The prosecutor must show that enough evidence exists to charge the defendant. Preliminary hearings are not always required, and the defendant can choose to waive it.

It must be held within 14 days of the initial appearance if the defendant is being held in jail. If the defendant is out on bail, it must be scheduled within 21 days of the initial appearance.

The preliminary hearing is like a mini-trial. The prosecution will call witnesses and introduce evidence, and the defense can cross-examine witnesses. However, the defense cannot object to using certain evidence, and in fact, evidence is allowed to be presented at a preliminary hearing that could not be shown to a jury at trial.

If the judge concludes there is probable cause to believe the crime was committed by the defendant, a trial will soon be scheduled. However, if the judge does not believe the evidence establishes probable cause that the defendant committed the offence, he will dismiss the charges.

Pre-trial Motions

One of the last steps a prosecutor takes before trial is to respond to or file motions. A motion is an application to the court made by the prosecutor or defense attorney, requesting that the court make a decision on a certain issue before the trial begins. The motion can affect the trial, courtroom, defendants, evidence, or testimony.

Only judges decide the outcome of motions.

Common pre-trial motions include:

➢ Motion to Dismiss—an attempt to get the judge to dismiss a charge or the case.

This may be done if there is not enough evidence, if the alleged facts do not amount to a crime.

- ➤ Motion to Suppress—an attempt to keep certain statements or evidence from being introduced as evidence. For example, if the police conducted a search without probable cause (in violation of the Fourth Amendment), it may be possible to suppress the evidence found as a result of that search.
- ➤ Motion for Change of Venue—may be made for various reasons including pre-trial publicity. If the local news has covered the case a great deal, it may be necessary to move the trial to another venue to protect the defendant's right to an impartial jury.

Trial

After many weeks or months of preparation, the prosecutor is ready for the most important part of his/her job: the trial. The trial is a structured process where the facts of a case are presented to a jury, and they decide if the defendant is guilty or not guilty of the charge offered. During trial, the prosecutor uses witnesses and evidence to prove to the jury that the defendant committed the crime(s). The defendant, represented by an attorney, also tells his/her side of the story using witnesses and evidence.

In a trial, the judge—the impartial person in charge of the trial—decides what evidence can be shown to the jury. A judge is similar to a referee in a game, he/she is not there to play for one side or the other but to make sure the entire process is played fairly.

Jury Selection

At trial, one of the first things a prosecutor and defense attorney must do is the selection of jurors for the case. Jurors are selected to listen to the facts of the case and to determine if the defendant committed the crime. Twelve jurors are selected randomly from the jury pool (also called the "venire"), a list of potential jurors compiled from voter registration records of people living in the federal district.

When selecting the jury, the prosecutor and defense attorney may not discriminate against any group of people. For example, the judge will not allow them to select only men or only women. A jury should represent all types of people, races, and cultures. Both lawyers are allowed to ask questions about their potential biases and may excuse jurors from service. Each side is allowed to excuse certain potential jurors without providing a reason by using a limited number of "peremptory challenges".

Opening Statements

Opening statements allow the prosecutor and the defense attorney to briefly tell their account of the events. These statements usually are short like an outline and do not involve witnesses or evidence. The prosecutor makes an opening statement first because the Government has the burden of proving that the defendant committed the crime.

Presentment of Cases

Witness Examination

Following opening statements, the prosecutor begins direct examination of his/her first witness. This is the prosecutor's initial step in attempting to prove the case, and it can last from a few minutes to several days. During direct examination, the prosecutor can introduce evidence such as a weapon or something from the crime scene.

Following the prosecutor's examination of a witness, the defense attorney has an opportunity to cross-examine or ask questions to the same witness. The purpose of cross examination is to create doubt as to the credibility of the witness.

After the defense attorney cross-examines the witness, the prosecutor asks the witness final questions to clarify any confusing testimony for the jury. This is called redirect examination. Once the process of direct examination, cross examination, and redirect of all the witnesses is complete, the prosecutor rests his/her case. After the prosecutor rests, no more witnesses can be called to the stand or evidence introduced by the government.

After the Government rests, the defense has the opportunity to present witnesses and evidence to the jury. The defense also has the option of not having the defendant testify. There is no burden upon the defendant to prove that he/she is innocent. It is the government's responsibility to prove the defendant committed the crime as detailed in the indictment. The fact that a defendant did not testify may not be considered by the jury as proof that the defendant committed the crime. The defense may also waive his/her case. If the defense does not put on any evidence, the jury cannot assume that the defendant is guilty simply because they did not put on a defense. The decision to put on a defense is solely up to the defendant and the defense attorney. However, the defense will usually present its own version of the case.

Objections

During direct or cross-examination, either attorney can make an objection to a question or a piece of evidence to the judge. For example, a prosecutor or defense attorney may object to the wide range of the direct examination because it is beyond the knowledge of the witness, the attorney may be arguing with the witness rather than asking questions, or the witness may be talking about things irrelevant to the case.

Common objections include:

➢ Hearsay—Statement by a witness who did not see or hear the incident in question but learned about it through secondhand information such as another's statement, a newspaper, or a document.

➢ Relevance—Testimony and evidence presented at trial must be relevant to the case.

The judge decides the outcome of an objection, sometimes after allowing attorneys on both sides to comment before making a ruling. The judge either "sustains" the objection so that the action stops, or he/she "overrules" the objection and allows the action to continue.

Closing Arguments

After the defense's direct testimony and cross examination by the prosecutor of all the witnesses, the defense rests, and the prosecutor and defense attorney prepare for closing arguments.

Closing arguments are the final opportunity for the prosecutor and the defense attorney to talk to the jury. These arguments allow both attorneys to summarize the testimony and evidence, and ask the jury to return a verdict of guilty or not guilty.

Jury Instructions

Following the closing arguments, the judge "charges the jury" or informs them of the appropriate law and of what they must do to reach a verdict.

Jury Deliberations & Announcement of the Verdict

After being charged, the jury goes into deliberation, the process of deciding whether a defendant is guilty or not guilty. During this process, no one associated with the trial can contact the jury without the judges and lawyers. If the jury has a question on the law, they must write a note to the judge, which the judge will read in court with all parties present. In federal criminal trials, the jury must reach a unanimous decision in order to convict the defendant.

After they reach an agreement on a verdict, they notify the judge, the lawyers, and the defendant in open court. Everyone is present in court for the reading of the verdict. The United States Marshals Service is present during trial to protect the judge and prosecutors from potential harm. If the defendant is found not guilty, they are usually free to go home.

Post-trial Motions

If the defendant is convicted, there are several motions that can be filed after the trial is over.

Common post-trial motions include:

- Motion for a New Trial—The court can vacate the judgment and allow for a new trial. This is rarely granted, but may be done "if the interest of justice so requires".
- Motion for Judgment of Acquittal—Court may set aside the jury's verdict and allow the defendant to go free.
- Motion to Vacate, Set Aside, or Correct a Sentence—Often successful for the purpose of correcting a clerical error in the sentence.

Sentencing

A few months after the defendant is found guilty, he/she returns to court to be sentenced.

The judge receives guidance and assistance from several sources in order to sentence a defendant. Congress has established minimum and maximum punishments for many crimes which the judge uses to craft a sentence. The United States Sentencing Commissions has produced a set of sentencing guidelines that recommend certain punishments for certain crimes while considering various factors. Further, the judge will look at a presentence report and consider statements from the victims as well as the defendant and lawyers.

The judge may consider a variety of aggravating or mitigating factors. These include whether the defendant has committed the same crime before, whether the defendant has expressed regret for the crime, and the nature of the crime itself.

Death Penalty

The death penalty can only be imposed on defendants convicted of capital offenses, such as murder, treason, genocide, or the killing or kidnapping of a congressman, the President, or a Supreme Court justice. Unlike other punishments, a jury must decide whether to impose the death penalty. Many states have stopped using the death penalty, though the federal government may still use it. The Supreme Court has found that imposing the death penalty on those under age 18 at the time of the crime or the mentally challenged to be "cruel and unusual punishment" under the United States Constitution.

Appeal

Even after a defendant is found guilty, he/she can appeal to the Circuit Court if he/she believes he/she was wrongly convicted or the sentence was too harsh. An appeal is not another trial but an opportunity for the defendant to try to raise specific errors that might have occurred at trial. A common appeal is that a decision from the judge was incorrect, such as whether to suppress certain evidence or to impose a certain sentence. Appeals are complicated and sometimes result in the case going back to the trial court. A specific conviction may be reversed, a sentence altered, or a new trial may be ordered altogether if the Appeals Court decides that particular course of action.

Even after an appeal is decided by a circuit court judge, a defendant can try to appeal that decision to the United States Supreme Court in Washington, D.C.

The United States Supreme Court, the highest appellate court in the American court system, makes the final decision concerning a defendant's appeal. The Court is not required to hear an appeal in every case and takes only a small number of cases each year.

Exercises

I. Identify the following statements as True or False.

1. The use of grand juries to charge defendants is a requirement in federal or state felony cases unless the defendant waives the grand jury indictment.
2. Criminal investigation done by the investigators at some agencies may also involve a search warrant issued by a "neutral and detached" judge.
3. Testimony of an eyewitness to a crime would be considered direct evidence because the person actually saw the crime.
4. The grand jury is a constitutional requirement for certain types of crimes and at least twelve jurors must concur in order to issue an indictment.
5. If a grand jury decides not to charge an individual based upon the evidence, all proceedings and statements made before a grand jury are sealed, meaning that only the people in the room have knowledge about who said what about whom.
6. Before the judge makes the decision on whether to grant bail, he/she must hold a hearing to learn facts about the defendant.
7. The prosecutor is not required to provide the defense with evidence that may hurt his/her case, called exculpatory evidence.

8. Once the defendant has entered a plea of not guilty, a preliminary hearing is always required and the defendant cannot choose to waive it.
9. Motion to Dismiss is an attempt to keep certain statements or evidence from being introduced as evidence.
10. A prosecutor may object to the wide range of the direct examination because the attorney may be arguing with the witness rather than asking questions.

II. Questions

1. Can you put forward some examples to show the differences between the state and federal criminal processes?
2. What are the important steps in the federal criminal process?
3. What is direct evidence? Can you put forward some example to show it?
4. What is circumstantial evidence? Please put forward some example to show it.
5. What is a witness? And how many types of witnesses do you know?
6. What are the important preparations that the prosecutor and the defense attorney should make before the trial?
7. What is plea bargaining in the U.S.?
8. How are jurors selected for a case?
9. What are the important steps in the trial process?
10. What motions may the defendant file after the trial if he or she is convicted?
11. How shall the judge sentence a defendant after he or she is found guilty?
12. What do you know about the death penalty in the U.S.?

Chapter 7
STATE CONSTITUTIONS AND COURTS

State Constitutions and Courts

A state constitution is the supreme law of that state. State constitutions establish certain organs of government for the state, vest these organs with their powers, and deny certain other powers.

Like the federal constitution, the written constitutions of the states do not comprise the entire "constitution" or fundamental law. In addition to the constitutions, each state government rests upon legislative enactments, executive decrees, judicial rulings, custom and habit. Often, the constitution of one state differs from that of another in various aspects. However, in their principal elements, state constitutions are all similar to one another.

The General Nature of State Constitutions
The Powers of State Governments

The general nature of state constitutions is based upon the type of powers that state governments possess and exercise. According to the Tenth Amendment to the federal constitution, "The powers not delegated to the United States by the Constitution, nor prohibited by it to the states, are reserved to the states respectively, or to the people."

Length of State Constitutions

State constitutions are quite long. The shortest is that of Vermont, which contains 8,295 words, while Alabama's sixth and most recent constitution, ratified in 1901, is 340,136 words long.

The Contents of State Constitutions

State constitutions resemble each other in general outline. The contents of most of the state constitutions can be summarized as follows:

Preamble

A state constitution usually opens with a preamble, which is a brief foreword setting forth the presumed reasons for which the constitution was drafted and adopted.

Protection of Rights

Every state constitution possesses a "bill of rights" or "declaration of rights".

Suffrage and Elections

State constitutions have considerable portions dealing with the suffrage and elections. They specify the various qualifications for the electorate. They set the dates for particular elections and establish the local administrative machinery for the balloting.

Organs of Government

State constitutions provide for the organs of the state government such as:

- Legislature
- The Office of the Governor
- Attorney General
- The Secretary of State
- The Judiciary

The constitution may contain other provisions endowing the organs with some of their powers.

Local Government

State constitutions include considerable portions devoted to the establishment and regulation of the various types of local government.

Taxation and Debt

The state constitutions set forth the power of the state government to levy taxes and to incur debt.

Powers of Government

The largest part of the state constitution is devoted to an enumeration of the general powers of the state government.

Amendment and Revision

A final portion of the state constitution provides means for amending and revising it. There are three methods usually appearing in state constitutions whereby the constitution may be amended or revised:

- Legislative proposal;
- Popular initiative;
- Constitutional convention.

Moreover, there is a fourth formal means of constitutional commission that is not specifically authorized by any state constitution but accepted by the courts.

State Courts

Background

The judicial powers of individual states are generally vested in various courts created by state constitution or (less frequently) state statute. Within the boundaries of each state and coexisting with state courts are numerous federal district and/or appellate courts that function independently. Also coexisting within state boundaries are various administrative tribunals that also hear and decide legal matters, such as worker's compensation boards, professional licensing boards, and state administrative tribunals. Yet, there are often local, district, and/or municipal courts within the community. At first blush, it may appear overwhelming and confusing to consider what legal matter may be decided in which forum. But for the most part, each of the above courts has its own separate function and role in applying the laws to the controversies brought before it and administering justice to all.

Function and Scope of State Courts

To understand the function and scope of state courts, it is necessary to consider them in relation to the federal court system expressly created in Article III of the U.S. Constitution. Article III also establishes the type of cases that federal courts may hear and decide (federal "jurisdiction").

Article VII of the Constitution declares that "This Constitution, and the Laws of the United States... and all Treaties made... under the Authority of the United States, shall be the supreme Law of the Land; and the Judges in every State shall be bound thereby, any Thing in the Constitution or Laws of any State to the Contrary notwithstanding." Later in the Constitution, the Tenth Amendment provides that "powers not delegated to the United States by the Constitution, nor prohibited by it to the States, are reserved to the States respectively, or to the people."

The ultimate effect these provisions have upon state courts is to reserve to them the right to hear and decide any legal matter not expressly reserved for the exclusive jurisdiction of federal courts, such as lawsuits between states. This matter mostly involves the "adjudication" of controversies concerning state laws, which impact the daily lives of citizens in a much greater manner than federal laws. State courts may also rule upon certain issues concerning federal law and the federal constitution.

State legislatures are therefore free to create—and state courts are free to enforce—any law, regulation, or rule that does not conflict with or abridge the guarantees of the federal constitution or the state's own constitution. The wide variance, from state to state, of both structure and procedure within the court systems is precisely due to the preservation of those independent powers to the states by the U.S. Constitution.

The Concept of Jurisdiction

A court's general authority to hear and/or "adjudicate" a legal matter is referred to as its "jurisdiction". In the United States, jurisdiction is granted to a court or court system by statute or by constitution. A court is competent to hear and decide only those cases whose subject matter fits within the court's jurisdiction. A legal decision made by a court that did not have proper jurisdiction is deemed void and nonbinding upon the litigants.

Jurisdiction may be referred to as exclusive, original, concurrent, general, or limited. Federal court jurisdiction may be exclusive over certain matters or parties (to the exclusion of any other forum) or may be concurrent and shared with state courts. In matters where both federal and state courts have concurrent jurisdiction, state courts may hear federal law claims (e.g., violations of civil rights), and parties bringing suit may choose the forum. However, when a plaintiff raises both state and federal claims in a state court, the defendant may be able to remove the case to a federal court.

General Structure of State Court Systems

The general workhorse of a state court system is the trial court. This is the lowest level of court and is usually the forum in which a case or lawsuit originates. It may be a court of general jurisdiction, such as a circuit or superior court, or it may be a court of special or limited jurisdiction, such as a probate, juvenile, traffic, or family court. Some states handle small claims in separate courts, while others handle such claims in special divisions of the general trial courts. This is also true for probate and juvenile matters. Although someone may broadly refer to juvenile court or small claims court, he or she may actually be referring to the juvenile or small claims division of the general circuit court.

> Probate courts primarily handle the administration of estates and the probating of wills. In many states, probate courts also handle such matters as competency hearings, applications for guardianships, adoptions, etc. In a minority of jurisdictions, probate courts may be referred to as surrogate's courts.

> Family courts hear cases involving (mostly) custody and child support, neglect and abuse cases, and, sometimes, juvenile crime or truancy. Most family courts do not handle divorces, which are generally handled by the courts of general jurisdiction.

> Traffic courts handle civil infractions and violations involving motor vehicles, petitions for reinstatement of driving privileges, and related matters. Some may handle minor (misdemeanor) criminal offenses related to motor vehicle-related violations. Most traffic courts do not handle automobile accident cases (as

between the parties involved in an accident).

- Housing courts, or landlord-tenant courts, handle exactly that. In many jurisdictions, landlords must choose to file their cases in one of two courts, depending upon whether they seek eviction, injunction, etc. (landlord-tenant court), or seek money damages (small claims court). Other jurisdictions handle all landlord-tenant related matters in a single court.
- Small-claims courts handle all civil matters in which the dollar amount in controversy does not exceed a certain amount. If a party seeks damages in an amount greater than the jurisdictional limit of the small claims court, the party must either waive his or her right to the exceeding amount or re-file the case in a court with greater jurisdiction. The maximum jurisdictional limit of small claims courts varies greatly from state to state but mostly falls in the range of $3000 to $7500.
- Juvenile courts handle truancy and criminal offenses of minors. The maximum age of the minor varies from state to state but generally is either 16 or 18 years. Older juveniles who have committed serious crimes may be "bound over" to a court of general jurisdiction for determination of whether they should be tried as adults.

Importantly, states may have separate courts for criminal and civil matters. Most often, a trial court of general jurisdiction will handle both, but often on separate dockets. Many local or district courts will have limited jurisdiction for criminal matters (e.g. misdemeanors only). In such circumstances, a person charged with a felony may be arraigned in the district court and then "bound over" to the next level court (having proper jurisdiction) for criminal trial. Again, this varies greatly from state to state.

Every state has its own system to handle appeals from the trial courts. Most states have a three-tiered court system in which there are intermediate "appellate" courts that review jury verdicts or the opinions of trial court judges on a limited basis and under strict criteria. These appellate courts may or may not be distinguished by separate buildings or courthouses. Often, what is referred to as a "court of appeals" is in reality a panel of justices who merely convene to hear and decide cases at the appellate level.

In a minority of states, trial court decisions receive only one appellate review at the level of the state's highest court or the court of last resort (generally referred to as the state's supreme court). Once a state's highest court has decided a matter, the only available appeal is to the U.S. Supreme Court. However, the Supreme Court is generally deferential to state supreme courts, and only reviews matters in very limited circumstances, e.g, where a state's highest court has ruled that a federal statute or treaty is invalid or unconstitutional, or where the highest courts of two or more states have ruled differently on federal issues. When a state's highest court has decided a matter that involves both federal and state issues, the U.S. Supreme Court will nonetheless refuse to review the matter if the non-federal question is decisive in the case.

Judges and Administrative Staff

Whereas most federal judges are appointed to their positions, the majority of state trial court judges are elected to their positions by the general populace. Appellate (especially supreme court) justices are often appointed by state governors or legislatures but may also be elected by voters.

What does vary greatly from state to state is whether judicial elections involve partisan politics. In some states, party politics play a direct role in judgeships; in other states, a judicial candidate's party affiliation is treated as private data (such as religious affiliation) not disclosed in campaign profiles. States also vary greatly in the extent to which they permit judicial candidates to "advertise" their candidacy and/or raise campaign funds.

State courts employ a large number of support staff, who are usually public employees paid by taxpayer funds. Generally, a judge's staff may include one or more private assistants, law clerks, court reporters, bailiffs and other court officers, and court clerks. The most important administrative office of the courthouse is that of the court clerk. This is the office that stamps and dates all lawsuits filed, serves process (or verifies the parties' service of process), posts legal notices, subpoenas witnesses, summons and prepares juries, and sends sheriffs or other court officials out to serve writs of execution to collect on unpaid judgments.

State Supreme Courts

The state supreme court is the highest state court in the U.S. state court system. The state supreme courts are known by various names in the states. State supreme courts' primary responsibility consists of correcting the errors of the inferior state courts. It exclusively hears appeals on legal issues from inferior state courts. Since it does not make any finding of facts, it holds no trials. In rare instances where the state supreme court finds that a trial court made any egregious error in its finding of facts, the state supreme court shall remand such case before it to the trial court for a fresh trial.

State supreme courts have a panel of judges appointed as per rules outlined by each state constitution.

State supreme court's interpretation of any state law is generally final and binding to both state and federal courts. Federal courts may overrule a state supreme court decision only when there is a federal question which springs up a federal jurisdiction. An appeal from any state supreme court decision concerning matters of federal jurisdiction shall directly lie to the supreme court of the U.S. state supreme courts exercise both mandatory and discretionary review of appeals from trial courts.

Exercises

I. Fill in the gaps with the appropriate words or phrases given in the box.

A. possess	B. reserved	C. resemble	D. Amendment and Revision
E. establish	F. elections	G. Preamble	H. federal Constitution
I. vest	J. deny		

A state constitution is the supreme law of that state. State constitutions 1_____ certain organs of government for the State, 2_____ these organs with their powers, and 3_____ certain other powers.

The general nature of state constitutions is based upon the type of powers that state governments 4_____ and exercise. According to the Tenth Amendment to the 5_____, "The powers not delegated to the United States by the Constitution, nor prohibited by it to the States, are 6_____ to the States respectively, or to the people."

State constitutions 7_____ each other in general outline. The contents of most of the state constitutions can be summarized as follows: 8_____, Protections of rights, Suffrage and 9_____, Organs of government, Local government, Taxation and debt, Powers of government, and 10_____.

II. Questions

1. Can you introduce state constitutions in the U.S. briefly?
2. What are the common methods whereby a state constitution may be amended or revised?
3. What is the function and scope of state courts in the U.S.?
4. What is the general structure of a state court system?
5. What do you know about the state supreme court?

Chapter 8
THE POLICE AND CRIME IN THE U.S.

There is no national police force in the U.S., where policing is organized on a state and local basis. The country has around 500,000 police officers and a total of 40,000 separate police forces, over half of which are simply one or two man sheriffs' offices in small towns.

The Police

Police forces include city police, possibly with separate departments to deal with schools, traffic and even refuse, county police, transport police, sheriffs' departments, state police (state troopers) and highway forces such as the California Highway Patrol. An ordinary policeman is usually called a patrolman.

In addition to regular full-time police officers, many towns have auxiliary, part-time police officers, special duty and volunteer sheriff's posses (which assist sheriffs' offices in some areas). The American response to increasing crime is usually to put more cops on the beat.

The division between federal and state law can be confusing; for example, murder is classified as a state crime, while less serious crimes such as taking a woman across state lines for immoral purposes is a federal crime although it may be dealt with by a local police force. City police are concerned with local crime, and offences outside their jurisdiction are usually dealt with by state police or federal investigators (the FBI). With the increased emphasis on fighting and preventing terrorism, more and more responsibility has fallen on the local police forces, and many jurisdictions are being stretched to the limit, with promised federal funds for fighting terrorism proving inadequate for the measures proposed.

All police are armed and popular weapons include 38 specials and shotguns. Police officers also carry truncheons (night-sticks), and some forces are issued with an electronic tazer gun administering a charge of 50,000 volts for around eight seconds (originally a cattle prod), used to knock out aggressive drug addicts. In many areas, police wear bullet-proof vests, although even these are no defence against the Teflon-coated bullets (known as cop-killers) used by some criminals. Police officers also carry mace, a riot gas similar to CS gas. Police officers are among the most frightening looking Americans you are likely to meet, with their carefully developed tough-men looks, truncheons and guns. In some states, police can legally shoot suspected criminals trying to evade arrest, so don't even think about it!

Variations Across Regions

As in most countries, the efficiency, honesty and politeness of police officers vary from city to city and state to state. Police corruption is reportedly widespread, particularly in the major cities such as New York, where many officers are involved in criminal activities such as selling drugs seized from pushers. Although some people claim to present their driving licence to a traffic cop along with a $20 bill, you should never attempt to bribe a police officer, even if he gives you an open invitation. As in many countries, most complaints against the police are dismissed out of hand by police review boards, and most people consider it a waste of time reporting cases of bad cops.

If you are stopped by a policeman, either in a car or when walking, don't make any sudden moves and keep your hands where they can be seen. Some policemen are extremely jumpy (often justifiably so) and may interpret any movement as an attempt to reach a concealed weapon. Always be courteous and helpful. It may not do any harm to emphasize that you are a foreigner (depending on your nationality) or to tell the officer you are a visitor or newcomer. If you have broken the law, you should apologise and stress that it was innocently and inadvertently done although they may not be convinced if you have just held up a bank with an AK-47.

In addition to federal and state police forces, there are around 75 federal law enforcement agencies such as the Federal Bureau of Investigation (FBI), who deal with interstate crime. The FBI has some 20,000 plain clothes agents who normally concern themselves with major offences such as murder, kidnapping and robbery. It publishes a list of the "ten most wanted fugitives" and provides state and local police forces with information.

In the last few years, however, the FBI has had its role expanded to include "homeland security" and there is talk of merging or at least coordinating the activities of the FBI with those of the Central Intelligence Agency (CIA). Each state also has a reserve national guard under the command of the state governor that can be called on to deal with civil unrest such as riots, as well as dealing with natural catastrophes, e.g. earthquakes, fires, floods and hurricanes. The National Guard has had its role vastly increased in recent years. Many companies and individuals also employ private armed guards.

Crimes

The purpose of this section is not to scare you, but to warn you about the high level of crime and violence in the U.S., which in the major cities is much higher than in many other countries, especially western Europe.

The "ground rules" are not the same in the U.S., as in many other countries. If you follow the rules, your chances of being a victim are as low as in most European cities, but break the rules and they rise dramatically.

Guns

The U.S. has always had an extremely high crime rate, due in no small measure to the vast number of guns. However, the trend over the last decade has been improving.

Most Americans support gun registration, although few favour a complete ban on the sale and possession of guns (Americans cannot understand why foreigners fail to grasp their obsession with guns). However, owning a gun is little deterrent against crime, as you must be ready and able to use it. Most people could never react quickly enough to a threatening incident, and statistics show that a gun is over 20 times more likely to kill a family member, friend or acquaintance than to kill an intruder.

Many children accidentally kill themselves or their playmates with guns that are left lying around homes (half the guns in the U.S. households are not kept under lock and key). Despite the statistics, the National Rifle Association (NRA) insists that any connection between gun ownership and crime is purely coincidental!

Black-on-black Crime

Black-on-black crime is the biggest problem in the U.S. and the middle-class U.S. has largely ignored the urban warfare raging in inner-city areas. Most whites live in rural areas and communities hermetically sealed from the trigger-happy chaos of the U.S.'s black urban life. However, there are increasing signs that the horror of the U.S.'s romance with the gun is spreading to small town, white America.

One of the most worrying aspects is the increase in violent crime committed by children: in recent years there have been a number of high-profile "massacres" perpetrated by children aged as young as eight. Schools routinely check children for weapons (using metal detectors), and many inner-city schools have armed security guards and a prison-like regime in order to reduce crime.

The crime rate varies considerably according to the region (the west has the most crime, the northeast the least) and city, although the recent application of a "zero tolerance" policing policy in many major cities has resulted in a dramatic reduction in crime rates, which are currently at their lowest for 25 years. In recent years, the right wing view has held sway, the majority believing that crime will go away if only they get tough, build more prisons, lock offenders away longer and execute more murderers.

Despite the statistics, the vast majority of Americans manage to get through the day without being molested, mugged, knifed or shot (or even witnessing such events), and most live to a ripe old age and die natural deaths (if over-consumption can ever be called natural!). Although crime and violence are among the most disturbing aspects of life in the U.S., it is important to maintain a sense of perspective, as heightened anxiety or paranoia about crime can be just as bad or worse than being a victim (and is a complete waste of time and effort).

Nevertheless, anyone coming to live in the U.S. would be wise to choose a low-crime, middle class suburb and avoid "high-crime" areas (e.g. most inner cities) at all times, as well as following the guidelines below.

Crime Prevention & Safety

Staying safe is largely a matter of common sense and you should observe the following guidelines.

At night, stick to brightly lit main streets and avoid secluded areas (best of all, take a taxi). Avoid parks and keep to a park's main paths or where there are other people during the day. If you find yourself in a deserted area late at night, remain calm and look as though you know where you're going by walking briskly. If you must wait for a train or bus at night, do so in the main waiting room, a well lit area, or where there's a guard or policeman. If possible, avoid using subways in the late evening or after midnight.

Walk in the opposite direction to the traffic so no one can kerb crawl (drive alongside you), and walk on the outside of the pavement, so you're less likely to be mugged from a doorway.

When you're in an unfamiliar city ask a policeman, taxi driver or local person if there are any unsafe neighborhoods (all major cities have "no-go" areas at night and some have areas that are to be avoided at any time) – and avoid them! Women should take care and should never hitchhike or accept lifts with strangers (rape statistics are extremely high and most go unreported).

Carry the bare minimum of cash with you, often referred to as "mugger's money", because in the event that you are mugged, it is usually sufficient to satisfy a mugger and prevent him/her from becoming violent (or searching further). In some cities, parents give their children mugger's money as a matter of course whenever they leave home. Never resist a mugger. It is far better to lose your wallet and jewellery than your life. Many muggers are desperate and irrational people (officially known as emotionally disturbed persons or EDPs) under the influence of drugs, and can turn violent if resisted. Some experts advise you to keep your cash in at least two separate places and to split cash and credit cards. Do not keep your passport, green card, driving licence and other important documents in your wallet or purse where they can be stolen. Anaesthetic sprays or ordinary hair or insect sprays are carried by some people to deter assailants (as are pepper sprays and mace). These are, however, of little use against an armed assailant and may increase the likelihood of violence. Many cities and states require registration or licensing for those carrying mace or pepper sprays and local police forces sometimes offer training classes in their use.

Warn your children of the dangers of American "street life", particularly if you have been living in a country where it is taken for granted that you can safely go almost anywhere at any time of day or night. It may be necessary to totally re-educate your family regarding all aspects of public life. Wherever you live and whatever the age of your children, you should warn them against taking unnecessary risks and discourage them from frequenting remote or high risk areas, talking to strangers, or attracting unwanted attention.

Do not leave cash, cheques, credit cards, passports, jewellery and other valuables lying around or even hidden in your home (the crooks know all the hiding places). Store anything of value in a home safe or a bank safety deposit box and ensure that you have adequate insurance. Good quality door and window locks and an alarm helps, but may not deter a determined thief. In many cities, triple door locks, metal bars and steel gratings on windows are standard fittings. Most city dwellers always lock their doors and windows, even when going out for a few minutes. Apartments are often fitted with a security system, so you can speak to visitors before allowing them access to your building. Luxury apartment buildings have armed guards in the lobby with closed-circuit TV and voice identification systems. In addition, most apartments have a peephole and security chain, so you can check a caller's identity before opening the door. Be careful who you allow into your home and always check the identity of anyone claiming to be an official inspector or an employee of a utility company. Ask for identification (ID) and confirm it with their office before opening the door.

If you live in a city, you should be wary of anyone hanging around outside your home or apartment block. Have your keys ready and enter your home as quickly as possible.

Never make it obvious that no one is at home by leaving tell-tale signs such as a pile of newspapers or letters. Many people leave lights, a radio or a TV on (activated by random timers) when they are not at home. Ask your neighbours to keep an eye on your home when you are on holiday. Many towns have "crime watch" areas, where residents keep an eye open for suspicious characters and report them to the local police.

If you are driving, keep to the main highways and avoid high-risk areas. Never drive in cities with your windows or doors open or valuables such as handbags or wallets on the seats. Take extra care at night in car parks and when returning to your car, and never sleep in your car. If you have an accident in a dangerous or hostile area (any inner-city area), police advise you not to stop, but to drive to the nearest police station to report it. In remote areas, accidents are sometimes staged to rob unsuspecting drivers (called highway hold-ups) and cars are deliberately bumped to get drivers to stop (again, seek out the nearest police station). If you stop at an accident in a remote area or are flagged down, keep the engine running and in gear and your doors locked (ready to make a quick getaway), and only open your window a fraction to speak to someone. In some states, hire car drivers are targeted by muggers (after a spate of attacks on tourists in Florida, rented cars are now indistinguishable from private vehicles) and you should be wary of collecting a hire car from an airport at night.

Police forces, the federal government, local communities and security companies all publish information and advice regarding crime prevention, and your local police department will usually carry out a free home security check.

Exercises

I. Fill in the gaps with the appropriate words or phrases given in the box.

A. legitimized	B. associated	C. separate	D. corruption
E. public	F. empowered	G. exercise	H. preservation
I. enforcement	J. protection		

A police force is a constituted body of persons 1_____ by the state to enforce the law, protect property, and limit civil disorder. Their powers include the 2_____ use of force. The term is most commonly 3_____ with police services of a sovereign state that are authorized to 4_____ the police power of that state within a defined legal or territorial area of responsibility. Police forces are often defined as being 5_____ from military or other organizations involved in the defense of the state against foreign aggressors; however, gendarmerie are military units charged with civil policing.

Law 6_____, however, constitutes only part of policing activity. Policing has included an array of activities in different situations, but the predominant ones are concerned with the 7_____ of order. In some societies, in the late 18th and early 19th centuries, these developed within the context of maintaining the class system and the 8_____ of private property. Many police forces suffer from police 9_____ to a greater or lesser degree. The police force is usually a 10_____ sector service, meaning they are paid through taxes.

II. Identify the following statements as True or False.

1. There is a national police force in the U.S., which is organized on a state and local basis.
2. Police forces in the U.S. include city police, county police, state police.

3. City police are concerned with local crime, and offences outside their jurisdiction are usually dealt with by state police or federal investigators.

4. If you are stopped by a policeman, either in a car or when walking, don't make any sudden moves and keep your hands where they can be seen.

5. Many Americans support gun registration, although most favor a complete ban on the sale and possession of guns.

6. The crime rate in the U.S. varies considerably according to the region; the northeast has the most crime, the west the least.

Chapter 9
U.S. LAW SCHOOLS

Getting into law school is the first step to becoming a lawyer. A law degree can also serve as a good foundation for other careers that require critical thinking.

In the United States, a law school is an institution where students obtain a professional education in law after first obtaining an undergraduate degree. Law schools in the U.S. issue the Juris Doctor degree (J.D.), which is a professional doctorate. Other degrees that are awarded include the Master of Laws (LL.M.) and the Doctor of Juridical Science (J.S.D. or S.J.D.) degrees(for international students). Most law schools are colleges, schools, or other units within a university. A total of 205 institutions are ABA-approved and confer the first degree in law (the J.D. degree).

Law School Accreditation

Accreditation is "to recognize an educational institution as maintaining standards that qualify the graduates for admission to higher or more specialized institutions or for professional practice". Law schools generally fall into categories of accreditation such as American Bar Association (ABA) accredited, and state accredited.

The ABA is the national accrediting body for law schools. It has enabled accreditation to become unified and national in scope with the potential for inconsistency, among the 50 states, the District of Columbia, the Commonwealth of Puerto Rico, and other territories. The Council of the ABA Section of Legal Education and Admissions to the Bar is the United States Department of Education recognized accrediting agency for programs that lead to the first professional degree in law.

State Accreditation

Each state has its own accreditation process. However, most of the states give accreditation status to ABA accredited schools. State requirements vary by state.

ABA Accreditation Process

Under Title 34, Chapter VI, 602 of the Code of Federal Regulations, the Council and the Accreditation Committee of the ABA Section of Legal Education promulgates the Standards and Rules of Procedure for Approval of Law Schools which law schools must comply in order to be ABA-approved. The law school approval process established by the Council is designed to provide a careful and comprehensive evaluation of a law school and its compliance with the Standards. An Accreditation Committee of 19 members assists the Council in evaluating schools seeking provisional or full approval.

A law school has to be in operation for one year before it may apply for provisional approval by the ABA. The applicant school is required to develop an extensive self-study including a critical evaluation of the school's strengths and weaknesses and establishing goals for the school's future progress. The school is required to complete a site evaluation questionnaire that provides much of the information that a site evaluation team needs to ascertain.

A law school must remain in provisional status for at least three years. However, a school may not remain in provisional status for more than five years. A school must demonstrate that it is in full compliance with each of the Standards, in order to be granted full approval. After provisional approval, a visit to the school by a full site evaluation team is conducted in years two, four, and five. Moreover, a limited site evaluation by one or two site evaluators is conducted during years one and three. Thereafter, a site evaluation report is submitted to the school and the Accreditation Committee. The Accreditation Committee reviews the site report and the school's response. The Committee sends the school a letter indicating any areas where the Committee concludes the school does not yet fully comply with the Standards.

Finally, after reviewing the findings, conclusions, and recommendations of the

Accreditation Committee, decisions on full approval are made only by the Council.

Getting into Law School

There is no single course of study required for admission into law school. Law schools accept applications from virtually all majors and every discipline. Law schools look for applicants with specific courses such as political science, philosophy, sociology, and history. Law schools also look for applicants with quantitative courses such as economics, business, math, and finance. A broad and varied undergraduate education is often considered as the best way to the legal profession.

An applicant must demonstrate:

➢ A solid academic record and an LSAT score;

➢ Professional commitment;

➢ Maturity and intellectual ability;

➢ Experience and purpose;

➢ Strong skills in analyzing, advocating, counseling, writing, speaking and negotiation.

The most important factor in law school admissions is an applicant's score on the LSAT. In addition, the candidate must have high GPA. GPA is a measure of a student's academic achievement at a college or university; calculated by dividing the total number of grade points received by the total number attempted. Most law schools require two or three letters of recommendation. Another significant factor in law school admission is the candidate's personal statement. It is also important that an applicant has a good financial credit record because law school is expensive.

Law School Degrees

Law school in the United States is a postgraduate level program which typically lasts three years and results in the awarding of Juris Doctor (J.D.) degree after successful completion of the program. J.D. is a professional law degree required by most states before a candidate can sit for the bar exam to become a licensed attorney.

In addition to the qualifications required to become a practicing lawyer, law schools also offer higher degrees such as doctorates for more advanced academic study. LL.M(for American students) is a research law degree obtained after earning a J.D. that allows a candidate to specialize in a particular area of law such as international law or taxation.

Majority of accredited law schools offer Joint Degree Program (JDP). JDP is a specified combination of degree programs or degree types in which a student is enrolled in two graduate degree programs concurrently. JDPs are developed and proposed by the relevant academic units with agreement of the deans of the schools affected.

LL.M

In the past decade, there has been tremendous growth in Americans legal education in the area of LL.M degree. The intent of law schools offering the LL.M is to enhance the skills and knowledge of individuals having their first degree in law. Essentially there are two principal variations of the LL.M degree. The first are those related to advanced study of specific subjects such as taxation, international and comparative law, business law, intellectual property, natural resources and environmental law, health law, real estate law, labor law, dispute resolution, maritime law and bankruptcy law.

The second type of the LL.M degree is one offered specifically for foreign trained lawyers. These programs usually consist of one or more required courses providing an introduction to American law and then a choice of various course topics usually from the courses offered in the J.D. curriculum.

The American Bar Association does not accredit or approve LL.M degree programs; rather it acquiesces in their establishment. The accrediting body permits an approved law school to offer the program. It does not approve the program; rather it is an approved law school, which offers an LL.M program about which the accrediting body has taken no action concerning the LL.M program academic content or quality.

There are no rules by the accrediting authority as to the number of credit hours required for the LL.M degree, whether there should be a substantial writing requirements associated with the degree or what specific courses should be taken to receive a LL.M degree in a specific subject matter area. These matters are determined by the law school offering the degree. Many law school programs require a written thesis produced under the supervision of a full-time faculty member, but some do not. Some programs provide opportunities or even require an internship experience, but others do not. Generally schools require between 20 and 24 semester credit hours for the degree earned over a period in residence of one year with a cumulative grade point average of B. Part-time students usually are allowed two calendar years to complete their study. For Americans students seeking an LL.M degree, most law schools require a J.D. from a law school, either approved by the Americans Bar Association, or a member of the Association of American Law Schools.

Bar Examination

Bar Examination is an aptitude examination for the law graduates from American Bar Association approved law schools in the U.S. to grant eligibility to practice law in a certain jurisdiction.

The Bar Examinations in the U.S. is administered by state owned agencies. A state bar licensing agency is associated with the judicial branch of government. This bar licensing agency may be an office or committee. The state's highest court or intermediate appellate court forms such a licensing agency. In some states, the bar licensing agency is part of the state bar association or its subunit.

The structure of Bar Examination is different in every state. However, there are some similarities. Normally the examination is broken into two to three days. There are two sessions daily.

The ethics exam, Multistate Professional Responsibility Examination (MPRE), designed by the National Conference of Bar Examiners (NCBE) is part of the Bar Examination in 47 states of the U.S. This examination is a prerequisite or corequisite to the Bar Examination. This is a multiple choice examination designed to evaluate the knowledge and understanding of professional conduct of lawyers.

The Bar Examinations of the U.S. states include essays, multiple choice essays, and multiple choice questions. The essay questions of the Bar Examination are aimed to evaluate the knowledge of general legal principles and state's own laws related to wills, trusts and community property. In some jurisdictions, the essay questions are from NCBC's Multistate Essay Examination (MEE). In certain other jurisdictions, they use essay questions from MEE and their own pool.

MBE

Multistate Bar Examination (MBE) is administered as part of the Bar Examinations in 48 states of the U.S. The MBE is not adopted in the states of Louisiana, Washington and Puerto Rico. This is a standardized examination designed by the NCBE. The MBE questions are aimed to evaluate the basic standard element for a particular field of law and general and accepted legal principles of common law.

The MBE is a multiple choice examination conducted in a single day with two sessions. Duration of each session is three hours with 100 questions each. There are 33 questions each in Contracts and Torts. There are 31 questions each in constitutional law, criminal law and procedure, evidence, and real property. Moreover, there are 10 pretest questions. Generally the questions may indicate the applicable statute, theory of liability, or comparable principle of law. Some questions require an analysis of legal relationships in a factual situation, or suggestions about interpretation, drafting, and counseling.

All questions are multiple choices with four alternatives. The Bar Examination score is based on the number of correct answers. Time management is an important factor in MBE.

The answer sheets of MBE candidates are centrally scored. The scores of candidate are based on raw scores and scaled scores. The raw score is the total of right answers. The scaled score is a conversion of a candidate's raw score to a common scale.

MPT

The Multistate Performance Test (MPT) is another written examination as part of the Bar Examination. This test is conducting in 33 jurisdictions of the U.S. The MPT is developed by the NCBE. The goals of the MPT are aimed to:

- Sort detailed factual materials and separate relevant from irrelevant facts;
- Analyze statutory, case, and administrative materials for principles of law;
- Apply the law to the relevant facts in a manner likely to resolve a client's problem;
- Identify and resolve ethical dilemmas, when present;
- Communicate effectively in writing;
- Complete a lawyering task within time constraints.

The MPT includes writing a legal memorandum, drafting an affidavit, or drafting a settlement offer letter to opposing counsel.

MEE

The Multistate Essay Examination (MEE) is a written examination to answer a collection of essay questions. The MEE is administered as a part of the Bar Examination in 26 jurisdictions of the U.S. This essay test is developed by the NCBE. The questions of essays can be from:

- Business associations such as agency and partnership, corporations, limited liability companies;
- Conflict of laws;
- Constitutional law;
- Contracts;
- Criminal law and procedure;
- Evidence;
- Family law;
- Federal civil procedure;
- Real property;
- Torts;

> Trusts and estates-decedents' estates; trusts and future interests;
> Uniform Commercial Code-Article 3, Negotiable Instruments; Article 9, Secured Transactions.

The MBE, MEE and MPT are administered on the same days across the country along with the state Bar Examinations.

Exercises

I. Identify the following statements as True or False.

1. The ABA is the national accrediting body for law schools.
2. Each state has its own accreditation process. However, state accreditation requirements are the same.
3. J.D. is a professional law degree required by most states before a candidate can sit for the bar exam to become a licensed attorney.
4. The LL.M degree is one offered specifically for foreign trained lawyers.
5. Law schools accept applications from virtually all majors and every discipline, no single course of study required for admission into law school.
6. The Bar Examinations in the U.S. is administered by American Bar Association.
7. Multistate Professional Responsibility Examination (MPRE) is designed to evaluate the knowledge and understanding of professional conduct of lawyers, which is an alternative examination to the Bar Examination.
8. Multistate Bar Examination (MBE) is a standardized examination administered as part of the Bar Examinations in 48 states of the U.S., which is aimed to evaluate the knowledge of general legal principles and state's own laws related to wills, trusts and community property.
9. The Multistate Performance Test (MPT) is another written examination as part of the Bar Examination. The questions are aimed to evaluate the basic standard

element for a particular field of law and general and accepted legal principles of common law.

10. The MBE, MEE and MPT are administered on the same days across the country along with the state Bar Examinations.

II. Fill in the gaps with the appropriate words or phrases given in the box.

A. profession	B. biographies	C. mock	D. fellow
E. honors	F. rewarded	G. admission	H. firms
I. law	J. minimum		

American law firms are often very credential-oriented. Apart from 1_____ the requirements of a J.D. and 2_____ to the state bar, there are certain credentials recognized within the 3_____ to distinguish lawyers from one another; those credentials are almost always mentioned in lawyer profiles and 4_____, which are used to communicate to both 5_____ attorneys and prospective clients. Chief among them are 6_____ such as being a member of their law school's law review, moot court, or 7_____ trial programs. Judicial clerkships after graduation or 8_____ clerk positions at prestigious law firms while in school are also distinguishing marks. This credential-based system is sown in law school, where high grades are frequently 9_____ with law review membership and much sought after summer clerkships with large private law 10_____.

Chapter 10
PRACTICE LAW IN THE UNITED STATES WITH A FOREIGN LAW DEGREE

When you look through online research on how to become a lawyer, it almost goes without saying that most of what you'll find is about how to become a lawyer in the United States through the typical path: law school, then the bar exam, plus additional requirements, then voila! You are a lawyer! It is a lot harder than it sounds, unfortunately, but that's the basic idea. But what about law professionals who were trained abroad?

While it can sometimes be difficult (depending on where you live) to practice law in the United States as a foreign-trained lawyer, it is not impossible.

Here are the steps you need to take as a foreign lawyer to practice in the United States.

Find Out About the State-Specific Regulations Regarding Practicing Law with a Foreign Degree

The most important thing to remember if you are thinking of practicing law in the United States with a foreign law degree is that each state has different requirements. The first thing you should do is to do some research into the state you are hoping to practice in, to see what your next steps should be. Here, California and New York will be talked about in depth, and then a short summary will cover the other states, which represent less commonly-used options but are not necessarily impossible.

New York

New York is a very popular destination for foreign-trained attorneys to practice, and the state requirements facilitate this process.

The New York Board of Law Examiners, who administers the New York Bar Exam, has a specific set of requirements for foreign-trained lawyers who wish to practice in New York. In a nutshell, a foreign-trained lawyer will fall into one of two categories: (1) their foreign education transfers to the U.S. system; or (2) their foreign education does not transfer to the U.S. system.

If a foreign-trained lawyer has completed a program that is at least three years long and is focused on common law, his or her education will usually transfer, and he or she can sit for the bar after receiving permission from the Board of Law Examiners. In all other cases, foreign-trained attorneys will need to complete an LL.M program with certain qualifications before they can sit for the bar exam.

If you plan to take the New York bar exam as a foreign-trained attorney, be sure to plan ahead! It is advisable to submit all of your materials at least six months to a year in advance of the date you plan to take the bar exam.

California

Another popular option for foreign-trained lawyers is California. Like New York, the California Board of Bar Examiners has relatively liberal admission requirements for foreign lawyers. In fact, if you meet the requirements, it may be even easier to sit for the bar exam in California than it is in New York. Under California regulations, foreign-trained lawyers who have been admitted to practice law in a jurisdiction outside the United States are often eligible to take the bar exam in California without needing to complete any additional requirements.

If the foreign-trained attorney has not been admitted to practice outside the United States, he or she can still be eligible to take the bar exam after completing an LL.M that covers four separate subjects tested on the California Bar Exam, and one of those courses must be a Professional Responsibility course that covers the California Business and Professions Code, the ABA Model Rules of Professional Conduct, and leading relevant federal and state case law.

Other States

As previously stated, each state has its own laws about how a foreign-trained lawyer can qualify to practice in the United States. Of the fifty states, plus the District of Columbia and five territories, there are thirty-four jurisdictions where foreign-trained lawyers have the opportunity to gain admission to the bar. Of these jurisdictions, Vermont is the only state that recognizes foreign law degrees with regularity, and there is a sort of apprenticeship program in place to help foreign-trained attorneys to prepare for the Vermont bar exam. In addition, there are four states (plus the territory Palau) where a foreign-trained attorney can take the bar exam after earning an LL.M.

Aside from New York and California—which have already been discussed—an LL.M degree would also allow a foreign-trained lawyer to take the bar exam in Washington state and Wisconsin. The remaining twenty-nine jurisdictions where foreign-trained lawyers can become eligible to take the bar exam feature a variety of different requirements before becoming eligible to sit for the exam. These include, but are not limited to, legal education in English common law, additional ABA-approved education, and practice of law in a foreign jurisdiction. The requirements for each state will be listed on the state-specific bar exam website and are summarized by the National Conference of Bar Examiners' Bar Admission Guide.

Go Back to School, If Necessary

In the states where only an LL.M is required in order to sit for the bar exam, completing the specified graduate education in your area of study should be high on your priority list. The states that allow a foreign-trained attorney to sit for the bar exam after earning an LL.M require specific courses and subjects covered, so it is advisable to look up the requirements in each state before settling on an LL.M program.

Some states offer accelerated J.D. degrees for foreign-trained lawyers in order to get them to the point of bar exam eligibility in that state. That option is useful in the thirteen states where additional education at an ABA-approved law school is needed in order to sit for the bar as a foreign-trained lawyer. In all other states where foreign legal education is not recognized, earning a J.D. at an ABA-approved law school is the only way you will be able to practice law in that state. While it would likely feel very repetitive to do so, practicing law in the U.S. is a competitive and closely-monitored profession—unfortunately, laws are laws.

Take Your State's Bar Exam

No matter which path you have to take in order to get here, every potential lawyer must sit for the bar exam in the state in which you hope to practice. Bar exam passage rates for foreign-trained lawyers are lower than the national average, unfortunately. The national average is around a 58% passage rate, while the average for foreign-trained lawyers is around a 30% passage rate. Law schools in the United States are rigorous, and students come out with a specific set of skills and a knowledge set that will help them study for and pass the bar. Foreign-trained lawyers may not have all of those same tools in their arsenals, and their passage rate may be lower for that reason. Foreign students should definitely plan to take a full commercial bar review course and may wish to explore private bar tutoring options as well.

Once You Have Passed the Bar

Congratulations! Passing the bar exam is the just step in becoming an accredited lawyer in the United States. There are other requirements that will need to be fulfilled at this point, such as taking the MPRE and passing the character and fitness requirements for your state's bar, but the most difficult part as a foreign-trained lawyer is now hopefully behind you.

Law is one of the most competitive professions to have in the United States; therefore, it is tightly regulated and difficult to break into for most foreign-trained lawyers. If you are striving to practice in one of the states that recognize training at foreign institutions of law, that is great news! You are already well on your way to becoming a U.S. attorney. If you have to go back to school in order to obtain your legal credentials, you will at least be able to decide whether practicing law in the U.S. is what you truly want to do. If it is, then dive in—you'll have earned your credentials in the end! However, there are also other ways to use your foreign law degree in the United States.

Using Your Foreign Law Degree in the U.S. Without Being an Attorney

There are a couple of ways to use your foreign law degree without becoming a fully admitted state bar member. One of the most common is to become a foreign legal consultant. A foreign legal consultant is, essentially, a foreign-trained lawyer who has set up a limited practice in the United States. There are foreign legal consultant rules in thirty-one states, plus the District of Columbia and the U.S. Virgin Islands, so it is essential to do your research before deciding to become a foreign legal consultant.

Other than becoming an FLC, there are also opportunities in some states for temporary transactional work, for pro hac vice admission to the state bar, and for foreign lawyers to be able to serve as in-house counsel, which could be very helpful for a global business. While earning bar admission would allow for the most opportunities for a foreign-trained attorney, these other opportunities to use a foreign law degree are important to understand as well.

Foreign-trained attorneys are at a definite disadvantage compared to students who have earned law degrees in the United States, at least when it comes to gaining state bar admission. There are many hoops to jump through and a good deal of communication needed between the foreign-trained lawyer and the state bar association if a foreign lawyer is seeking admission to the bar.

If you are a foreign-trained lawyer seeking bar admission, the information provided here should hopefully help you decide whether it makes sense to seek full admission to the bar in the state you are living in. Luckily, there are several options for foreign-trained lawyers who choose not to seek full admission to the bar, including jobs as foreign legal consultants and in-house counsel. No matter what you decide, be sure to do your research, since each state has a different set of requirements, and the stringency of the regulations is sure to be high. Law is a very competitive field, but if it is what you love, keep working toward your goals! Good luck!

Exercises

I. Fill in the gaps with the appropriate words or phrases given in the box.

A. proceedings	B. lawyer	C. documents	D. agents
E. paralegals	F. computer-assisted	G. construct	H. assistants
I. notary	J. advice		

In its most general sense, the practice of law involves giving legal 1_____ to clients, drafting legal 2_____ for clients, and representing clients in legal negotiations and court 3_____ such as lawsuits, and is applied to the professional services of a 4_____ or attorney at law, barrister, solicitor, or civil law 5_____. However, there is a substantial amount of overlap between the practice of law and various other professions where clients are represented by 6_____. These professions include real estate, banking, accounting, and insurance. Moreover, a growing number of legal document 7_____ (LDAs) are offering services which have traditionally been offered only by lawyers and their employee 8_____. Many documents may now be created by 9_____ drafting libraries, where the clients are asked a series of questions that are posed by the software in order to 10_____ the legal documents.

II. Questions

1. What steps are foreign lawyers recommended to take to practice law in the U.S.?
2. What are the most common ways to use your foreign law degree without becoming a fully admitted state bar member in the U.S.?

Chapter 11
LEGAL CAREER OVERVIEW

Overview

Although television dramas might have you believe that you only need good looks and a fashionable wardrobe to succeed as a lawyer, in reality, completing three years of law school and passing a tough bar exam barely prepare you for the practice of law.

Law is the way society regulates its behavior. It creates rules of conduct that are widely understood and gives us parameters for resolving disputes and defining acceptable codes of conduct. The federal, state, and local laws regulate everything from how people do business with each other to how they act in public to where they can park their cars. Because law is considered a technical profession not easily comprehended by the untrained individuals and companies hire professionals—lawyers—to help them comprehend it and conduct the procedures it defines.

The law is an integral part of nearly every area of our lives from the environment, trade and commerce, and civil rights to national security, the Internet, and entertainment and sports.

People who enter this demanding and all-encompassing profession do so for many reasons, not the least of which is the desire to work in an intellectually rigorous field that can have a significant impact on the world around them. Of course, in most legal careers, the pay is great, too, but most lawyers will tell you the money is not enough to sustain one's commitment to a job that can be incredibly challenging, with long hours and high stress. If you want to be a lawyer, you'd better love the law.

Lawyers can work for law firms, which can range in size from less than a dozen people to thousands, in government agencies, in legal departments of public or private corporations; or they can hang out their own shingles. Lawyers can work on behalf of their own employer, if they are in-house counsel, or on behalf of clients. Everyone from the largest company to the average John Q. Citizen is likely to have a need for an attorney at some point. Large corporate transactions are almost always reviewed by legal counsel. Starting a new business often requires advice from a skilled lawyer. Individuals may need advice on everything from managing estate issues from the death of a loved one to obtaining advice about a divorce or fighting a local zoning ordinance.

What You Will Do

In broad terms, lawyers apply their interpretation of the law (the codified rules of their society) to advise their employers or clients on completing transactions in compliance with the law or resolving disputes based on current understanding of the law.

In more specific terms, lawyers can have a broad range of responsibilities depending on the specific area of law they practice. But if you think being a lawyer mainly involves making speeches and grilling witnesses in a courtroom, think again. Even trial lawyers—those who specialize in courtroom litigation—spend surprisingly little time before a judge or jury. For every hour in the courtroom, many more are spent doing research, conducting interviews, or writing documents in preparation for litigation. Many lawyers, in fact, never set foot in court.

At its most basic level, a lawyer's role is that of an advocate and adviser. Attorneys use specialized knowledge to research and interpret the intent of the law and apply it to whatever circumstances their clients face. It is an imperfect practice, as interpretations of the law may vary significantly based on the circumstances of the situation.

The legal profession can be divided into two major categories: litigation and transactions. Litigation, which concerns both civil and criminal law, is the process of arguing a dispute between two parties. Transactions relate to business and personal matters that usually do not require courtroom argumentation. For example, a lawyer may counsel a client in the transactions of preparing a will, contract, or lease, to help secure venture capital for a new company, or to prepare a patent for a new technology. However, if the will is contested or if the venture capitalists sue the business owner for fraud, that would then require an attorney with litigation skill.

Litigation and transactions have specializations of their own, such as tax, antitrust, bankruptcy, labor, real estate, insurance, international trade, environmental regulation, and mergers and acquisitions—to name just a few. Lawyers can also specialize in specific industries such as health care, high tech, life sciences, entertainment, or even nonprofits.

Depending on the type of law they practice, lawyers will spend their time on paperwork; researching, preparing for, or participating in trials; and advising clients. They spend hours in law libraries and with online databases researching legal precedents. They prepare contracts, briefs, and other documents, assembling boilerplate paragraphs or writing from scratch.

They plan and conduct depositions, or interviews with witnesses. In complicated cases, these can generate thousands of pages of testimony, all of which have to be read, analyzed, and refined into usable information. They present their evidence—the information they have gathered about a case and about the laws relevant to a case—in a court of law, arguing before a judge and/or jury. Alternatively, they may present their research findings to clients, advising them on business or other issues.

Who Does Well

Working as a lawyer requires excellent and persuasive oral and written communication skills. (English majors: Here is a chance to prove Grandpa wrong and use your degree for something useful and lucrative!) You will be required to interpret complicated, and sometimes ambiguous, laws in such a way that backs up your clients or company, while doing your best to maintain the integrity of the legal system. Lawyers must be detail-oriented, natural negotiators who enjoy research. And they must also have a high tolerance for tedium—there can be a lot of paperwork and poring over dry case law involved.

Requirements

Becoming a lawyer is an arduous process. After completing a bachelor's degree, you take the Law School Admission Test (LSAT), complete involved applications, gather the appropriate recommendations, and go through interviews to gain admission to law school.

Once you have been accepted into law school, you will spend three years striving to outdo your classmates by way of test scores, law review membership, Socratic method success stories, and summer associate positions before you earn your J.D. degree. Upon graduation, you must be admitted to your state's bar association, which requires you to pass a written bar exam and often a written ethics exam.

All that work done, you are still not guaranteed a job. However, if you earn your J.D., you gain membership to a highly educated group of professionals that includes doctors, university professors, and the like. The skills you learn in law school and in the workplace can take you a long way in your career. Even if you never practice law, you will earn the right to the title of Esquire, be known as a natural negotiator, and have credentials that invariably position you as a capable and talented candidate in the landscape of job opportunities. In fact, a legal background is great experience for many skilled industries or professions. Those who do want to work in traditional law jobs can choose to work in a number of settings, but positions at large law firms remain the most coveted, especially for recent law graduates.

Private Practice

Law firms host on-campus interviews at law schools and offer summer associate programs for interested 1Ls and 2Ls (first-and second-year law students, for the uninitiated). During the summer, law students can get a feel for associate life and make valuable contacts within the firms. These summer programs are integral to firms' hiring practices—they usually hire around 85 percent of their summer associates as full-time attorneys upon graduation. Major firms maintain websites with recruiting contacts and smaller firms can be contacted directly with inquiries.

Assistant District Attorney, Assistant U.S. Attorney, and Public Defender

Most government agencies do not actively recruit, and hiring programs vary from office to office. If you are interested in working for the government, you need to initiate contact. It is a good idea to research a specific agency thoroughly (most of them maintain websites) and gather information first by arranging briefings or informal meetings with people who work there.

Public Interest

Equal Justice Works hosts an annual job fair in Washington, D.C. It is a great place to network as hundreds of employers participate. Summer internships are key to breaking into this area of law. Most of them are unpaid, but there are a lot of fellowships available to finance the undertaking.

Law Professor

If you want to teach law, you will attend the American Association of Law Schools' (AALS) annual faculty recruitment conference in November in Washington, D.C. Commonly known as the "meat market", the conference is a great chance for aspiring professors and law-school administrators to mix and mingle.

About Lawyer Referral Services

In many areas, lawyer (or attorney) referral services are maintained by local (e.g. county) bar associations, whose members provide legal representation for a reasonable fee. Before retaining a lawyer, ask exactly what legal representation costs, including fees for additional services such as medical experts, transcripts and court fees. Most importantly, hire a lawyer who is a specialist and experienced in handling your type of case. If you cannot afford a lawyer and your case goes to court, a court-appointed lawyer represents you.

An unusual feature of the U.S. legal system is plea bargaining, which involves the prosecution and the defence making a deal where the defendant agrees to plead guilty to a lesser charge, thus saving the court time and leading to a reduced sentence. This has made the U.S. legal system something of a lottery, often with victims' lives at stake, and in high profile cases, such as the O.J. Simpson case, a media circus. In the U.S., you are normally considered guilty until proven innocent, at least in the eyes of the general public, and you may be tried and convicted by the media (there are virtually no reporting restrictions in the U.S.), long before your trial comes to court.

Penalties are often harsh, particularly for less serious crimes, while professional and white-collar criminals who can afford the best defence often get off with a light sentence or a fine. Many American judges are elected, rather than appointed from qualified members of the legal profession, which often results in bad legal decisions and a lack of consistency in sentencing (at the lower court levels, corrupt judges are not unknown).

Job Outlook

According to the Bureau of Labor Statistics, the long-term outlook for lawyers is that employment will grow about as fast as the average for jobs overall between 2004 and 2014 (meaning: about 14 percent). The pace of overall job growth for lawyers will depend on the performance of the economy; better economic performance typically results in more activity among businesses of the type that requires legal assistance, e.g. mergers & acquisitions, corporate securities being brought to market, and so on.

Certain areas of the law are expected to grow faster than others. Among these is elder law. As Baby Boomers are increasingly entering their 60s, the demand for attorneys versed in the issues of senior citizens will increase. In addition, as the Internet changes the way that people communicate and transmit information, there will be more demand for intellectual property law specialists, as well as those versed in international law, as business becomes more globalized. Environmental law will continue to be in high demand as issues surrounding so-called "green" initiatives and environmental remediation of sites that have been neglected or damaged by toxic substances.

Competition among recent law grads will continue to be stiff thanks to the large number of graduates every year. Further reducing opportunities is the trend among many businesses to rely on accounting firms and paralegals that perform the same functions lawyers do, but more cheaply. Lawyers who want to set up their own practice should find it easiest in small towns and expanding suburban areas, where there is less competition from established firms and more chances to get to know potential clients. Lawyers with specialized expertise will also find it easier to set up shop.

Those who are interested in becoming judges will be sad to hear that the BLS projects judicial career growth to be slower than the average rate of growth for all jobs between 2004 and 2014. The main reason is tight government budgets.

Paralegals, who cost less than attorneys to employ, will enjoy more of a boom employment market than their colleagues with J.D.s; job growth in this area is expected to exceed the rate of growth in jobs overall between 2004 and 2014.

Career Tracks

Lawyers who go into private practice follow a relatively fixed path up the corporate ladder. Many lawyers, however, choose to leave private practice to work in business or other law-related careers. Skills gained through the practice of law are highly transferable to other industries and functions, such as business development, consulting, and investment banking.

Firm Associate

Firms offer associate positions to recent law school graduates and laterals, or lawyers who change firms. Associates work long hours—70 to 80 per week is not uncommon at the large firms—and do the bulk of the grunt work, from producing documents and doing due diligence, such as reviewing and substantiating claims, to writing briefs and overseeing deals.

Associates either work as transactional, or corporate, lawyers or litigators. Transactional lawyers deal with business issues—corporate financing, contracts, acquisitions, or bankruptcy to name a few—with the goal of completing deals and avoiding future legal problems. Litigators, on the other hand, deal with legal problems after they occur—breaches of contract, securities law problems, class action suits, antitrust actions, employment-related problems, white collar crime, and the like.

In-house Counsel

In-house counsel refers to one or more attorneys hired to work within a company's legal department. Attorneys in such positions advise management on legal issues ranging from accounting compliance to merger-and-acquisition negotiations. They generally work more reasonable hours than attorneys in big firms, and positions are typically filled by transactional attorneys with three or more years' experience.

Solo Practitioner

Attorneys deterred by the hierarchical structure of law firms sometimes start their own practices. This is an option more commonly chosen by seasoned veterans with solid client bases, although ambitious recent law school graduates have been known to try their hand at it. Starting your own firm is an exercise in entrepreneurship—in addition to practicing law you are running a business. Flexible hours and the freedom to choose interesting projects are the perks, while the lack of administrative personnel and resources are a couple of the disadvantages.

Public Defender

Public defenders are appointed by the court to conduct criminal defenses for people who cannot afford representation. Federal defenders are located in most major cities, with the plum jobs in Washington, D.C., as well as San Francisco and New York. States and counties provide publicly funded defense lawyers for those charged in nonfederal cases. Although the salaries for these positions are lower than most private sector lawyers', they are often not the poverty-level offerings that many people think they are. But dealing with a lot of hopeless cases and jaded judges can sour a young lawyer's idealism about the system very quickly. The work is stressful, but new cases every day make for an interesting career. There is stiff competition for these jobs and they can be tough to come by.

Assistant District Attorney

Assistant district attorneys aid district attorneys in prosecuting criminal cases in a city or county's municipal or superior courts. The office of the district attorney presents evidence to grand juries in order to obtain criminal indictments. The fast-paced days in court and high-profile trials are highlights of this job, but the work can be draining. As with most government jobs, these jobs tend to not pay as well as the private sector.

Legal Aid Lawyer

Legal aid lawyers defend indigent clients in civil cases. Funded by the federal Legal Services Corporation and some states, salaries are often low, but the work is meaningful. While this position offers a lot of responsibility from the outset, many legal aid attorneys burn out on the job quickly after representing too many unsavory defendants or seeing how cold or inefficient the justice system can be.

Assistant U.S. Attorney (AU.S.A)

AU.S.As are appointed to work with state law-enforcement officials to put together federal cases against individuals or institutions. Such jobs are relatively specialized; different AU.S.As will work on, for example, DEA cases, securities law cases, and racketeering cases.

Public Interest Attorney

Among the most prestigious jobs for lawyers are positions with impact litigation advocacy organizations. These include the American Civil Liberties Union, the National Center for Youth Law, NOW, NARAL, the Lambda Legal Defense and Education Fund, the NAACP Legal Defense Fund, and the Environmental Defense Fund. The work usually involves a great deal of brief writing and advocacy. In some cases, there is a great deal of client contact, too. Because these positions are both intellectually stimulating and socially meaningful, competition for landing one of these coveted posts is high, despite the relatively low pay. One exception is environmental law organizations, which tend to be better funded.

Law Professor

Law professors are attorneys who teach their trade to law students. Working on a tenure-track or adjunct basis, professors spend most of their time teaching in the classroom and researching legal issues. They may run clinical programs, giving students hands-on experience representing underprivileged clients, or teach classes such as constitutional law, tax law, and intellectual property law. Competition is fierce for these positions, and spots usually go to experienced practitioners.

Exercises

I. Identify the following statements as True or False.

1. The legal profession in the U.S. can be divided into two major categories: litigation and transactions.
2. Even if you never practice law, with a degree in law you will earn the right to the title of Esquire, be known as a natural negotiator, and have credentials that invariably position you as a capable and talented candidate.
3. In-house counsel refers to one or more attorneys hired to work within a company's legal department.
4. Legal aid lawyers are appointed by the government to conduct criminal defenses for people who cannot afford representation.
5. Public interest attorneys aid district attorneys in prosecuting criminal cases in a city or county's municipal or superior courts.

II. Questions

1. What are the requirements for becoming a lawyer in the U.S.?
2. Except for being a lawyer who go into private practice, there are some other law-related careers. What are they?

Chapter 12
MAJOR DIFFERENCES BETWEEN THE U.S. AND UK LEGAL SYSTEMS

Attorneys probably already know legal systems in both the UK and the U.S. share the same historical common law roots, and are for that reason quite similar. The purpose of this section, though, is to highlight a few of the key divergences in order to give attorneys a sense of how the U.S. and UK legal systems differ.

A Note on States

Much like the main subdivisions of the UK, i.e. England, Wales, Scotland, and Northern Ireland, the states of the U.S. have their own laws, court systems, and bar associations. In the U.S., federal law and court decisions generally take precedence over these state laws and decisions. Powers not granted to the federal government are instead specifically reserved to the states in the U.S. Constitution.

Court Systems

Court systems in both countries are quite similar. Minor criminal offenses and small civil disputes are handled by special magistrate courts tasked with resolving such disputes. In the U.S., these are cases for state courts almost exclusively.

More serious crimes and civil cases in both countries are then subject to a three-level court hierarchy. In the U.S., at the federal level, criminal cases and civil cases are not heard by separate courts; at the state level, however, many states do have separate court systems for these two types of cases. Cases begin in lower courts (Crown Court in the UK, District Court in the U.S.), then move on to Courts of Appeals, and are finally resolved in a single Supreme Court, if necessary.

It is important to note that the U.S. does not have a "Tribunal System" as the UK does for certain disputes. There are, however, niche courts for certain types of cases (e.g. bankruptcy court is a separate type of federal court). In the U.S., parties may also agree to submit to binding arbitration or mediation as a means of alternative dispute resolution in certain cases. This often provides a less costly, more streamlined, and less adversarial way to conclude conflicts.

Sources of Legal Authority

Much like courts in the UK, courts in the U.S. rely mainly on past judicial opinions as authoritative precedent when resolving litigation. In the U.S., these are often referred to as "opinions" or simply "cases", while the phrase "law report" has become somewhat archaic.

As readers will also likely know, for legislation, the U.S. has two centralized federal bodies, the House of Representatives and the Senate, together known as the Congress, which are similar to the Houses of Parliament. Each of the 50 states in the U.S. is afforded two senators, while representatives are allocated proportionally based on each state's population.

In order to become a law in the U.S., a bill under discussion must be approved by a majority of both congressional bodies, and then signed into law by the President. If the President refuses to sign the bill into law, his or her veto can be overridden by a two-thirds majority vote in Congress.

Roles of Lawyers

Aside from differences in nomenclature, the roles of lawyers in both countries are quite similar. The terms "barrister" and "solicitor" are not commonly used in the U.S., and litigators and non-litigators are not separately licensed. Instead, once an attorney is admitted to the bar in a particular state, he or she may generally practice any kind of law. For the sake of clarity, court-going barristers are known as "litigators" in the U.S., and solicitors are called "corporate" or "transactional" attorneys, or are referred to in accordance with their area of specialization e.g., a health care attorney, a real estate attorney, a family law practitioner, etc.

Legal Education

Unlike in the UK, there is not a requirement to pursue further courses and apprenticeships beyond law school in the U.S. Instead, all prospective lawyers take a three-year course at an accredited law school and receive a Juris Doctor (J.D.) degree upon graduation. Then, students must pass the bar exam in a state of their choosing. After licensure, they may generally practice law in any field of their choosing.

Legal Terms & British Spelling

Although UK lawyers share a common language with their American counterparts, they sometimes employ different terminology. For example, insider trading is referred to as insider dealing in the UK.

When searching for materials published in the UK, be mindful of variations in spelling between British English and American English. These seemingly minor differences can have an enormous impact on search results.

To conduct a thorough search for books or articles about labor law in the UK, you should include both the British and American spellings ("labour law" or "labor law").

As you can see, the systems are more alike than they are different. Hopefully, this section can serve as a basic guide so that attorneys can get a sense of how the two systems compare.

Exercises

I. Identify the following statements as True or False.

1. Legal systems in both the UK and the U.S. share the same historical common law roots, and are for that reason quite similar.
2. Much like the main subdivisions of the UK (i.e. England, Wales, Scotland, and Northern Ireland), the states of the U.S. have their own laws, court systems, and bar associations.
3. In the U.S., federal law and court decisions generally take precedence over the state laws and decisions.
4. In the U.S., minor criminal offenses and small civil disputes are handled by special magistrate courts tasked with resolving such disputes.
5. In the U.S., at the federal level, criminal cases and civil cases are heard by separate courts.
6. The trial court in the UK is Crown Court, in the U.S. District Court.
7. The U.S. has a "Tribunal System" as the UK does for certain disputes.
8. For legislation, the U.S. has two centralized federal bodies, the House of Representatives and the Senate (together, known as the Congress), which are similar to the Houses of Parliament.
9. Court-going barristers in the UK are known as "litigators" in the U.S., and correspondingly, solicitors in the UK are called "corporate" or "transactional" attorneys or are referred to in accordance with their area of specialization, e.g., a health care attorney, a family law practitioner, etc.
10. Like in the UK, there is a requirement to pursue further courses and apprenticeships beyond law school in the U.S.

II. Topic for Discussion

The major differences and similarities between the UK and the U.S. legal systems.

Part III

Selective Readings

Chapter 1
OVERVIEW OF THE CANADIAN LEGAL SYSTEM

Common Law Versus Civil Law

As a former British colony, Canada's judicial system hails from the British common law tradition, which is a system of rules based on legal precedents—decisions made by judges. These precedents then become the foundation on which other judges base their decisions.

Quebec is the only province that does not go by common law, embracing a more structured civil law system that stems from Roman law. The statutes are clearly defined and the judges enforce the law strictly as it is written. It relies less on case law and more on broad legal principles that have been codified, hence Quebec goes by its own Civil Code. Therefore judgments are more prescribed and cases are less open to interpretation from judges.

The Quebec Act of 1774 turned Canada into a "bijural" country—one with two types of law. Since then common law has been applied outside Quebec in matters of private law, while similar matters in Quebec are dealt with under civil law. In criminal, or public, cases, on the other hand, the common law is applied throughout Canada.

Civil Versus Criminal Cases

The main distinction here is that civil law governs relationships between individuals, while criminal law governs relationships between individuals and the state, or Crown, which represents all Canadians.

Combined with the previous definition of "civil law" above, the term can be more than a little confusing. The Justice Canada website further clarifies:

"In its other sense, civil law refers to matters of private law as opposed to public law, and particularly criminal law, which is concerned with harm to society at large. It is usually clear from the context which type of civil law is intended."

Only the federal government has the ability to make criminal laws. The federal, provincial, and territorial courts all have the power to make civil laws.

Legal Structure

Canada's legal system is divided into three tiers. The government makes and administers the laws through its executive (Cabinet), legislative (Parliament) and judicial (courts) branches.

The process of making laws starts with the Cabinet, or ruling party, which then presents the legislation to Parliament, composed of the House of Commons and Senate, for debate and approval. The final step involves the Governor General, or Queen's representative, who must give the bill official "assent".

The same process applies provincially, but the Queen's representative is called the Lieutenant Governor.

Parliament can make laws for all Canada, but only about matters assigned to it by the Constitution. A provincial or territorial legislature, likewise, can make laws only about matters over which it has been assigned jurisdiction. This means these laws apply only within the province's borders.

The government usually makes laws related to issues that apply to all Canadians, including constitutional rights, crime, aboriginal rights, national defence, trade and patents.

The provinces handle laws concerning education, property, civil rights, the administration of justice, hospitals, municipalities, and other matters of a regional importance.

The Constitution Act, a successor to the British North America Act of 1867, establishes Canada's dual legal system and enshrines the provinces' jurisdictional rights over property and civil, or private, rights.

Once a law is enacted, it is the role of the judiciary—judges who preside over cases in the courts—to interpret and apply it. While judges cannot make their own laws, their decisions can create legal precedents—a new way to interpret the law for future cases.

The Courts

The judicial system is made up of various levels of courts that fall under federal or provincial/territorial control. Here are the different types of courts:

Provincial/Territorial Courts

These courts exist in every province or territory, except Nunavut, and deal with most criminal offences, family law matters (except divorce), young persons 17 and under in conflict with the law, traffic violations, regulatory offences, and claims involving money.

Provincial/Territorial Superior Courts

Each province and territory, including Nunavut, has superior courts. These courts have different names and most provinces have their own supreme court that is separate from the Supreme Court of Canada. Some, like Alberta, even have a division called the Court of Queen's Bench. These courts hear serious criminal and civil cases. They also are specialized to deal with certain family law matters such as divorce and property claims. The judges are appointed and paid for by the federal government and superior courts serve as the first level in the appeals process.

Provincial/Territorial Courts of Appeal

These appellate courts hear appeals from decisions rendered in the provincial/territorial regular and superior courts. They usually sit as a panel of three judges, which are all federally appointed.

Federal Courts

These courts, which consist of the Federal Court and Federal Court of Appeal, only deal with matters related to federal laws. Decisions by the Federal Court that get appealed are heard by the Federal Court of Appeal. These courts mostly try cases stemming from inter-provincial and federal-provincial disputes, intellectual property proceedings, citizenship appeals, trade and competition cases, and cases involving Crown corporations or government departments. The Tax Court of Canada and military courts are specialized arms of the Federal Court.

Supreme Court of Canada (SCC)

This is the top court in Canada and the final court of appeal and has the final and binding interpretation of Canadian laws. The Supreme Court has jurisdiction over disputes in all areas of the law, including constitutional law, administrative law, criminal law and civil law, but only hears the most important cases. While the panel of nine judges, including a Chief Justices and eight fellow judges, are appointed by the Prime Minister, they are independent and often make decisions counter to the government's will. Under the Supreme Court Act, three of the nine judges must come from Quebec. The SCC also decides on key questions regarding the Canadian Constitution and the Charter of Rights and Freedoms. The Court also serves an advisory role to the government, which can ask for its opinion on important legal matters.

Department of Justice

The role of the Department of Justice (DOJ) is to ensure that Canada's justice system is as fair, accessible and efficient as possible. The DOJ works with the federal government to develop policy and to make and reform laws. It also acts as the government's lawyer, providing legal advice, prosecuting cases under federal law, and representing the government in court. These responsibilities reflect the double role of the Minister of Justice, who is also the Attorney General of Canada.

Chapter 2
AUSTRALIA'S LEGAL SYSTEM

Australia's legal system, also known as common law system, is based on the model which was inherited by those countries whose development was influenced by British colonialism in particular the commonwealth countries and the U.S. Under the Australian legal system all people whether domestic or international are treated equally before the law and safeguards to ensure the fairly judgment by government or officials. Australian courts work on adversarial system, which innate within the English legal system. This system comprises of two parties presenting their case against each other, where the third party known as judge or magistrate presides the case directly. Whereas in the adversarial system, witnesses are not handled by the judge directly. The judge listens to each side's discussions and after the cross-examination of witnesses by both sides then only the judge makes the decision. But in other countries like France, inquisitorial system of courts operates, where the judge plays an active role in examining evidence and questioning witnesses.

The Australian Constitution

Australia operates in a constitutional monarchy. At a federal (Commonwealth) level, the first institution of law in Australia is the Commonwealth Constitution. The Constitution comprises of rules which control the power, authority and operation of a Parliament. In Australia, each state has its own constitution. The Commonwealth Constitution consists of federal government, the federal parliament, and the federal courts, the territories, and the creation of new states. Thus, the Commonwealth Constitution is the fundamental document of empowerment in the Australian political and legal systems.

It establishes that, where the Commonwealth and a state pass conflicting laws, any valid Commonwealth law trumps (overpowers) the state legislation. States can pass laws on any subject matter.

The federal government has the power to enact legislation about certain areas given by the Constitution. In activities such as marriage, immigration and taxation, the Commonwealth has the power to order the law. But in the buying and selling of property and criminal laws constitutional capacity of the Commonwealth Parliament could not do anything.

Division of Powers

"The law making powers which are not stated in the constitution as belonging to the commonwealth remains with the state." A federation involves a division of powers between the constituent elements in Australia that is between the states and the federal body, the Commonwealth of Australia. One of the most important roles of the constitution is the division of powers between the federal and state legislatures. The constitution confers a limited number of exclusive powers such as defence, foreign trade and immigration etc., but most of the Commonwealth's powers, granted under s. 51, are concurrent powers. These powers can be exercised by the Commonwealth and the states but, in the event of conflict, the Commonwealth law will prevail (s. 109). Powers which are not expressly mentioned in the Constitution—residual powers—remain with the states.

Separation of Powers

Governing Australia needs lots of power. The Constitution says that this power is divided between three groups of people so they can balance each other. Each group checks the power of the other two. This division of power stops one person or group of people taking over all the power to govern Australia.

Thus, legislative involves in making laws, executive administering laws and judicial applying laws to individual cases. "Under the Commonwealth Constitution, legislative power is formally allocated to the Commonwealth Parliament, executive power to the Crown (the Governor-General acting through the Federal Executive Council, effectively the government) and judicial power to the courts."

The Federal Parliament

The Australian Federal Parliament consists of two houses: the House of Representatives and the Senate. The House of Representatives is called as the "lower house", whereas the Senate is as the "upper house".

The House of Representatives

At present, the House is made up of 150 single member electorates. There are 50 electorates in New South Wales, 37 in Victoria, 26 in Queensland, 15 in Western Australia, 12 in South Australia, 5 in Tasmania, 3 in the Australian Capital Territory and 2 in the Northern Territory.

The Senate

The Senate has 76 members composed of 12 from each state, plus two each from the territories. Thus, the two houses of Parliament comprise the legislative arm of the Australian political system. The government is drawn from the party or parties that command a majority in the House of Representatives. At present, the Liberal Party and the National Party govern in coalition. Legislation has to pass both houses in order to become law and, except in the case of money bills, the Senate has equal power with the House of Representatives.

Distinguishing Features of the Australian Legal System

Legal system by definition refers to the process of making and implementation of laws. This system primarily describes the type of laws created and implement among

States. This reflects the manner on how people, governments and organizations behavior in accordance with the observance of the laws.

The Australian legal system has been created based on the legal system of Britain due to the European settlement in Australia. When the British Parliament has granted the permission of putting up government in their colonies including Australia, laws have been created which follows the establishment of the legal system. It was during the 19th century that the six states of Australia created a movement for the creation of central government. The creation of the Australian Constitution that took effect in January 1,1901 has marked the beginning of an independent Australian legal system.

Chapter 3
SINGAPORE'S LEGAL SYSTEM

Jurisdiction & Law

As a Commonwealth nation, Singapore's legal system has its roots in English law and practice. Founded in 1819 by Sir Stamford Raffles, the once sleepy island was transformed into a major entrepôt along the shipping route between Europe and the Far East. With the arrival of the British, English law and customs were adopted.

Since self-governance in 1959 and independence from Malaysia in 1965, Singapore has developed its own autochthonous legal system, establishing legislation and case law that are unique to its social and economic circumstances.

Despite forging its own path suited to Singapore's requirements, there is one inherited British legal foundation that remains intact, albeit just: common law. Singapore inherited the English common law traditions, especially in contract, tort and restitution, and thus the stability, certainty and acceptance that such law enjoys among other Commonwealth nations. While Singapore courts still refer to case law emerging from England, it has made significant departures in the past 30 years, especially in statute-based areas such as company law, criminal law and evidence, in favour of local jurisprudence.

The Singapore legal structure comprises the Legislature, Executive and Judiciary. The Legislature is made up of the Parliament and an elected President. The Parliament is tasked with enacting laws of the land. Singapore has a unique parliamentary composition. Besides elected Members of Parliament (MPs), non-elected MPs also sit in Parliament but their voting rights are restricted to matters that do not concern the Constitution, finance bills and votes of no-confidence in the government.

The Executive is helmed by the President and comprises the Cabinet which is responsible for the general direction of the Government and accountable to Parliament. Cabinet ministers are drawn from MPs and as such there is no complete separation of powers between the Legislature and the Executive.

Singapore has a comprehensive judicial system. The State Courts, previously known as Subordinate Courts, form the first tier in the judicial hierarchy to administer justice amongst the people. It comprises the District Courts, Magistrates' Courts, specialised courts—Family Court, Juvenile Court, Coroner's Court—Small Claims Tribunals and the Court Mediation Centre. The District Courts, Magistrates' Courts and Small Claims Tribunals can hear civil matters where disputed amounts do not exceed $250,000, $60,000 and $10,000 respectively.

The second tier is the Supreme Court, made up of the High Court and Court of Appeal, the latter being the highest court in the land. Both courts hear criminal cases and civil claims exceeding $250,000. The Chief Justice, Judges of Appeal, Judges and Judicial Commissioners are appointed by the President on the advice of the Prime Minister.

While the judicial system has been efficient in dispensing justice, the government has found it necessary and expedient to complement the courts with other modes of alternative dispute resolution (ADR), namely, arbitration and mediation. Having established itself as a major international commercial centre, Singapore has made giant leaps to cater to the demands of business for cheaper, quicker and, at times, confidential dispute resolution. It has positioned itself as a competitive arbitration centre to match that of London and Hong Kong. Major law firms in Singapore now offer arbitration services, and institutions with state-of-the-art hearing facilities are in place to meet the arbitration needs of disputants.

For smaller claims, mediation has been promoted as an alternative method of resolving disputes. The State Courts via their Primary Dispute Resolution Centre and the Singapore Mediation Centre are the two main mediation avenues. The rest are initiatives spearheaded by the government or industry, namely, Maintenance of Parents Tribunal,

Community Mediation Centre and Consumers' Association of Singapore.

Supreme Court of Singapore

The Supreme Court is made up of the Court of Appeal and the High Court, and hears both civil and criminal matters. Led by the Honourable the Chief Justice Sundaresh Menon, the Supreme Court Bench consists of the Judges of Appeal, Judges and Judicial Commissioners of the Supreme Court.

The High Court has jurisdiction to try all offences committed in Singapore and may also try offences committed outside Singapore in certain circumstances. In criminal cases, the High Court generally tries cases involving capital offences or cases involving imprisonment terms that exceed 10 years. Generally, except in probate matters, a civil case must be commenced in the High Court if the value of the claim exceeds $250,000. Probate matters are commenced in the High Court only if the value of the deceased's estate exceeds $3,000,000 or if the case involves the resealing of a foreign grant. In addition, ancillary matters in family proceedings involving assets of $1,500,000 or more are also heard in the High Court.

Since 2002, various specialised courts like the Admiralty Court, the Intellectual Property Court and the Arbitration Court have also been set up in the Supreme Court in response to the increasing complexity of commercial cases reaching the judiciary. The establishment of dedicated specialist commercial courts underscores the Supreme Court's depth of expertise and experience in these areas, and its commitment to position and promote Singapore as a premier centre for dispute resolution and as a jurisdiction of choice for the resolution of both domestic and international commercial disputes.

Singapore International Commercial Court (SICC)

Building on Singapore's reputation of having a world-class judiciary that is well-known for its efficiency, competence and integrity, the Singapore International Commercial Court (SICC) was established specifically to provide parties with a prime destination for international commercial dispute resolution. The SICC offers parties an efficient dispute resolution process adjudicated by a panel of experienced judges comprising specialist commercial judges from Singapore and international judges from both civil law and common law traditions.

The SICC is a division of the Singapore High Court. It offers the option of a court-based dispute resolution mechanism focused on international and commercial disputes, even where the dispute has no connection with Singapore and is not governed by Singapore law.

The SICC has a number of key features, like a diverse panel of eminent international and local jurists, which differentiate it from other Courts.

Others include:

More options for representation: A party to proceedings may, in certain circumstances like offshore cases, be represented by foreign counsel, who must be registered with the SICC and be subject to a Code of Ethics. Foreign counsel may also appear to address the SICC on matters of foreign law.

More flexible court procedures: Court procedures in the SICC follow international best practices for commercial disputes. However, due to the international and commercial nature of disputes and the parties, the SICC's court procedures are flexible in various respects.

Confidentiality: The Court generally takes a more liberal approach in granting confidentiality orders for offshore cases.

Rules of evidence: Ability to apply to the Court to adopt rules of evidence that you are familiar with.

Determination of foreign law: Questions of foreign law may be determined on the basis of submission instead of proof.

Document production or discovery: The document production rules are similar to that in the International Bar Association Rules on the Taking of Evidence in International Arbitration.

Costs: Costs are at the discretion of the Court, with the general principle that the unsuccessful party shall pay the reasonable costs of the proceedings to the successful party.

State Courts of Singapore

The Judiciary is one of the three constitutional pillars of government along with the Legislature and the Executive. As an organ of state, the Judiciary's function is to independently administer justice. The Chief Justice is the head of the Judiciary which comprises the Supreme Court and the state courts (originally called subordinate courts).

The state courts of Singapore include the district courts, the magistrates' courts, the specialised courts, i.e., family courts, juvenile courts, etc., and the small claims tribunals. As a critical component of the Judiciary, the state courts handle more than 95% of the Judiciary's caseload.

The Presiding Judge has overall responsibility for the leadership and management of the state courts.

The Presiding Judge of the state courts is assisted by the Deputy Presiding Judge who concurrently heads the Corporate Services Division as Registrar of the state courts. The Presiding Judge and Deputy Presiding Judge are supported by the Leadership Team comprising the Principal District Judges/Heads of Division, senior judicial officers and senior court administrators. The leadership is supported by court administrators from the six divisions in the state courts.

Attorney-General's Chambers

The Attorney-General's Chambers (the "AGC") is an organ of state led by the Attorney-General of Singapore. The Attorney-General plays an important role in upholding the rule of law in Singapore. He/she is the Principal Legal Advisor to the government in both domestic and international law and his/her office is responsible for the drafting of written laws. In addition, the Attorney-General is the Public Prosecutor, and has control and direction of prosecutions for criminal offences.

The Attorney-General discharges his responsibilities and duties through 6 legal divisions, namely, the Civil, Criminal Justice, State Prosecution, Economic Crimes and Governance, International Affairs, and Legislation and Law Reform Division.

Ministry of Law

The Ministry of Law's mission is to ensure a sound and progressive legal infrastructure, intellectual property infrastructure and insolvency regime, and to optimise land resources, to support national goals. The Ministry plays a key role in formulating and reviewing legal, intellectual property, land and insolvency, as well as legislation and strategies under its purview; providing legal and policy input for other Ministries' proposed bills and programmes; and developing the legal services, alternative dispute resolution and intellectual property services. Departments, statutory boards and agencies under the Ministry of Law include the Community Mediation Centre, Insolvency & Public Trustee's Office, Legal Aid Bureau, Intellectual Property Office of Singapore, Singapore Land Authority and the Land Surveyors Board.

Law Society of Singapore

Established in 1967, the Law Society of Singapore is a body established under the Legal Profession Act. It carries out various statutory functions prescribed under the Legal Profession Act, including maintaining and improving the standards of conduct and learning of the legal profession in Singapore, the facilitation of the acquisition of legal knowledge by members of the legal profession, and protecting and assisting the public in all matters ancillary or incidental to the law. Law Society has also established a Pro Bono Services Office as part of its mission in ensuring access to justice for the needy.

Singapore Institute of Legal Education

The Singapore Institute of Legal Education ("the Institute") is a statutory body established under the Legal Profession Act.

The Institute is entrusted with maintaining and improving the standards of legal education in Singapore, and has powers to review the implementation of initiatives, programmes and curricula relating to legal education in Singapore, including diploma, undergraduate and postgraduate programmes, and continuing professional development. The work of the Institute includes conducting the Singapore Bar Examinations and the Foreign Practitioner Examinations, and coordinating the mandatory Continuing Professional Development Scheme.

The Institute is managed by a Board of Directors which includes members of the Supreme Court judiciary, the Attorney-General, the President of the Law Society of Singapore and the Deans of the National University of Singapore Faculty of Law and the Singapore Management University School of Law.